1953

The Crowning Year of Sport

Also by Jonathan Rice
available from Methuen

One Hundred Lord's Tests

The Fight for the Ashes 2001

1953

The Crowning Year of Sport

JONATHAN RICE

Methuen

Published by Methuen 2003

1 3 5 7 9 10 8 6 4 2

First published in 2003 by
Methuen Publishing Ltd
215 Vauxhall Bridge Rd
London SW1V 1EJ
www.methuen.co.uk

A CIP catalogue record for this book is available from the British Library.

Methuen Publishing Ltd. Reg. No. 3543167

0 413 77239 X

Designed by Geoff Green
Printed and bound in Great Britain by The Bath Press

The Publishers thank the following for their kind permission to reproduce illustrations in this book:

HULTON ARCHIVE pages 2, 6, 8, 11, 15, 42, 53, 64, 72, 80, 84, 89, 94, 100, 102, 106, 110, 114, 120, 123, 132,
138, 141, 143, 144, 150, 156, 159, 162, 164, 166, 170, 184, 187, 189, 191, 194, 195, 202, 206, 209, 213, 217, 220,
226, 230, 233, 250, 253, 256, 260; DAILY MIRROR pages 18, 28, 31, 36, 38, 44, 57, 69, 77, 134, 147, 149, 152,
160, 173, 236, ,244, 258; D C THOMSON & CO LTD pages 169, 174, 176, 178, 182; DAVID FRITH pages 117,
119, 130, 198; THE FOOTBALL ASSOCIATION pages 23, 25, 26; TOPHAM PICTUREPOINT pages 35, 163;
ROYAL GEOGRAPHIC SOCIETY, LONDON page 47; POPPERFOTO page 92; the picture on page 21 is repro-
duced from "The Story of the Football League, 1938".

The publishers thank Epsom Racecourse for providing racecard details for the 1953 Derby Stakes,
shown on page 87.

Contents

The events in 1953 are engraved on my memory and some of my most vivid recollections are of the great sporting achievements of that year.

In May, Stanley Matthews provided a typically magical performance in the FA Cup Final; then in June all racing fans were delighted when Sir Gordon Richards at last won the Derby. In August it was the turn of cricket enthusiasts to celebrate the return of the Ashes for the first time since the 1932/1933 series of Test Matches in Australia. The greatest thrill came, appropriately, on the morning of the Coronation, when we were woken with the news of the British Everest Expedition's success in reaching the summit of the world's highest mountain. This gave me very particular pleasure as I had agreed to be Patron of the expedition.

Each of these achievements, and all the others described in this book, have a common thread. They are all distinguished by good sportsmanship and good grace and I hope that these qualities will continue to be a mark of British sporting achievements long into the future.

Introduction

The Summer 1953 edition of the Magazine of Aldwickbury School in Harpenden, Hertfordshire contained this particularly incisive contribution:

> *Coronation Day*
>
> On Coronation Day we went into the sittingroom and swiched on the Television. My brothers and I saw the Queen and Duke of Edinburgh in the State Coach. As well as that we saw the Beef eaters and the Household Cavalry. Mummy watched it in Piccadilly.
>
> *By Jonathan Rice (aged six years four months)*

That was my first ever published writing, and in many ways my best. It was short and to the point, and I spelled 'Piccadilly' correctly for perhaps the only time in my life before the invention of Spellcheck. We can pass over the missing 't' in 'swiched' because I made up for the error, and proved my prescience as a social commentator, by using a capital letter for 'Television', emphasising its position as the most powerful weapon of the second Elizabethan age. The set in question had been acquired by my father especially for the Coronation. It was state of the art technology – two knobs, one for volume and one for brightness – and it came with a vast magnifying glass on wheels that turned the twelve-inch screen into Todd-AO widescreen wall-to-wall pictures – at least that is how it seemed to this six-year-old. I remember standing to attention and saluting the screen at key moments in the ceremony, while my grandmother sat on the sofa sipping a large gin and tonic. We all tried to spot Mummy in Piccadilly as the State Coach processed past, but the picture was never clear enough to pick out individual faces in the crowd. Mummy returned wet through, so we knew she had been in Piccadilly somewhere.

1953 proved to be a memorable year for the British people, for many reasons beyond the pomp and circumstance of the Coronation. There were floods, the death of the new Queen's grandmother, and the first performance, in America, of a new song called 'Rock Around The Clock', by a chubby, smiling country-and-western style guitarist called Bill Haley. For sports fans, however, 1953 was a very special year. By the time Christmas came around, British fans had been able to enjoy the recapture of cricket's Ashes after 19 years in Australian possession, and the winning of the highest trophy in table tennis, the Swaythling Cup, for the first and so far only time; they had shared in the joy of Stanley Matthews' first and only Cup Winner's medal and of Sir Gordon Richards' only Derby victory; they had been thrilled by Mike Hawthorn's victory in the French Grand Prix, the first Grand Prix victory by a British driver since the 1920s; they had gnawed their fingernails to the quick as our golfers just failed to retake the Ryder Cup from the Americans after 20 years; and they had witnessed the footballing magic of the Hungarians at Wembley, where Puskas, Hidegkuti and the rest ran rings round the English to win by six goals to three. They had also been able to puff out their chests with pride as a British team of mountaineers were the first to reach the summit of the world's highest mountain, Mount Everest. Never mind that the two men who actually reached the top were a New Zealander and a Nepalese – it was still a British triumph.

This is the story of that sporting year. I have not been able to rely on too many of my own memories of 1953 for this book (although I do remember being Tom Graveney in back-garden cricket while my brother was Lindwall), so I am very grateful to the many people who have helped me in my research. Much of the raw material has been gleaned from contemporary reports taken from newspapers and magazines stored at the British Newspaper Library at Colindale, but I have also been able to speak to a number of people whose first-hand accounts of their contributions to the sporting year of 1953 have added massively to my understanding of the atmosphere of the time.

Among those who have helped me are Peter Alliss, Sir Alec Bedser, Richie Benaud, Christopher Brooker, Sir Christopher Chataway, Ian Craig, Ron Crayden, Alan Davidson, Dick Francis, Tom Graveney, Neil Harvey, Johnny Leach, Jimmy Lindley, Cliff Morgan, Arthur Morris, Jan Morris, Sir Stirling Moss, Sir Peter O'Sullevan, Bill Perry, Aubrey Simons and Derek Ufton. Thanks also must go to those who helped me reach some of these famous names, notably Michael Campbell Bowling, Harold Caplan (Maidenhead junior table tennis champion 1949 and wicketkeeper extraordinaire), Felix Francis, Jim McGrath, Ken Muhr, Bob Radford, Alex Rice, Tim Rice, Audrey Snell, Peter Tummons and Ian Wooldridge.

I would also like to acknowledge with thanks the kind permission of *Wisden Cricketers' Almanack* to let me quote from their 1954 edition, and to thank Eleanor Rees for her usual brilliant and thoroughly organised editing of my sometimes shambolic prose. Most of all, I would like to thank my wife Jan who consistently tolerates my abstractedness while putting books together, and even listens without falling into a deep coma when I read out extracts of the manuscript for her comments.

Without the help of all these people I could not have written the book, but any mistakes are mine.

JONATHAN RICE

I · *1953*

I t was the best of times, it was the worst of times. The year in England began with hope and despair in roughly equal measures. An Englishman waking up on 1 January 1953 would have looked around him and thought that things might be getting better, but that they were starting from a pretty low point. He would not have had much of a hangover, because in 1953, 1 January was not a holiday, just a working Thursday like any other. No one would celebrate the new year too wildly if he had to be fit to work his lathe, drive his bus or sell his wares in the morning.

The Britain our working man awoke to was a country still in the grip of post-war greyness. The Labour Party, which had so overwhelmingly been elected to power in the closing days of the war, had been voted out again after six years, and in October 1951 Winston Churchill, then almost 77 years old, had become Prime Minister once again. His was a cabinet largely made up of old men who looked backwards more naturally than forwards. Rationing, which had been a necessity during the war years, was still in place for certain foodstuffs, notably sugar, eggs and sausages. The war may have lasted for six years of actual fighting, but another seven and a half years later its legacy was still felt daily by everyone in Britain.

London, Coventry, Liverpool and many other cities were still scarred by the effects of the German bombing of a decade before. These bomb sites doubled as playgrounds or car parks, as there was still not the money to rebuild all the houses, offices and factories of the 1930s. There was almost no foreign currency available either, so people could not easily take holidays abroad even if they wanted or could afford to. Nobody could subsist overseas for long on the few pounds that were allowed to be taken out of the country. And anyway, much of Europe was even more scarred by the war and its aftermath than Britain.

Around the world, the political situation was unstable and apparently getting worse by the day. The war in Korea, the first of what many expected to be a series of wars between East and West, between Communism and Capitalism, was raging into its third year, with British

troops fighting alongside Americans, Australians and many other nationalities to defend the rights of the peace-loving Koreans in the south of
the peninsula against the belligerent intrusion of the Communist-backed
Koreans from the north. In America, General Dwight D. Eisenhower
had just been elected president, and there was little expectation that a
man who had served as supreme commander of the Allied forces in the
Second World War would expect anything less than a military solution in
Korea. The French, too, were becoming increasingly involved in a war in
Asia as a Communist-backed guerrilla movement in their colony of
Indo-China threatened to hasten the break-up of French authority east
of Suez.

Even the elements seemed to conspire against Mr Average Briton.
Although the winter was in general a mild one, unlike the severe winter
of 1946/47 when Britain had shivered in sub-zero temperatures for weeks,
the end of January brought disastrous floods to the east of England. On
the night of 31 January 1953 a peak spring tide coincided with a sea surge,
brought on by a change in air pressure, of about eight feet. This combination proved too great for the sea walls along much of the East Anglian
coast and the Thames Estuary, and in the resulting floods more than 300
people in Britain lost their lives, as did 1,800 in the even more defenceless
Netherlands. Vast areas were flooded: about a thousand people in the
town of King's Lynn had to be evacuated, as were all 13,000 inhabitants
of Canvey Island in Essex. The new Queen spent much of February
assiduously touring the stricken parts of her country, and must have won-
dered what more would be thrown at her beleaguered people.

Another major news story at the beginning of 1953 was the trial,
conviction and execution of Derek Bentley for the murder of a policeman. Now that the unfortunate Bentley has been granted a posthumous
pardon, we tend to feel that British justice must have been grossly in
error to convict such a man, and it is certainly true that the case had a
major influence on the subsequent abolition of the death penalty. But,
looking back on the case with 50 years of wisdom to influence our opin-
ions, the most astonishing thing is the speed at which it all happened.
The events for which Bentley was hanged took place on 11 December
1952. Bentley did not even fire the shot that killed PC Miles: it was his

Cambridge win the ninety-ninth University Boat Race on 28 March, gaining revenge for their defeat in 1952.

partner in crime, Christopher Craig, who fired the gun, in response to a cry of 'Let him have it!' from Bentley, who may well have been asking Craig to hand over the gun, not to fire it. Craig was a minor and, though found guilty, could not hang, but a policeman had been killed so somebody had to pay the ultimate price and Bentley was the unfortunate victim. It had not taken the police long to catch the criminals. Bentley was already under arrest when the fatal shot was fired and Craig was captured soon afterwards. What is still quite incredible is that the process from crime to execution took only 48 days, including the Christmas holiday period. Bentley was hanged on 28 January 1953, the day after the Labour MP Sidney Silverman tried to urge the Home Secretary, David Maxwell Fyfe, to reconsider his decision not to grant mercy. The Speaker refused to allow a debate on the grounds that the case was still *sub judice*. That meant in effect that Parliament could not discuss whether or not Bentley should be hanged until he had been hanged, which he was the next day.

Winter began to give way to spring, and with it came the first signs of an improvement in the Englishman's lot. On 4 February, the government announced the end of sweet rationing. Now the children of Britain could gorge themselves until they were sick on pineapple chunks, Spangles, gobstoppers and sweet cigarettes. Many did just that. Then on 1 March sausage rationing ended. At last we could all enjoy a full plate of bangers and mash (potatoes had been freely obtainable for years). Mr Churchill had resolved to abolish all rationing if he could during Coronation year, but dismantling the final controls was not as easy as that: no Prime Minister, not even Churchill could put a whole bureaucracy out of work with the stroke of a pen. Rationing had to be dismantled stage by stage because the civil service departments that ran it could only be disbanded gradually. On 26 March, eggs were decontrolled. Sausage, egg and chips at last! The British working man was coming back into his own.

In this grey and sometimes frightening world, people found that one way of forgetting the dreariness of their everyday lives was through sport. In the first few years after the war, British sportsmen and -women had not, in general, distinguished themselves on the international stage, although the Olympic Games of 1948, held in London, had been a triumph of good humour over austerity. British athletes won no gold medals in track and field events, but nevertheless the games were considered a great success. Our only gold medals in 1948 were won on the water, by Richard Burnell and Herbert Bushnell in the double sculls, George Laurie and John Wilson in the coxless pairs and Stewart Morris and David Bond in the Swallow class yachts. Rule Britannia, Britannia rule the waves, but not much else.

In the same year our cricketers had been swamped by the mighty

Australian touring team, the last one led to England by Don Bradman, which was one of the best sides, if not the very best, ever to leave Australia. The England cricket team had even managed to lose to India for the first time, in a Test played in February 1952, during the course of which King George VI had died. Our golfers, led by Henry Cotton and Max Faulkner, Open champions both, were fighting a losing struggle against the Americans, who were able to hone their skills on the regular weekly professional tournament circuit. Our tennis players could at least easily remember the great years of Fred Perry and Bunny Austin before the war, but our men had no real hopes in any of the major tournaments. Our women were certainly better placed, with several players, led by the young Angela Mortimer, capable of a big upset, but it was still the Americans who dominated. In football, England maintained their unbeaten record at home against teams from beyond the British Isles, but it was not a vintage period for British football as the players readjusted after the war. This did not stop the crowds from turning out in their millions to cheer on their teams, but there were few players of genuine world class – Stanley Matthews and Tom Finney always excluded.

The Five Nations Rugby Union tournament, which traditionally livens up the beginning of the year, began on 10 January, when France played Scotland at the Stade Colombes. France won this opening encounter by 11 points to five, in the process scoring what would prove to be their only try of the entire tournament. The pitch was very poor after a dreadful week of snow and freezing temperatures, and the play was scrappy at best. By the end of the tournament these two countries were at the bottom of the table, so, given the conditions and the talent on show, it was hardly surprising that the match was no great advertisement for the Union code. The next weekend, Wales played England at Cardiff Arms Park, and Ireland played France at Ravenhill in Belfast. Wales had swept all before them in 1952, but England were improving rapidly, and this was perhaps the key game of the tournament.

Early Mist, ridden by Bryan Marshall, leaps Becher's Brook on his way to a 20-length victory in the Grand National.

However, to defend their title Wales had to do without their regular halfbacks, as both scrum half Rex Willis and fly half Cliff Morgan were injured. 'I was coming back from an injury,' says Morgan. 'I played at Bath the day of the international, but I hadn't been to practice, so they picked Roy Burnett and W. A. Williams in our place.' The Newport pair did their best, but England emerged from the day with a tightly fought victory, by eight points to three. Burnett and Williams never played again for Wales.

Meanwhile in Belfast Ireland were beating France by 16 points to three. Today the margin would have been much greater, as the points were made up of four Irish tries, two of which were converted, against a solitary French drop goal, 24–3 in modern currency. Whichever way you add up the score, it was Ireland's biggest victory over France for 40 years, and it left England and Ireland as the teams setting the pace. At Murrayfield two weeks later, Wales, with Cliff Morgan and Rex Willis back in the side, beat Scotland 12–0, despite Willis going off injured early in the game so that Morgan was forced to take over at scrum half. A week later the big match took place at Lansdowne Road. Ireland and England fought to their first ever draw in Dublin, ending with nine points all, a try and two penalties to each side. This left England still without a win at Lansdowne Road since the end of the war, and it meant that nobody would achieve the Triple Crown, but it was also enough to install England as favourites for the Championship, with home matches against the two weakest sides, France and Scotland, to come.

The last Saturday of February saw England beat France easily, thanks in large part to Jeff Butterfield who scored a try and made another on his international debut. The 11–0 scoreline, a goal and two tries, would be 17–0 today. Up at Murrayfield, Scotland continued their supporters' misery by losing 26–8 to Ireland, for whom winger Sean Byrne scored three of his side's six tries. Scotland's selectors went into overdrive in 1953, picking and discarding players like cards in a game of rummy. All in all, they chose 29 players for the four matches, of whom 16 were backs. The only men to play all four games were the forwards Wilson, Henderson, Hegarty and McMillan, but even as the changes grew more frequent, and selectorial whimsy more apparent, the team showed no improvement.

Arsenal coach Leslie Compton (far left) and manager Tom Whittaker (far right, holding the League championship trophy) show off some of their 1953 silverware to the club apprentices.

Scotland managed a unique if unwelcome double by losing to England by 26 points to eight, exactly the same score by which Ireland had humbled them three weeks earlier, and once again they conceded six tries in a game. The victory was enough to give England the Five Nations title and Scotland the wooden spoon. Wales merely had their pride to play for as they took on France at the Stade Colombes. The host nation's inability to cross the try line proved crucial as Wales won a low-scoring match by two tries to a penalty goal, 6–3.

England, the undefeated 1953 champions, had come so near and yet so far. They still had not won the Triple Crown since 1937, nor completed a Grand Slam since 1928. They did not, in the event, have long to wait before their next Triple Crown, which they secured in 1954, but by losing their final match of that year to France they missed out on both the Championship and the Grand Slam. Their next Grand Slam would have to wait until 1980, 52 years after the last.

On Friday 6 March, while the Five Nations tournament was bubbling up nicely towards its resolution, something happened which was probably the most important single event of the year, even for rugby enthusiasts: Josef Stalin, the leader of the Soviet Union, died. Stalin, ruler of the only nation to have been allied both to Nazi Germany and later to the Western powers, was in most ways a monster. His passing was not mourned, except officially in the Soviet Union, where the eulogies were fulsome and hollow. The struggle to succeed him, and to define the relationship between East and West, which would persist for another 35 years, took up the rest of the year and more.

Eighteen days after the death of Stalin, and two days before eggs were decontrolled, the new Queen's grandmother, Queen Mary, died at Marlborough House in London at the age of 85. It was no surprise, as her health had been gradually worsening for some months, but it cast a shadow on the preparations for the Coronation, already set for 2 June. At the time, the lady born Princess Victoria Mary Augusta Louise Olga Pauline Claudine Agnes on 26 May 1865 was the longest-lived consort in the history of the British royal family, a record eventually beaten by her daughter-in-law Queen Elizabeth the Queen Mother. Queen Mary lived on as two of her sons became kings, one abdicating and one dying, before finally her granddaughter became her queen. She was respected more than loved ('a proud, charming queen, a lady of vigour to the last,' was how Pathé News described her), and her passing was seen as the end of an era. A first-hand connection with Queen Victoria, Queen Mary's grandmother-in-law who had died 52 years earlier, was now consigned to history. The second Elizabethan Age was safely under way and it was to be an age of progress and change, not one of harking back to the good old days of the recent past.

Queen Mary died just four days before a sporting event that would acquire a royal link through the efforts of the late Queen's daughter-in-law. The Grand National of 1953 was run on 28 March, to perhaps less fanfare and expectation than for many a year. The problem was a lack of top-quality steeplechasers. The Cheltenham Gold Cup had been won by one of the few genuinely good horses of the season, the Irish-bred and trained Knock Hard, whose brilliant running had been enhanced by a jumping style that improved as the season progressed. But Knock Hard did not run in the National. Nor did Teal, the 1952 winner, who had led until half-way in the Gold Cup but then had tailed off and returned home very distressed. It turned out that he had ruptured his bowel, and sadly he died during the operation to correct it. Other horses failing to line up at the start of the National included the previous year's runner-up, Legal Joy, and the twice placed Wot No Sun. The race looked to be very open, even by the standards of one of racing's greatest lotteries. The betting reflected this, with no particularly short-priced runner. The favourite bore the remarkable name – for today – of Little Yid, and among the other fancied runners were Early Mist and Mont Tremblant, winner of the Gold Cup in 1952.

The race itself lived up to all expectations: it was as dull a Grand National as anybody could remember. Dick Francis, still hoping to win the big race after coming second on Lord Bicester's Roimond in 1949, was riding another of his lordship's horses, Senlac Hill. As Francis remembers it, 'Senlac Hill was a notoriously bad jumper who had a habit of putting his feet into the open ditches and turning end over end, giving his jockey a nasty fall. Somehow I had managed to stay on long enough to win a three-mile steeplechase at Lingfield and hence qualify the horse for the Grand National. I began to think that was a mistake!' Francis could have ridden Irish Lizard, a horse he had earlier won the Topham Trophy on, but his commitment to Lord Bicester came first. Senlac Hill's chances were dismissed not only by his jockey but by all knowledgeable commentators, one writing that his chance of even completing the course seemed extremely remote.

Thirty-one horses started, and at the half-way point 13 were still in the race, including Senlac Hill. 'I expected only to reach the third fence, which is an open ditch,' remembers Francis. 'I thought that Senlac Hill would do his usual trick of planting his feet firmly in the ditch and that would be that – I would be eating grass. Amazingly the horse jumped the obstacle and on we went.' While more fancied horses including Cardinal Error, Parasol II, Knuckleduster and Whispering Steel fell by the wayside, Senlac Hill hacked on. The favourite, Little Yid, gave its backers a run for their money, but eventually pulled up four fences from home, looking exhausted. From the twentieth fence, when Ordnance had fallen while in the lead, there was only one horse in it, the 20–1 shot Early Mist, ridden by Bryan Marshall. All he had to do was to clear the final few fences, complete the run in and the prize would be his. He did and it was. He cantered home a winner by twenty lengths ahead of Mont Tremblant, who was carrying 12 st. 5 lbs, 17 pounds more than the winner and no less than 27 pounds more than the third-placed horse, Irish Lizard.

Only five horses finished the race: Overshadow came in fourth, and fifth was Senlac Hill, 'a long way back from the other four' according to Francis. 'The racecourse commentator, who I believe was Raymond Glendenning, was heard to say, "Here comes Dick Francis hacking in on Senlac Hill. He must have fallen somewhere out in the country." It was years before the race was televised or filmed by the racecourse security services as it is nowadays, and I had quite a task to convince the stewards that I actually finished the race having jumped all the obstacles.' Three years later, he would fail to finish because his horse appeared to jump an extra obstacle, but that is another story.

Early Mist, bred in England but now owned by the Dublin businessman J. H. Griffin, had fallen at the first fence in the 1952 National, so the contrast between the two rides could not have been greater. A year earlier, he had been owned by J. V. Rank, a notable racehorse owner from the Rank flour-to-films dynasty, who had never won the Grand National despite years of trying. Rank died in 1952, and his horses were sold. Griffin bought Early Mist, who then came good a year too late for his original owner and began a sequence of three consecutive winners for trainer Vincent O'Brien.

Somebody else who came good around this time was Marilyn Monroe, whose first starring film, *Niagara*, opened in Britain on 23 April, St George's Day. The film got mediocre reviews, which were no more than it

Early Mist is led in after winning the Grand National on 28 March. Early Mist was trained by Vincent O'Brien – the first of three consecutive Grand National winners.

deserved, but regardless of the merits of the film that was her vehicle: the film star who took the role of the sex symbol in the movies to previously unconsidered heights had launched her career. 'Can she act?' asked Donald Zec in the *Daily Mirror*. 'Brother, I wouldn't know. That seemed to be the only thing she was not allowed to reveal.' Zec knew, like the rest of the world, that Monroe's acting did not really matter. The glamour she brought to the filmgoers of Britain (and there were millions of them in those days before television took its grip on the pulse and throat of the nation) was what they cared about – a welcome antidote to post-war life.

In Britain April is the transition month between seasons, both meteorologically and in sporting terms. Even these days, when football, tennis and golf go on all the year round and rugby league is played in summer, April represents the climax of most of the winter sports and the beginning of the summer ones. In April 1953 the English football league season finished with a flurry of vital results. The struggle against relegation was very tight, with at least six teams contesting the two places of ignominy, which finally went to Derby County and Stoke City. Six years after selling Matthews, the Potters slipped out of the top division, much to the relief of the other clubs on the edge of the drop, Manchester City, Chelsea, Sheffield Wednesday and Liverpool. Derby and Stoke were to be replaced by Sheffield United and Huddersfield Town, who had been quite well ahead of all challengers in the Second Division for some weeks, making the divisional race for promotion about as exciting as the Grand National had been.

As 1952 turned into 1953, the struggle for the First Division title seemed to be between Arsenal and Preston North End, Tom Finney's club. Arsenal were chasing their seventh title, which would be a record, while Preston were looking for their first League championship since they won the title in the first two years of the League's existence, in 1888/89 and 1889/90. It would finish as one of the closest-run title chases in the history of the League.

All season, Arsenal just looked to have the edge over their rivals. Their team was built around a very solid defence, featuring Wally Barnes and Joe Mercer as the stars, but it was their forwards who made the difference, scoring 97 goals during the campaign, 11 more than the next most prolific team, third-placed Wolverhampton Wanderers. The Footballer of the Year Award went to Bolton's Nat Lofthouse, but the leading League goalscorer was not Lofthouse, he was not one of the Wolves and he was not a Gunner. It was Preston North End's Charlie Wayman, with 24 goals. Preston were the team chasing Arsenal hardest, and by chance the structure of the fixture list meant that everything would be decided in the final match of the season, Preston North End against Arsenal at Deepdale.

Before the kick-off, Arsenal had 54 points from 41 games, having won 21, drawn 12 and lost eight. Preston had 52 points from 41 games, with 20 wins, 12 draws and nine losses. If Preston could beat Arsenal,

the teams would be level on points. In 1953, the Football League awarded two points for a win, and teams equal on points were separated by
means of calculating their goal 'average', that is to say goals scored divid-
ed by goals conceded. Arsenal had already scored 97 goals while conced-
ing 62, giving them a goal average of 1.56. Preston had scored 83 goals
and let in 60, so their goal average was just 1.38. However, if Preston
were to win by enough goals, they could reverse the situation and claim
the title. Some quick maths showed that 5–0 would be enough. Their
goal average then would be 88/60, 1.47, while Arsenal's would be 97/67,
1.45. By today's rules of three points for a win, the teams would still be
tied on points, but with today's goal difference rules, even 5–0 would not
have been enough for Preston, who would then have had a goal difference of 28 to Arsenal's 30. A scoreline of 6–0 would have tied the goal
difference as well but given the title to Arsenal on goals scored, so today,
a score of 7–0 would have been needed. Even 5–0 was a very tall order,
but theoretically possible.

The ground at Deepdale was full to bursting, even though it did not
quite match the record crowd of 42,684 that had turned up to see the
exact equivalent fixture against Arsenal on 23 April 1938. That season had
ended with Arsenal as champions and Wolves and Preston in the next
two positions, and, sadly for Preston's fans, 1953 proved to be a case of
déjà vu. The game never really reached any pitch of excitement, because
Arsenal were just content not to concede five goals, and Preston, despite
their best efforts, could not break down the mighty Arsenal defence often
enough. They scored twice, and 2–0 was an honourable result, but it still
left Arsenal as champions on goal average, 1.52 against 1.42. Preston
North End have never come so close to the title again. When they were
runners-up to Wolves five years later (while Arsenal languished in
twelfth place), they were five points adrift. The long cold football season
can be cruel when it ends in sudden death like this.

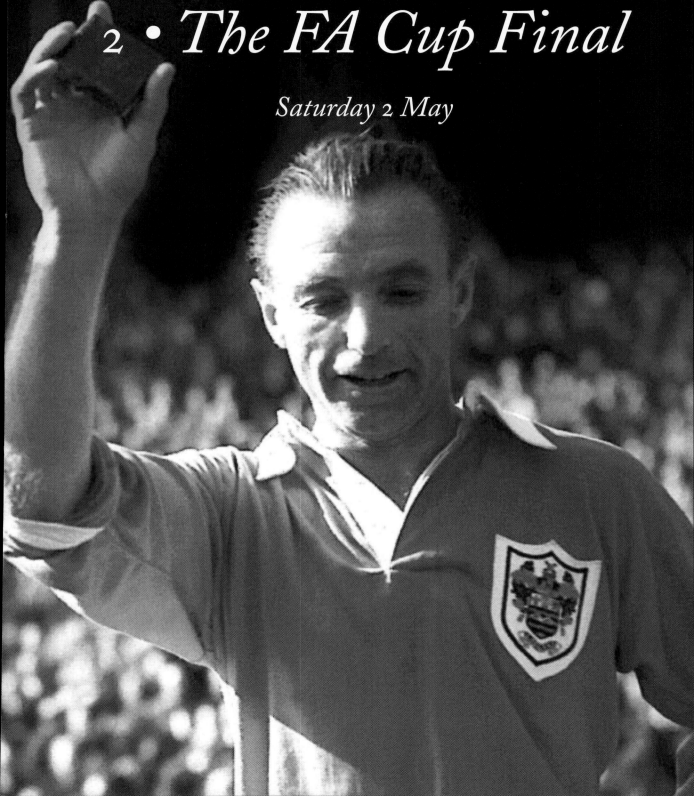

It was Lawrie McMenemy who said, 'The last player to score a hat-trick in an FA Cup Final was Stan Mortensen. He even had the game named after him – The Matthews Final.' 1953 was the year that Stanley Matthews finally won his FA Cup Winner's medal, a trinket that had taken him so long to earn and had been so well deserved by virtue of his long and distinguished career for two not particularly distinguished clubs, that it was inevitable that it would be 'his' match, even if Stan Mortensen or anybody else on the pitch scored a hatful of goals. The FA Cup was the pinnacle of footballing achievement in those pre-Europe days, and whether or not Stanley Matthews considered this match to be the peak of his career, for millions of football lovers it will always be the game for which he is remembered and by which he is defined. Everybody in Britain who was at all interested in the game, apart from a few thousand Bolton Wanderers fans, wanted Matthews and Blackpool to win.

Stanley Matthews was already 38 years old when he came to Wembley for his third Cup Final appearance. With the exception of the referee and Stan Hanson, the Bolton Wanderers goalkeeper, who was just 10 months Matthews' junior, he was at least three years older than everybody on the pitch. Doug Holden, the man with the impossible task of matching up to the maestro as Bolton's outside right, was born two days after Matthews had made his Stoke City debut, playing as an amateur for their second team in the Central League. From that very first match, Stanley was singled out for praise by the newspapers. While Doug Holden was still yowling or sleeping in his mother's arms in Manchester, the *Staffordshire Sentinel* reported that 'Matthews frequently gained the applause of the crowd by some very pretty movements' as Stoke City beat Burnley 2–1. From that day, the life of the 15-year-old Stanley Matthews became public property. He made his first team debut for Stoke City six weeks after turning professional, on 19 March 1932. His team beat Bury, away from home, by one goal to nil in a late season Second Division game.

Back Row : JOHNSON, ROBERTSON, SELLARS, SPENCER, JOHN, BEACHILL, TURNER, MAWSON, LIDDLE.
Middle Row (players only) : WARE, DAVIES, PALETHORPE, SALE, MATTHEWS.

Second Division Champions 1932-33. Stoke City and the youthful Stanley Matthews.

The next season Stoke City were promoted to the First Division, although it must be admitted that Matthews did not play a particularly big part in their Second Division championship season. He played 15 League games that winter, enough to earn a Championship medal, and the official team photograph that year shows a smiling Matthews standing on the far right of the front row of players – the same position he took on the pitch. The odd thing about the team photo is that the players are all standing in the back two rows. The entire front row is taken up by seven seated men in suits, the directors claiming their moment of glory.

A year later, the 19-year-old prodigy, who was on the way to his best ever scoring season with 15 goals, 11 in the League, was selected to play for The Rest against England in an international trial at Roker Park. Matthews was playing for the first time alongside the Sunderland inside forward Raich Carter, and the right-side pair took the England defence apart. Carter, 15 months older than Matthews, scored four goals as The

Rest beat the senior side 7–1. Both players were praised to the skies by the newspapers, who decided that here were two men for the future, and both in due course made their England debuts. The selection committee nevertheless lived up to its reputation for failing to spot a good thing even when it bit them in the backside and didn't pick them both in the same England side for another two years.

Matthews first played for England against Wales at Cardiff in September 1934, and England won 4–0. From then on, he began to experience the strange love-hate relationship that English sport seems to have with men of true genius, and he found himself left out of the England side almost as much as he was in it. But at least he was at the heart of the Stoke City side, and it was largely because of his brilliance on the right wing that the Potters remained in the top division until the war came along.

In those pre-war seasons, the best Stoke City could manage in the FA Cup competition was in the quarter-finals in 1933/34, when they lost 1–0 to Manchester City, the eventual Cup winners. Matthews scored four goals in the three Cup matches before Stoke's defeat that season, including one against Blackpool, whom they beat 3–0 in the fourth round. In the 1934/35 season they lost 4–1 in the third round against Swansea Town. Matthews scored Stoke's only goal, but did not add to his tally in the Cup for a further 12 years and three days. In fact, he only scored four more goals in the FA Cup in his entire career after 1935: the winner against Spurs for Stoke City in the third round of 1946/47, one for Blackpool against Sheffield Wednesday on 10 January 1953, and two more when he was back at Stoke in the long twilight of his career, against Leicester City in 1962 and against Swansea Town on 15 February 1964, a fortnight after his forty-ninth birthday.

Matthews was not in the side to score goals. He was there to help others score. When he transferred to Blackpool in 1947 for the massive sum of £11,500, he came into a team that already contained one of the great goal-scorers of the immediate post-war era, Stan Mortensen. Morty was coming

Front cover of the official programme for the 1953 FA Cup Final.

THE FOOTBALL ASSOCIATION CHALLENGE CUP COMPETITION

FINAL TIE

BLACKPOOL v
BOLTON WANDERERS

SATURDAY, MAY 2nd, 1953   KICK-OFF 3 pm

EMPIRE STADIUM

WEMBLEY

Chairman and Managing Director: SIR ARTHUR J. ELVIN, M.B.E.

OFFICIAL PROGRAMME · ONE SHILLING

up to his thirty-second birthday at the time of the 1953 Cup Final, and was in his prime. He had already played 23 games for England, scoring 21 goals, a strike rate unmatched except by one regular England forward in football history, but of course that did not make him a certainty for the England side. He had not played since scoring both goals in England's 2–1 victory over Argentina at Wembley in May 1951: his place in the England team had gone to Bolton's centre forward Nat Lofthouse and in truth the England team was not weakened by this change. Lofthouse, dubbed 'The Lion of Vienna' after his brilliant winning goal against Austria in May 1952, scored 30 goals in his 33 internationals, and was the only man whose strike rate could match Mortensen's. What's more, Lofthouse was four years younger. By the time the teams reached Wembley, Mortensen knew he had something to prove to the watching England coach and selectors, not to mention the Queen, the Duke of Edinburgh, several members of the visiting Australian cricket team and the rest of the 100,000-strong crowd that packed Wembley as usual for the showpiece game of the season.

Blackpool had never won the FA Cup in their long history, although since Matthews' arrival they had already been losing finalists twice. In 1948, they were up against Manchester United, runners-up to Arsenal in the League, but it was United who ran out winners by four goals to two. This was a particularly traumatic final for Blackpool, because they not only scored first, from a penalty by Eddie Shimwell when Mortensen was tripped, but were also leading 2–1 at half time. Manchester United scored three times in the second half and Blackpool became the first team to have led twice in a Cup Final and still lost. That statistic probably did not interest Matthews, who was never one for the facts and figures of the game apart from the result of his latest match.

Three years later Blackpool were back at Wembley, having just finished the League season in their highest ever position, third behind Tottenham Hotspur and Manchester United. Their opponents, Newcastle United, had finished one rung lower than Blackpool, but the Tangerines ran into Jackie Milburn on peak form and lost 2–0. Of the 1953 team, four players were appearing for the third time in a Blackpool shirt in the final:

Bolton Wanderers – the team photograph taken from the 1953 Cup Final programme.
Back row, left to right: W. Ridding (Manager), G. Higgins, N. Lofthouse, R. Hartle, S.
Hanson, M. Barrass, D. Holden, H. Hassall, E. Bell, D. Sprotson (Trainer). Front row,
left to right. J. Wheeler, R. Banks, W. Moir, T. Sell, R. Parry, R. Langton, J. Ball.

right back Eddie Shimwell, centre half and captain Harry Johnston,
Mortensen and Matthews. Four others were playing for the second time:
goalkeeper George Farm, left back Tom Garrett and the left-hand-side
forwards Jackie Mudie and Bill Perry. That left just three who were playing for the first time for Blackpool in a final, right half Ewan Fenton, left
half Cyril Robinson and inside right Ernie Taylor. Robinson was in for
the injured Hughie Kelly, who had played in the two previous Blackpool
finals but now had a chipped ankle bone and had to watch from the
terraces. Ernie Taylor had already appeared in a Blackpool final, but on
the other side. In 1951 he had played for Newcastle and was thus the only
member of the Blackpool side who already had a Cup Winner's medal on
his sideboard. Taylor would go on to play in the final again in 1958 with
Manchester United, the other team Blackpool had faced in the final, and
once again the opponents would be Bolton Wanderers.

'The public wanted Matthews to win the final,' remembers
Blackpool's outside left, Bill Perry. 'We players also wanted him to win
this final honour. We were pulling for him as we had in 1951.' They did
not want a repeat of those losing performances. 'It's the most devastating

Blackpool in 1953 – the forward line is seated, the half backs and defence have to stand. Back row, left to right: H. Johnstone, F. Fenton, F. Shinwell, T. Garrett, A. Brown, G. Farm, H. Kelly, J. Crosland. Front row, left to right: Mr J. Smith (Manager) S. Matthews, R. Taylor, S. Mortensen, J. Mudie, W. Perry, J. Lynas (Trainer)

feeling to lose at Wembley, a horrible feeling coming off the pitch, walking with heads bowed back to the tunnel.'

The Cup Final came at the end of a very exciting League programme from which Arsenal emerged as champions by virtue of a better goal average than runners-up Preston North End. The outcome had not been decided until the last game of the season so after a thrilling chase for the League title, much was expected of the FA Cup Final. Bolton Wanderers were probably the underdogs, having finished seven places lower in the League than Blackpool, with eight points fewer than their opponents and only five more than Matthews' old club Stoke City, who were relegated that year. However, Bolton had made it to the final despite a difficult run through the early rounds, and Lofthouse had scored in every round, just as Jackie Milburn had done in the year Newcastle had beaten Blackpool. Bolton were a slightly younger side than Blackpool, although their outside left, Bob Langton, formerly of Blackburn Rovers and Preston North End, was coming up for 35.

The press generally forecast a close final, with popular sentiment heavily on Blackpool's side, but when heads ruled hearts many sound judges opted for Bolton. What they did not know at the time was that there was a very real doubt about Stanley Matthews' fitness. He had strained a knee earlier in the season and it had troubled him on and off for several months, but now, as the Cup Final approached, he knew all was not right. To cap it all, he picked up a slight thigh injury and, in those days before substitutes were allowed, he knew it would be wrong to jeopardise his team-mates' chances of winners' medals for the sake of his own personal glory. It was a risk, but in the end his manager, Joe Smith, decided that the psychological advantage of having the great Stanley Matthews on the pitch would outweigh the risk of his breaking down during the game. It was a gamble that paid off.

The guest of honour, Her Majesty Queen Elizabeth II, was attending a football match for the first time in her life a month before her Coronation. At the first Cup Final of her reign, in 1952, the Cup had been presented by the Prime Minister, Winston Churchill. As she looked in her engagement diary for that morning, the Queen might have thought that there were more productive ways of spending a Saturday afternoon, but the sun was shining and, as it happened, she was about to witness one of the great football matches of all time. Had she never seen another game the Queen might have assumed that all football matches were played on perfect turf in beautiful spring sunshine and that they all ended in a flurry of goals.

Before the match, the teams were introduced to the Duke of Edinburgh on the pitch, but the Queen waited up in the Royal Box. By this time the nerves of all the players were on edge, and perhaps the Blackpool side, with so many who had been there already, were a little bit calmer than the Wanderers. Matthews, who never showed much emotion at all, looked serene as always, and nobody could have guessed at the problems with his thigh and knee.

The match itself is almost too well known to report on. The film of Matthews jinking past Bolton's hapless left back, Ralph Banks, and crossing the ball to where Mortensen and Perry are waiting for the kill has been shown on television a thousand times. The ineptitude, to our sophisticated

Bolton's goalkeeper Stan Hanson gathers the ball to stop another Blackpool attack.

eyes, of poor Stan Hanson in the Bolton goal has been run and rerun over the years until there is hardly a football supporter in the country who can understand how the poor chap ever made a living out of goalkeeping. The shy smile of Matthews as he is lifted on to the shoulders of his team-mates for the lap of honour after the Cup has been presented is another enduring image, so enduring that we almost begin to imagine we were there ourselves. And you can bet that many more than the 100,000 who were there have since claimed they saw Stanley Matthews at Wembley in 1953.

The key moment in the Final was probably the injury to Bolton's left half, Eric Bell. Bolton Wanderers were already a goal up by this time, Nat

Lofthouse having shown the crowd after only 90 seconds why he was England's centre forward in preference to Stan Mortensen. In truth, it was a shot more in hope than expectation, but George Farm in the Blackpool goal failed to get behind the ball and it ricocheted off his arm into the goal. One–nil to Bolton. Would Matthews be going home empty-handed again? But mid-way through the first half Eric Bell tore a muscle, and it was immediately evident that he would struggle to retain any mobility, especially as his role was to try and contain Matthews. So Bolton regrouped. They switched the hobbling Bell out to the left wing, moved inside left Harold Hassall to left half, and brought Bob Langton, the outside left, inside to take over from Hassall.

To start with this looked like a sensible move. Matthews, clearly testing his injuries, had a quiet first half, and Bell, the passenger on Bolton's left wing was able to carry on without getting too involved in the match. The action was all taking place elsewhere on the pitch. With 10 minutes to go before half-time, Mortensen hit an undistinguished left-foot shot towards the goal, where Hassall, now having to play out of position in defence and covering Mortensen's run, could only deflect the ball past Hanson and into his own net. One all. With Bolton down to 10 fit men, that should have been it.

But Bolton scored again just four minutes later, and once again George Farm was at fault. A cross from Langton, still displaying his winger's skills despite playing at inside left, evaded Farm, who was too slow coming off his line to collect the ball, and Bolton's captain Billy Moir was there to meet it with his head and regain the lead for Bolton. This was not a great match for the goalkeepers. So the half-time score was 2–1 to Bolton, and most of Britain assumed that even with ten men Bolton were likely to see off the challenge of a curiously lacklustre Blackpool team.

The second half merely seemed to add to Blackpool's misery. Ten minutes in, Bolton scored for the third time, thanks to their injured man on the left wing, Eric Bell. Doug Holden, the baby of the match, put in a great cross and Bell, despite his injury, managed to climb high enough to beat Farm and head the ball into the net. With scarcely more than a third of the game to go, Bolton had apparently locked the door on Matthews' ambitions, and only had to defend well to carry home the Cup.

At this point, however, the game went through an amazing transformation. Matthews at last came to life and in doing so revealed the flaws in the thinking behind Bolton's reshuffle after Bell had been injured. If there was one thing that upset Matthews' rhythm on the right wing, it was an opposing left winger who tackled back at him. Matthews had even been known to get so frustrated that he would tell wingers to get on with their own job and leave the tackling to the halves and full backs. Langton would have tackled back against Matthews if he had been on the left wing, but instead the injured Bell was there, able to act as noth-

After 20 years of trying Stanley Matthews receives his Cup Winner's medal from Her Majesty the Queen.

ing more than a traffic island, motionless and negotiable. To make matters worse, Bolton's left back, Ralph Banks, came down with terrible attacks of cramp, so that Bolton's left flank became a hundred yards of open territory in which Matthews could disport himself. The injuries to the two left-side defenders undoubtedly were a very significant factor in Bolton's eventual collapse, though we should take nothing away from the astonishing performance by the Blackpool forward line in the final 20 minutes of the game. Today, of course, substitutes would have replaced the injured players, and things might have been very different. What is more, most pundits at the time felt that Bolton manager Bill Ridding made a tactical error by not moving John Wheeler, their right half, over to the left-hand side to try to handle Matthews, rather than merely rejigging their left-hand-side trio. Certainly, when two of the three men were limping it seemed almost suicidal not to play fit men up against the one real threat to Bolton's lead.

By now the hot afternoon sunshine was sapping the strength of all the players, not just Banks and Bell. There were signs of cramp affecting several of the players on both sides, but Matthews, despite his doubts before the match began, seemed immune. 'Stan was a loner,' says Bill Perry. 'He was very popular with the rest of the players, but he liked to do his own type of training. The manager let him keep himself in tune.' His 'own type of training' was certainly far more punishing than anything his younger colleagues put themselves through, and it was on days like this that it paid off. Crucially, the rest of the Blackpool forward line kept going as well as their right winger, and the flagging Bolton defence had no answer. Little Ernie Taylor, playing inside Matthews, was also benefiting from the displaced and injured Bolton left side, and he caused huge problems for Hassall, Langton and Bell. It was clear that despite their 3–1 lead Bolton suddenly felt far from secure. The crowds in the terraces may have sensed their unease, but surely not even a side with Matthews on the right wing could score three goals in 20 minutes?

It was a pass from Taylor to Matthews that began the fightback. Anticipating the way Matthews would move for the pass, Taylor delivered the ball to his winger's feet just as the 38-year-old Matthews accelerated past poor Eric Bell. Bell was no match for anybody that day, but Matthews, even at an age when most men have long since taken off their shinpads for the last time, was as quick over 10 yards or so as anybody in the game. No defender would ever back himself to turn and catch Matthews once he had gone past. The trick was not to let him past, but that dip of the shoulders, that shake of the hips had been inducing the best in the world to let him past for almost a quarter of a century, and today Matthews was going past. Nothing could stop him.

With the ball at his feet, Matthews raced to the goal-line and crossed the ball towards the far post, where he knew Mortensen would be waiting. Hanson, completing a day of disaster for the goalkeepers, flapped at the ball as it flew past, just getting enough on it to touch it to the feet of the onrushing Mortensen, instead of leaving it and letting it drift harmlessly out of play for a goal kick. Mortensen stuck out a foot and bundled the ball inelegantly but highly effectively over the line. It was 3–2, and game on.

That was how it stayed for the next 17 minutes, even though Blackpool were clearly the superior team. Bolton looked to be hanging on. Banks was off the pitch getting treatment for his cramp almost as much as he was on it, but still the tangerine shirts could not break through. Then, with just three minutes to go, Jackie Mudie, the Blackpool inside left, was tripped just outside the penalty area. Stan Mortensen stepped forward to take the free kick. Mortensen had an immensely powerful and accurate dead ball kick, and considering the weight of the heavy leather ball even on a dry day like this, it was a brave man who stood in the defensive wall only ten yards from his boot. But the entire Bolton team was prepared to be brave: after all, they were just three minutes from winning the Cup. Eddie Shimwell, Blackpool's canny right back, drifted out to take up a position by the left-hand post in case of the unlikely event that Mortensen decided to pass rather than blast. Shimwell's move was noticed by the Bolton wall, and one man moved from the right-hand end across to the other side to cover him. It was all the help Mortensen needed. Now he could see the goal. His kick was hard and dead straight through the tiny gap that had been opened up. The ball was in the back of the net before anybody on the pitch had had a chance to react. The reaction on the terraces was rather quicker. A huge cheer went up to mark the fact that Blackpool were level; hats were thrown, rattles were spun, newspapers waved and tangerine scarves raised high in the air. In all the excitement it was easy to overlook the fact that this was Mortensen's hat-trick, the first ever in a Cup Final at Wembley and indeed in any Cup Final of the twentieth century. The Blackpool players ran quickly back to the centre circle. They knew the game was there to be won, although even the most hardened optimist among them was assuming the match would go to extra time.

It very nearly did. With the referee looking at his watch, Taylor slotted another precise and perfect pass through to Matthews, who once again raced for the goal-line. He shimmied past one, two, then three Bolton men, dropping his shoulders to put them off balance and then racing past them as though they had never existed. It was the sheer wizardry of his game that so demoralised his opponents. They kept thinking they had his measure, and at the last moment discovered they did not. Matthews' cross was this time aimed towards Bill Perry, Blackpool's South African-born outside left. 'As he crossed the ball, he fell,' says Perry. 'The ball came along the ground to me round about the penalty spot. I was a left winger, but I am right-footed really, and I hit it with my right foot. I was just happy to see it hit the back of the net.'

At this point reality bade farewell to Wembley Stadium and the fairy tale kicked in. The crowd went crazy. The crescendo of noise lasted for well over five minutes, until long after the final whistle had been blown and the teams were accepting their medals from the Queen. The crowd had every reason to celebrate, even the Bolton supporters who had seen their dream shattered in five minutes of supreme artistry. Not only had the greatest hero in the history of British football now won his FA Cup Winner's medal at long last, but they had all witnessed one of the truly great football matches of all time. It may not have touched the heights for the full 90 minutes, but in the second half at least it had been played at a great pace and a very high level of skill. The result had been in doubt until the final kick; more accurately, the wrong result had been a foregone conclusion until almost the final kick. The final scoreline, 4–3 to Blackpool, beggared belief.

As Harry Johnston led his team up the steps to receive the Cup from the Queen (he had first rushed to collect his teeth from the Blackpool reserve, Johnny Crosland), the accolades began. Derek Dooley, the brilliant centre forward who had lost a leg to gangrene just a few months before, commented that 'the FA Cup was won by a shrug of the shoulders'. Bob Ferrier in the *Daily Mirror* wrote that 'this was the ultimate in sport, the limit of human endeavour. I do not hope to see anything finer than this, and that includes the gallantry with which Bolton took their stunning defeat. It was a privilege to be there.' Geoffrey Green, in *The Times*, called Matthews a superb artist who 'paints, as it were, in water-colours and not oils … He has it within him to turn mice into horses and nothing into everything.' Even the greatest writers were unable to make sense of it for themselves.

The effect of the Cup Final on the British public was equally remarkable. It was to be expected that there would be a huge sense of relief and enthusiasm for the great man. What was not expected was the outburst

Stanley in action, Wembley, May 1953.

of affection for this reserved and gentle professional who had at last attained the pinnacle of his career. A letter from a Mr George Edgar of Crawley to the *Daily Mirror* was typical of the reaction: 'Stanley Matthews has become as much a part of this island as Loch Lomond or the Cliffs of Dover … There is something else that can be done and must be done – Sir Stanley Matthews! He is the shining example of a life's dedication to the sport which beyond all doubt is our national game.' Mr Edgar had to wait until 1965 before he got his wish. When the knighthood finally came, Matthews was still playing for Stoke City. He was the first professional footballer to be knighted, and even in the era of Sir Bobby Charlton, Sir Tom Finney and Sir Geoff Hurst he is still the only playing professional ever to have been so honoured.

Most people in the crowd on 2 May 1953 thought they were watching the

Stanley Matthews and Harry Johnston, the Blackpool captain, are chaired around the pitch by their team-mates after the match.

last great match of a brilliant career. Few realised that Matthews would carry on playing for another twelve seasons and in just six months' time would take part in an even more significant game at Wembley Stadium. He was one of the three great English professional sportsmen of the pre- and post-war era, and it was fitting that all three should reach the heights in the same year, the first full year of the new Elizabethan era. Stanley Matthews dominated the game of football as much as Gordon Richards dominated flat racing and probably even more than Len Hutton dominated cricket, but all three men achieved their lifetime's ambitions within the space of four months that summer.

The Australian cricketers, who were up against Hutton's side in 1953, had the opportunity of sampling all the sporting delights of that summer, and many of them took that opportunity. Neil Harvey, for example, was and still is a huge racing fan, and had his money on Pinza for the Derby even though his playing commitments meant he could not attend the meeting in person. On Cup Final day the Australians were playing at Leicester, so most of them were unable to get to the match. As Richie Benaud remembers, 'I didn't make it to Wembley even though I was the only player in the team who actually played soccer in Australia. I was twelfth man that day in the game against Leicestershire. My good luck was that Jack Walsh, the wonderful Australian spin bowler who played at Leicester, took us back to his place for dinner and to watch the Final on television. It was one of the most thrilling things I have ever seen. When Matthews started his runs down the right and then went looking for the ball, the atmosphere at Jack's place was electric, and we already knew the result!'

Blackpool have never scaled the heights again. Three years later they were runners-up to Manchester United, but they were no fewer than eleven points behind the champions, and never really serious challengers for the title. Since 1953 they have never gone beyond the quarter-finals of the Cup, and only once to the semi-finals of the League Cup. Bolton Wanderers, on the other hand, came back to Wembley five years later to take on Manchester United just three months after the Munich air crash. Yet again, public sentiment was overwhelmingly against them, but this time they won. Of the 1953 side, only two men, Nat Lofthouse and Doug Holden, would remain in the side five years on.

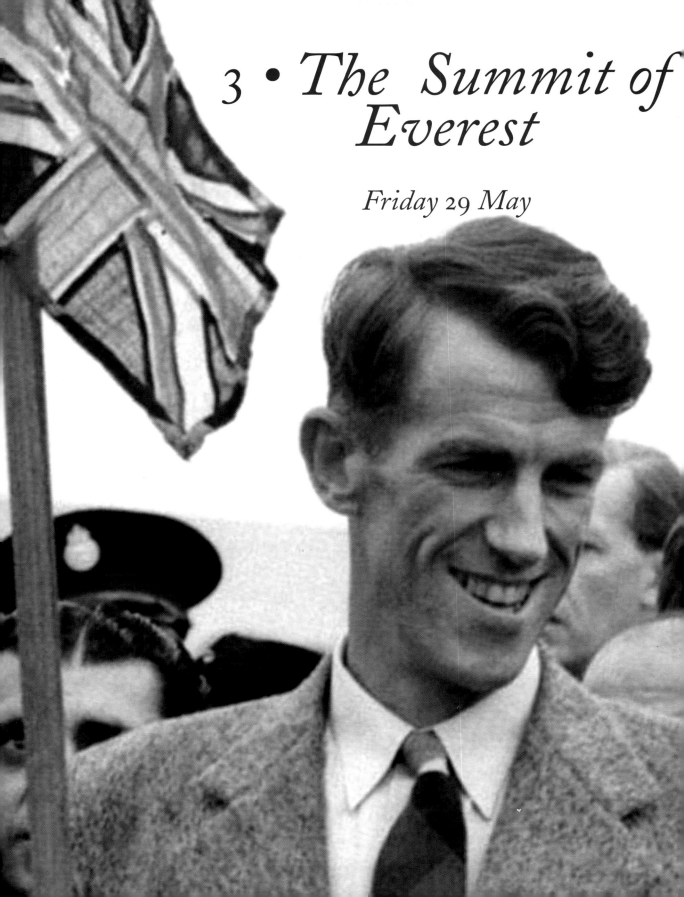

3 • *The Summit of Everest*

Friday 29 May

The crowds that lined the streets of London on Coronation Day expected the rain – after all, it was June in England – and they expected Imperial splendour as the leaders of the world, crowned heads and presidents alike, gathered for the ceremonies. The 30,000 people who spent the night in the Mall expected discomfort and they expected a bit of the wartime spirit that seems to emerge whenever the British people have to make the most of a difficult situation: it's a hybrid of their traditional reserve and a touch of mass hysteria, as the class barriers come tumbling down for a few hours or so.

What they did not expect was the news that made it to page six of *The Times* that morning, and which became headline news in the three London evening papers, the *Evening Standard*, the *Evening News* and the *Star*. 'Everest Climbed,' proclaimed *The Times* on the top right-hand corner of its front page. Page six confirmed the paper's exclusive scoop to the crowds packed on to the pavements and the statuary, and hanging out of the windows of all the houses, shops and hotels. The loudspeakers along the route were commandeered to relay the same magnificent story: a British expedition, led by Colonel John Hunt, had reached the summit of the highest mountain in the world.

The two men who actually stood on the roof of the world, at what was then thought to be 29,002 feet above sea level, were Edmund Hillary, a bee-keeper from New Zealand, and the Nepalese Sherpa Tenzing Norgay, two men whose lives had already revolved around the mountain for many years, but who for ever after would be the Men Who Climbed Everest.

The summit had been reached on 29 May, but news of the ascent took time to reach London because it first had to be taken by runners from the base camp at a monastery in the village of Thyangboche to Kathmandu. As *The Times* explained, 'Because the long journey from the mountain to Kathmandu could be covered only by runners on foot, several days had to elapse between the writing of despatches and their arrival in London. The suspense has been rewarded, if only by the apt timing of the announcement on the eve of the Coronation.' *The Times* had its own correspondent with the party, James Morris, who wrote the despatches carried by those hardy Nepalese 'runners on foot', so it was *The Times* that broke the news exclusively on 2 June. The other papers all followed as quickly as they could, although the *Daily Telegraph* of 3 June filled its front pages with these headlines: 'Elizabeth II is Crowned', 'Splendour In Abbey Seen By Millions', 'Queen 6 Times On Palace Balcony: Vast Crowds' and, inevitably, 'Bakerloo Chaos'. But no mention of Everest, Hillary or Tenzing on the front page.

It is difficult to say when planning for the successful assault on Mount Everest, the world's highest mountain, began. It was certainly well before 1953, and one could argue that the seed was sown in the minds of all mountaineers in the 1920s when two great climbers, George Mallory and Sandy Irvine, were lost as they approached the peak of Everest. It was Mallory who had given the famous response to the question, 'Why climb Everest?' 'Because it's there' was all the inspiration they and the climbers who followed in their footsteps needed.

Mount Everest is named after Sir George Everest (1790–1866), surveyor-general of India at the height of the Raj. Its Tibetan name is the rather more romantic Chomolungma, which means 'Goddess Mother of the Snows'. Western assaults on Mount Everest were not possible until the 1920s, when for the first time a reconnaissance party was allowed to reach Everest on the Tibetan side. This led to the first serious attempt to climb Everest, by a British expedition led by C. G. Bruce in 1922. The highest point they reached, climbing with oxygen, was around 27,300 feet, but the cost was high: seven sherpas were killed in an avalanche. Two years later, the Norton expedition reached 28,150 feet without oxygen before a final attempt was made by Mallory and Irvine, who were using oxygen. They were last seen at about 28,000 feet, still climbing in clear weather, but they never returned. There is no doubt that

Michael Westmacott tries out the open circuit oxygen equipment in Snowdonia in January, assisted by Tony Rawlinson, one of the reserves for the final team.

they died on Everest, but there was never any proof of whether they died before reaching the summit, or after. It was not until three-quarters of a century after he disappeared that Mallory's body was finally found on Everest, but even the discovery of his well-preserved corpse did little to solve the riddle of whether he made it to the top or not. Wishful thinking says yes but realism has to say no.

The next major expedition was mounted in 1933, led by Hugh Ruttledge. Three members of the party reached about 28,150 feet, the same height as had been achieved in 1924. One of these three men, Frank Smythe, later published an account of their ordeal. He and Eric Shipton spent two nights in a raging blizzard at 27,400 feet. Shipton fell sick, so Smythe went on alone. They had got this far without oxygen, without high-technology lightweight weatherproof clothing and without knowing what sort of terrain they were stepping into. The strength, bravery and sheer foolhardiness, bordering on lunacy, of these men is hard to imagine. Another who reached that height on this expedition, Wyn Harris, discovered an ice-axe on his way down at about 27,600 feet. It could only have belonged to Mallory or Irvine.

In 1936 Ruttledge led another expedition, but this was a failure largely because the monsoon season arrived early, and made climbing impossible. They abandoned any attempts to climb higher than the North Col, about 26,000 feet. Another expedition two years later was also cut short by the early monsoon, which forced the team to turn back at 27,200 feet.

The war intervened, and for over a decade no major attempts were made to climb Everest. Then in 1949 Nepal allowed foreigners into the country for the first time, and thus a new route to Everest was opened up. In 1950 an Anglo-American team made a brief reconnaissance of the mountain from the south, but they did not have enough time to achieve any real progress and, indeed, reported that they could not find a way to climb Everest from this new aspect. This report merely encouraged others to take a look, and in 1951 a team led by Eric Shipton, the veteran of Ruttledge's 1933 party and several other pre-war attempts, spent enough time there to be able to test out possible routes from the south. Their expedition was a remarkable success. Having gone with little expectation of finding a way to get to the top of this mysterious mountain, they came back not only with a possible route to the summit mapped out, but also with the experience of having

The complete Everest party with their high altitude Sherpas at Advanced Base Camp two days after Hillary and Tenzing had reached the summit.

climbed up one of the most difficult sections of their proposed route, through the West Cwm.

This new information was not only of interest to the British. Every climber in the world wanted to be the one to conquer the highest peak, and the Swiss in particular felt they could succeed. In 1952 a Swiss party fought their way through winter hardships to a position above 28,000 feet, roughly the same height, on a different part of the mountain, as Norton – and possibly Mallory and Irvine – had reached a quarter of a century earlier. One of the two men who reached that height was Tenzing Norgay. A few months later another Swiss party followed in their compatriots' footsteps, but similarly had to admit defeat. But all the time, the experience each party gained was being studied and learned from: the great mountain was slowly and reluctantly yielding up its secrets.

At roughly the same time that the Swiss were attempting to beat Everest, a British training expedition led by Eric Shipton was climbing in the Himalayas, not to have a go at Everest but to test out their equipment and to study the physiology of climbing and living at extreme altitude. By the time they came back, having climbed another Himalayan peak, Cho Oyu (26,860 feet), they had learnt a great deal about the effectiveness of their equipment – especially their oxygen systems – and had also found out what sort of men were required to make a successful attempt on this mountain. Suddenly Everest seemed climbable.

Getting two men to the top of Mount Everest is hardly less complicated than getting two men on to the surface of the moon and, to the sceptic, no less pointless. However, the point of the climb is not the issue: 'because it's there' is justification enough. The purpose of the expedition was to conquer Mount Everest, and that end result required meticulous planning, brave and skilful execution, and not a little luck.

The planning began in earnest on 1 September 1952, when Charles Wylie began work as the Organising Secretary of the expedition. The leader of the team, Colonel John Hunt, did not arrive in London to join Wylie and his embryonic organisation until six weeks later, and the complete party did not get together until 17 November, when there was a day of clothing measurements, division of responsibilities and renewal of old friendships. It was also a day on which the full glory of British Army bureaucracy revealed itself to the mountaineers.

The expedition was run jointly by the Alpine Club and the Royal Geographical Society, and it was they who chose John Hunt to be its leader. Henry Cecil John Hunt was born in 1910, so was already 42 when he was appointed leader. He had been mountaineering since 1925, when he climbed his first Alp. As a regular soldier, he had been seconded to the Indian police for much of the 1930s, which had given him ample opportunity to indulge his love of climbing. He took part in three Everest expeditions during that time. By 1952 he was a colonel on the general staff of HQ1 (British) Corps, with a wartime DSO and an urge to become involved in the latest attempt on Everest. His climbing pedigree made him a strong candidate to be leader; his organisational skills as a staff officer clinched the matter.

The party consisted originally of 10 climbers and a doctor, as well as a number of reserves. The Sherpas, who would be the ones to transport much of the equipment up to Base Camp and beyond, were not considered part of the team at this stage, and the one journalist, James Morris of *The Times*, had not yet been brought into the reckoning. The ten men were Hunt, Hillary and Wylie, George Band, Tom Bourdillon, Charles Evans, Alfred Gregory, George Lowe, Wilfrid Noyce and Michael Westmacott. The team doctor was Michael Ward. They were soon joined by Griffith Pugh, a physiologist from the Medical Research Council, and Tom Stobart, who was there to make a film of the expedition.

These 13 men (who became 14 when Morris joined and 15 when Tenzing was officially added to the climbing party) had between them a vast amount of mountaineering experience, of the Himalayas in particular. Tom Bourdillon, for example, who was recognised as perhaps the most technically brilliant climber in the party, was only 28 years old but had already climbed Cho Oyu with Eric Shipton, as had Charles Evans, who was in many ways the physical opposite of Bourdillon, being short and wiry as opposed to huge and bear-like. Evans had also worked as a surgeon at the Walton Hospital in Liverpool. His waiting lists must have been spectacularly long.

Alfred Gregory was another from Shipton's Cho Oyu venture. He was even smaller than Evans, and was the oldest member of the party, at 39, apart from Hunt himself. One of his roles was official photographer for the team. Gregory was a travel agent from Blackpool, an incongruous background for a leading mountaineer, but he more than anybody might

Tenzing Norgay at the summit of Everest on 29 May – the achievement of every mountaineer's dream.

have predicted the state of Everest half a century on: all tourists and trash among the snowfields. More conventional were the pedigrees of Michael Westmacott and George Band, past presidents of the Oxford University Mountaineering Club and its Cambridge counterpart respectively. Westmacott had served in the Royal Engineers at the end of the war, so had the military background to appeal to Hunt. Band, tall and, like Westmacott, bespectacled, was the baby of the party, just 23 when the team was chosen and with no Himalayan experience.

Charles Wylie had spent much of the war in a Japanese prisoner-of-war camp. He was a serving officer in the Brigade of Gurkhas, although his wartime internment had meant that he had had very little experience of climbing in the Gurkhas' home ranges. His attention to detail was remarkable. He proved to be the perfect Organising Secretary, making sure that no issue, however seemingly unimportant, was overlooked, and also satisfying Hunt with the quality of his work. This second part of his job might well have been the more onerous. Wilfrid Noyce, a schoolteacher, had been a brilliant Alpine climber before the outbreak of war, and during the war he had worked for a while with Hunt, training soldiers and airmen in mountain warfare and snow survival in Kashmir. Another schoolteacher was George Lowe, who had also been on Shipton's Cho Oyu expedition with his fellow New Zealander Edmund Hillary. Hillary kept bees in Auckland, a strange and poorly paid occupation for a mountaineer, but his reputation as a climber was already of the highest order. He had been climbing in New Zealand since his schooldays at Auckland Grammar School and, despite being badly burned in a wartime accident while he was with the Royal New Zealand Air Force, had taken part in many of the most important and difficult expeditions since the war. Hunt and Hillary knew each other's strengths and weaknesses well: they had conducted a lengthy correspondence on a wide variety of mountaineering issues for some time before they met.

These were the climbers selected for the greatest challenge left on earth. These were the men who would take the romantic dreams of millions of less adventurous, and certainly less fit, men and women with them to the top of the world. Yet the way they did it was in many ways so prosaic and so just plain organised that the romance was plucked from the achievement like feathers from a dead goose. The book that Hunt wrote about the conquest, *The Ascent of Everest*, is possibly the least enthralling account of any great athletic achievement ever written. He emphasises the planning, he details the organisation charts and every man's diet, he even reproduces memos written to all and sundry in the planning phase. But, being the British soldier that he is, he cannot bring himself to write more than a few words about the romance of the expedition, and he cannot revel in the excitement and adulation that his team's brilliant achievement brought to the people of Britain. The only time we sense the real thrill, as well as the hardships, of climbing in the Himalayas is in the one chapter written by Hillary, 'The Summit'. Half a century later, Hunt would have been an astronaut – a technocrat in an explorer's clothing.

The equipment they took with them fell into three main categories – their breathing equipment, their nutrition and their tents. We should also mention the 30-foot rope ladder they were given by the Yorkshire Ramblers Club 'to deal with any vertical ice pitches', as Hunt explained it: the sort of vertical ice pitch, one assumes, that Yorkshire Ramblers come across on an almost daily basis.

Breathing at 29,000 feet was something that had never been attempted before. Everyone was agreed that oxygen would be essential, the accepted wisdom being that at any height above about 27,000 feet the heart and respiratory system were likely to stop functioning without supplementary oxygen. Tests had been carried out on the Cho Oyu expedition, and details of how other campaigns had approached the problem were thoroughly picked over, but still no final decision had been made about whether to use a 'closed' oxygen system or an 'open' one. Without going into too much technical detail, the essential difference between the two options was that with the open system the climber inhaled the outside air enriched by added oxygen, and he breathed out into the atmosphere. With the closed system, the climber inhaled a high concentrate of oxygen from a breathing bag. He then exhaled through a soda lime canister, which absorbed the carbon dioxide and allowed the oxygen to go back round the circuit into the breathing bag. The closed system was much less well proven at high level, but what tests there had been seemed to show that this was the more efficient method of breathing at high altitude. But the expedition did not commit itself one way or the other. Officially it would rely on the open system, on the basis that it had the track record, at least up to 28,000 feet, but it is easy to read between the lines and detect a strong undercurrent of feeling that the closed system might prove to be the party's trump card. The key thing was to try to limit the weight of the system, whichever one was chosen. This was far easier said than done: the average weight of oxygen equipment carried by each climber was around 40 lbs. The closed system weighed 35 lbs with one cylinder attached and 47 lbs with two; the open system weighed 41 lbs with three cylinders. With only one cylinder attached the weight of the open system was reduced to 18 lbs, but the range of the climber was massively restricted.

All sorts of ideas were considered to find a more efficient way of transporting oxygen up the mountain. One ingenious suggestion was to fire the bottles of oxygen up the mountainside by means of a mortar, which would have to be more powerful than the two-inch variety already supplied to the party by both the Indian Army and the War Office. The disadvantages of this idea became clear when nobody could guarantee that the mortar could shoot straight enough to prevent the need for a high-level game of Hunt the Thimble whenever the bottles were fired up; there was also every likelihood that the bottles would break on impact, and a further danger that the noise of the mortars could set off avalanches. Aircraft of the day could not be flown at altitudes high enough to allow supplies to be dropped for climbers to pick up as they reached them, and anyway the final route was not yet known. Carrying the supplies up was the only possible option, and even on the very final assault, both open and closed systems were in use. The advantages and disadvantages of each would continue to be debated after 29 May.

One thing that in retrospect might have eased the problem a little would have been for the expedition to have smoked a little less. The problems of smoking and its effects on the lungs were not as well known in 1953 as they are 50 years on, but all the same it was quite an eye-opener to find on the list of official suppliers to the expedition no fewer than six purveyors of tobacco and cigarettes. Carreras Ltd, Imperial Tobacco (Ogden Branch), Richard Lloyd Ltd, Stephen Mitchell and Son, John Player and Sons and W. D. & H. O. Wills easily outnumbered the suppliers of stoves and cooking equipment (four), photographic equipment and materials (four) and soap (one).

The diet of the expedition was studied and prepared in the minutest detail. All sorts of tests were made beforehand, working out how to prepare the most efficient foods in the most efficient ways, to be eaten at the most efficient times. One need only glance at the list of suppliers to the party to realise that this was not a gourmet's paradise. Ready Mixes Co. Ltd supplied scone mix, A. Wander Ltd supplied Ovosport blocks, and Bovril Ltd supplied pemmican. This was a time of rationing in Britain, of course, so any diet would have been acceptable, but even the rum was bought on the same principle that was to get Neil Armstrong to the moon 16 years later — the lowest bid wins the contract. The rum was supplied by the Indian Army.

A thoroughly detailed menu of each day's meals for each man was drawn up, and the contents were packed carefully so that the climbers could work out which bit was breakfast and which bit was lunch, which box was for Thursday and which for Sunday. For Wylie, the Organising Secretary who had spent so many years in a prisoner-of-war camp, it must have seemed like luxury. For the ex-presidents of the Oxford and Cambridge University Mountaineering Clubs, it must have been less mouth-watering. Breakfast was the same every day — one 12-ounce tin of oatmeal biscuits, bacon, butter, jam, marmalade and cheese, along with 10 ounces of chocolate and two and a half ounces of sweets for the day's march — but the main meal of the day was a little more varied. Stewed steak only appeared twice a week (Thursday and Sunday), as did pork luncheon meat (Wednesday and Saturday). Friday was, of course, fish (salmon). Dessert was tinned fruit or 'rich cake' every day. Another vital issue was that of toilet paper, just five sheets per man per day, so it was probably fortunate that prunes were left off the menu. The institutionalised British public schoolboy and Army officer was coming into his own on the southern slopes of Mount Everest.

Yet Tenzing did not share this diet, preferring the Sherpa's traditional rice-based provisions, and he made it to the top as easily as Hillary. It cannot be denied that the diet worked, because the expedition was successful, but the legacy of this strict regime was not a wide range of tasty food ideas for future climbers. What the Everest expedition menus led to was the development of food science as a major part of any athlete's preparation, and this is perhaps the biggest lasting contribution that the 1953 expedition made to the sporting history of the second half of the twentieth century.

The tents were of a standard two-man design, with few specific adaptations for the extreme conditions on Everest. There was much discussion in memos before the party set out as to whether two-man tents were the ideal, but the consensus was that they were light enough to be easily portable and small enough to be pitched in a restricted space, yet still promoted the congeniality required in a team venture such as this. The tents were lined with nylon, which, the precise Hunt delighted in noting, gives 'an extra four degrees of warmth'. They also took with them two 12-man domed tents, which weighed around 50 kilograms, and one five-man pyramid tent at about 40 kilos, to be erected at the Advanced Base Camp. Hunt stated that 'our Sherpas were gregarious and found no discomfort in sleeping on the sardine-tin principle', which also provided for greater warmth in the same way that soldiers on both sides in the American Civil War used to sleep 'spooned', each man lying right up against the next like spoons packed in a drawer to keep as warm as possible. The record, reported by Charles Wylie, was 60 Sherpas sleeping in a 12-man tent, and eight in a two-man tent.

Tenzing, incidentally, held a different view about the tents. 'In the English expedition,' he said in an interview a few years after his climb, 'I

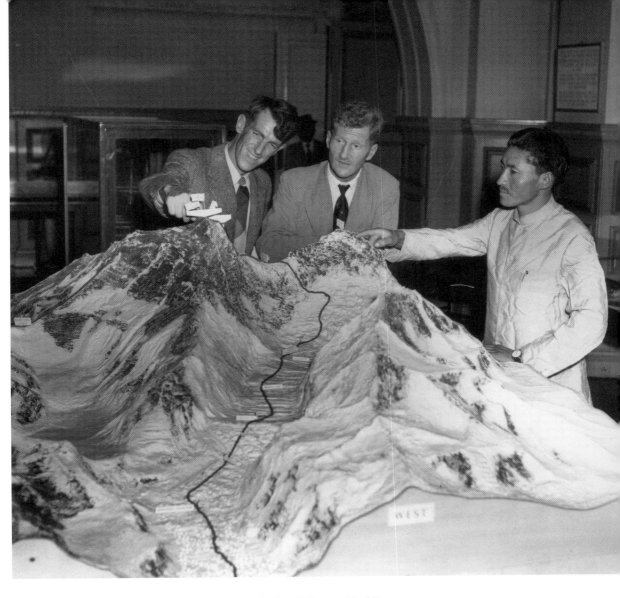

On 3 July, Hillary, Hunt and Tenzing explained to the Royal Geographical Society, sponsors of the expedition, how they reached the summit of Everest.

had to live alone in my tent until the last night when Hillary and I shared night-quarters. By the way, he was the only one who did. Other people, other customs. Nothing more to say about it.' Tenzing was not fully correct in this statement, as there are photographs of him sharing tents with other climbers during the final few days. All the same, he certainly felt that as a full member of the climbing team it was odd that he was not sharing the living arrangements of his fellow climbers. The tent that he and Hillary shared on the last night before the summit was an even smaller tent than the standard two-man issue: this 'assault tent' had to be as light as possible, and the final design proved to be barely half the weight of the six-kilo two-man tents. One of the big worries of the party before they reached Nepal was that there might never be quite enough tents to go round, so in a stream of further memos and meetings a complicated system of moving the tents up the mountain was worked out.

The planning period, which had begun on 1 September 1952, continued until early February 1953, a period of 23 weeks. This compares with the total period of less than 15 weeks that elapsed from the time the party left Kathmandu to begin the assault on Everest to the day they arrived back in Kathmandu, having achieved their goal. There is absolutely no doubt that Hunt's genius for planning was one of the most important reasons why this expedition succeeded where others had failed. It may not have been adventurous, but it repaid every moment spent examining every contingency.

On 5 February, the party held its final gathering in London, and a week later it set sail for India on SS *Stratheden*, bound for Bombay. Even on board ship the preparations continued, with Wylie, a fluent Nepali speaker, giving lessons in the language to the rest of the party. By 8 March the entire party and all the kit had made it to Kathmandu. This was the moment when the expedition began in earnest. Around 350 local bearers were recruited to transport the kit from Kathmandu to the base at the monastery at Thyangboche, a village 16 days' march away to the east and higher up into the Himalayas.

It was at the outset of this trek that Tenzing Norgay joined the party, meeting Hunt and many of the rest of the team in the garden of the British ambassador to Nepal, Christopher Summerhayes. Tenzing was at this time the most experienced Himalayan climber of all. He was 39 years old, and had begun his serious mountaineering career 18 years earlier as a porter on an Everest reconnaissance expedition in 1935. He had participated in every major Everest attempt from that time on, including most recently in 1952 when he had reached over 28,000 feet with the Swiss mountaineer Raymond Lambert. His health had been affected by that climb, and there had been some doubt about whether he would be able to join the British team, but by the time the party arrived in Nepal he was back to full fitness.

The Thyangboche headquarters was set up by the end of March. The monastery is about 12,000 feet above sea level, three times as high as any mountain in Britain but still less than half the altitude of Mount Everest. All the same, it was felt essential that everybody should become fully acclimatised to the altitude before beginning the main assault. Many days of marching, in teams led by Hunt, Hillary and Evans, were undertaken at heights of up to 20,000 feet. In this they were helped by generally favourable weather, with no sign of an early monsoon, which could have upset even the best laid plans (and these *were* the best laid plans). It was not until mid-April, therefore, that the first party arrived at the spot chosen for the Base Camp.

The operation called for a series of camps: Base Camp, on the Khumbu Glacier, was established at about 17,900 feet and Camp II was set up by Hillary, Lowe and Band by the Ice Fall on the Khumbu Glacier leading to the West Cwm. These three went on to establish Camp III at 20,200 feet, above the Ice Fall. Camp IV, the Advanced Base Camp, brought the party up to 21,200 feet, very much in the footsteps of the Swiss expedition of 12 months earlier. Camp V was to be set up at 22,000 feet as a stores depot at the foot of the Lhotse Face and Camp VI at 23,000 feet. Camp VII, at 24,000 feet, and Camp VIII, at 26,000 feet on the South Col, were to enable the final assault party to establish the final Ridge Camp IX, at 27,900 feet, from where the summit could be reached. The process of establishing these camps and bringing men and supplies up to them was to continue over a period of about four weeks, at the end of which they would be ready to climb Everest. The date by which everything was to be ready for the final assault was 15 May. The fact that so little went wrong during this period is a measure of the party's success. Logistically it was almost as great an achievement as it was in mountaineering terms.

The Ice Fall on the Khumbu Glacier was the first immediate obstacle in their path, and without doubt one of the most difficult barriers to cross on their way to the summit. Eric Shipton's party had been the first to negotiate this treacherous stretch of the glacier, in 1951, and their efforts in proving that the Ice Fall could be overcome gave heart to all those who came later. The Ice Fall, which Hunt called 'this staircase leading to the first floor of the mansion that is Everest', is a fault in the glacier which means that, instead of a steady upward ascent, climbers are faced with a precipice from which massive chunks of ice the size of an out-of-control truck split off and crash down hundreds of feet to the ground below. It is a frozen waterfall, and it must be crossed. Up and around is the only way. You cannot trust the ice flow at any time.

Hillary was of the opinion that the general condition of the Ice Fall was far more dangerous than it had been when Shipton had worked his way around it, but the success of the 1953 party in taming its horrors can be seen by the fact that despite almost constant comings and goings past the Ice Fall over a six-week period there were no accidents to report. The motto of another hero of 1953, the golfer Ben Hogan, springs to mind. 'If I miss one day's practice, I know it; if I miss two days the spectators know it, and if I miss three days the whole world knows it.' The preparation and practice put in by the Everest expedition was the reason why there were no disasters. The era of the athlete as an efficient machine was coming of age.

The final plans for the assault on the summit were drawn up on and around 14 May at the Advanced Base Camp. It was decided that there would be two assaults on the summit, the first, by Bourdillon and Evans using the closed breathing system, to take place on 26 May. If that failed, on 28 May a second attempt would be made by Hillary and Tenzing, using open-circuit oxygen. Bourdillon was the closed-circuit expert: he had been involved in the design and development of the system, but it had suffered a number of setbacks during the expedition, and Hunt was

Hillary, Tenzing and an ice-axe decorated with the Union flag.

not particularly optimistic about the chances for the first assault team. In the event, they achieved far more than Hunt had expected, but they still did not reach the very summit.

Bourdillon and Evans came within a few hundred feet of becoming world-famous names for all time. They failed partly because of the weather, which was not particularly favourable, and partly because of their breathing system. They climbed efficiently and well to around 28,000 feet, the same height reached by Tenzing and Lambert a year earlier, but it was at this stage that they realised they would need to change the soda-lime canisters that were an integral part of their breathing system. Each canister had a life of about three and a half hours, and they had by now been going for nearly three hours. They were then at the only place on the route where there was space enough to change canisters safely, but in changing them now they were limiting their total range, and also risking the possibility of the apparatus freezing up with the introduction of the new, cold canisters. In the end they did decide to change their canisters there, and despite Evans having trouble with his breathing apparatus, and the snow becoming more flaky and unsafe with each step, they pressed on to reach the South Summit of Everest, around 28,700 feet. This was the primary objective of this assault, and they achieved it brilliantly. They had now gone beyond the height that any man had reached before, but it was obvious they had too little oxygen to carry on. To reach the summit, which they could see across the final ridge, might take another three hours, and by the time they had come back along the same route there would have been no chance of getting back to camp safely. They had to abandon the attempt, having all but reached their goal.

When finally they made it back to Camp VIII on the South Col, they were able to describe the route in detail to Hillary and Tenzing, and it was this extra information, along with the open-circuit breathing systems, that made the final attempt a success. But the next morning, 27 May, dawned to strong winds and extreme cold. At the camp, there were ten men hoping to help mount the second attempt: Hillary, Gregory, Lowe, Hunt, Evans, Bourdillon, Tenzing and three Sherpas, Ang Temba, Ang Nyima and Pemba Norbu. It did not take long for Hunt to realise that it would be suicidal to make an attempt on the summit in such powerful winds and at temperatures of around minus 25 degrees centigrade, but they still had to prepare for the climb to the Ridge Camp from where Hillary and Tenzing would make their assault. Matters were not helped by the sickness of Ang Temba and the exhaustion of Bourdillon and Evans after their exertions of the previous day. Hunt decided to accompany Evans, Bourdillon and Ang Temba back to Camp VII, leaving the other six up on the South Col to sit out the storm all day. The situation looked pretty hopeless. The sense of isolation, of discomfort and of despair as they watched their leader go down the mountain was almost tangible. They were so close to the goal that everybody had been striving for – after all, Evans and Bourdillon had seen it – but now it looked as though it would be taken from their grasp by the forces of nature, over which they had no control. Maybe Everest was truly unclimbable after all.

When the party awoke the next morning, 28 May, the wind was still blowing strongly, making an immediate attempt as impossible as it had been the day before. To make matters worse, they learnt that Pemba had been sick all night and was in no state to carry on. With only two of four Sherpas left in the team, the party had to rethink how much they could carry up to the Ridge Camp, which involved unpacking their kit and reluctantly deciding how much to leave behind. In 25 degrees of frost neither the mind nor the muscles can cope easily with such decisions. Then, of course, they had to repack their rucksacks with what they could not do without.

But then the Goddess Mother of the Snows relented. At around 8 a.m. the wind died down, and the sky cleared. It would be possible to move that day. Within the hour Lowe, Gregory and Ang Nyima set out for the Ridge Camp, carrying over 15 kilos each. Tenzing and Hillary stayed behind with the sick Pemba, but their purpose was not merely to act as nursemaids. They needed to conserve their energy for the final assault, and therefore they were waiting until the path to Ridge Camp had been cut by the three in front of them, so they could climb as efficiently and as quickly as possible. An hour after the lead trio had set out, Hillary and Tenzing left for the Ridge, leaving the ailing Pemba on his own.

After a couple of hours' climbing, during which they had to take regular evasive action as chips of ice rained down on them from above where Gregory and Lowe were cutting a path across the South-East Ridge, Hillary and Tenzing caught up with their companions. Nearby were the remains of the Swiss tent which Tenzing and Lambert had used a year before. On that occasion the climbers had had to spend the night without sleeping bags, but at least this time the effort of bringing the equipment up would mean that the most basic of comforts would be provided. However, they now realised that this ridge was not high enough to be effective as a starting point for the next day's climb. They needed to move up another 150 feet or so, to where John Hunt and Da Namgyal had made a dump of further kit a couple of days earlier. When they got there, they found that even this site, at 27,350 feet, was too low. They decided to move still higher up, carrying not only what they had brought up with them in the morning but also many of the vital items that Hunt had left behind. This meant that each man was now carrying a load of between 25 and 30 kilos, with all that that implied in terms of effort and balance at such an altitude. For two hours more they climbed, but when they reached a height they considered close enough to the summit to make the next day's target attainable, they could not at first find a level ridge on which to pitch a tent. It was only thanks to Tenzing's memory of the previous year's climb with the Swiss party that they could traverse some steep slopes to their left and find a small and relatively level area to pitch the tent. They were now at around 27,900 feet. This was Camp IX.

It was now time for Lowe, Gregory and Ang Nyima to make their way down again, which they did as quickly as possible so as to be back at the lower camp, where the sick Pemba was still waiting, well before nightfall. Hillary and Tenzing watched them go with mixed emotions. Hillary checked their very limited oxygen supplies and calculated that there was still a chance that they could succeed. Sleeping with oxygen, however, would have to be restricted to four hours each at one litre of oxygen per minute. This was hardly the best way of preparing for the morrow, the day on which the world would, with luck, finally be at their feet. As the sun set, they crawled into their tent, put on every item of clothing available and squeezed into their sleeping bags. They drank as much liquid as they could and tucked in to whatever was left of the food stocks so carefully and scientifically planned all those months ago in the calm of London. What they managed to find was soup, sardines on biscuits, tinned apricots, dates, jam and honey.

At four o'clock in the morning, it was time to begin the day. Hillary and Tenzing got their cooker going and set to breakfast with as much gusto as one can manage at 27,900 feet when confronted by nothing more exciting than a tin of sardines and yet more biscuits. Looking on the bright side, it was at least their last tin of sardines. They also made sure that they took in as much liquid as they could – a mixture of lemon juice and sugar – to prevent dehydration and to give them the energy they would surely need for their momentous day's work.

It is worth noting what Hillary wore to reach the summit, a clothes list carefully compiled for the official account. On his head he wore a skull cap, to which his oxygen mask was attached. He also wore a down hood and a windproof hood, and protecting his eyes was a pair of sunglasses in aluminium frames. On his torso, he wore a string singlet under a short-sleeved woollen vest, which in turn was underneath a long-sleeved Shetland pullover. Over this he wore a woollen tartan shirt described as 'New Zealand type', though it is not clear whether this describes the shirt or the tartan. This was covered by the down jacket attached to the down hood, which was underneath a windproof jacket attached to the windproof hood. Both jackets were zipped to the neck. Six layers of clothing to combat Everest's deadly cold.

His lower half was encased in short cellular underpants followed by long woollen underpants. Over these he wore down trousers with elasticated ankles, and over them windproof trousers with elastic straps under the insteps. Only four layers of protection for the legs, two pairs of socks and high-altitude boots for the feet, and three pairs of gloves (silk, woollen and windproof in ascending order). Around his waist was threaded a thin nylon line on to which the climbing rope was clipped. He carried an ice-axe, and in the large pouch pocket at the front of his windproof jacket there was a camera, spare gloves and 'a few English coins which just happened to be there'. On top of it all, he carried his open-circuit oxygen equipment, which weighed almost 15 kilos. While history does not record in such detail exactly what Tenzing was wearing that fateful day, we must assume that he had as many layers of clothing, even if it seems less likely that one was a New Zealand tartan shirt. The temperature was minus 27 degrees centigrade.

At 6.30 a.m. they began the climb. They took a few deep breaths of oxygen, looked up at the South Summit and set off. It took them two and a half hours, but by nine o'clock they had reached the place where Bourdillon and Evans had stood a couple of days before. The difference was that this time the climbers did have enough oxygen to continue. Hillary estimated that with one full bottle – 800 litres – left, they had perhaps four and a half hours. It would be a close-run thing, but it was certainly possible.

They left the South Summit, and immediately realised that the Goddess Mother of the Snows was smiling on them. As they made their way along the ridge to the summit the snow beneath them, never before trodden by man, proved to be firm. It was a narrow ridge, but passable with care, if care is an adequate word to describe the way in which they had to traverse a narrow snow and ice-packed ridge of rock with a sheer drop of over 10,000 feet for the unwary. Hillary would cut a 40-foot line of steps while Tenzing belayed the rope. Then he would return the compliment, using his ice-axe as an anchor for the line and allowing Tenzing to move up to join him. Progress was slow but steady. Hillary remembers enjoying the climb, even though there was no room for error or lapses in concentration.

At about 10 a.m., one hour after they left the South Summit, they hit a major obstacle: a 40-foot rock step, which at first sight seemed smooth and without holds, and too difficult for men to overcome at 28,000 feet and more. Fortunately, upon further investigation, Hillary found a narrow crack running upwards, and using all the skills he had learnt in the New Zealand Alps and on Cho Oyu he cramponed his way backwards up it. It was the most difficult part of the final assault, but when Hillary reached the top there was a narrow ledge, on to which he collapsed gratefully, gasping for air. Within a few minutes Tenzing had joined him, and as they lay there like two beached whales they both began to feel that now they would reach the summit. After a brief respite, they set out once more, Hillary again cutting the steps as Tenzing belayed the rope. It became a grim struggle, men against mountain, with the men feeling ever more sure of a hard-won victory. Then suddenly the ridge stopped rising. Almost without knowing it, they had made it. It was 11.30 a.m. on Friday 29 May 1953, five hours since they had left the Ridge Camp.

Which of the two was the first man to step on to the summit of Everest? At first the question was coyly sidestepped, with neither wishing to take more of the credit than the other. Hillary's officially published account simply says, 'A few more whacks of the ice-axe in the firm snow and we stood on top.' Tenzing's account states, 'At last we stood on the top of the world, Hillary and I hugging each other the best we could with our inconvenient equipment.' From the description of the way they had climbed the final section, the logical conclusion was that Hillary got there first, but it was not until 1955 that Tenzing confirmed in an interview that Hillary had been the first to reach the eyrie of the Goddess Mother of the Snows. Many years later, after Tenzing had died, Hillary confirmed this by saying, 'I moved on to a flattish exposed area of snow with nothing but space in every direction. Tenzing joined me, and we looked around in wonder.' In wonder indeed, at a view that no man had known before, under (or was it above?) beautiful clear skies with the wind at manageable levels. Below them there was the South Col and the Rongbuk Glacier, the peaks of Changtse and the unclimbed Makalu, Lhotse and Lho La. In the distance glistened Kangchenjunga,

the third highest mountain in the world, Chomo Lonzo, their training ground Cho Oyu, Pumori and Gyachung Kang.

They stayed at the summit for 15 minutes, long enough for Tenzing to bury some gifts to the Buddhist deities who inhabit the top of Mount Everest. He left a few biscuits (no doubt he'd been trying to get rid of them for days), some chocolate and a blue pen that his daughter Nima had given him to take to the top of the mountain. Hillary put beside them a crucifix which John Hunt had given him two days earlier to take to the top, and then took some photographs, including one of Tenzing with his ice-axe acting as flagpole to the flags of Britain, Nepal, India and the United Nations. It is that image which has become the symbol of the conquest, the photograph which appeared in every newspaper and every magazine that reported the climb, then and later.

They could not delay at the top. The oxygen supply was limited, they were both very tired after the exhilaration of their triumph and they had to get going as quickly as possible. As it turned out, their progress down was much faster than they had expected. When Evans and Bourdillon had looked across the ridge from the South Summit, they had estimated it could take three hours to reach the summit proper from there, and two more to come back. In fact, Hillary and Tenzing did the journey to the top in under two and a half hours and took barely one hour to get back. They pressed on to arrive back at their tent at Camp IX by 2 p.m., so the journey that took five hours altogether on the way up was completed in only just over two hours on the way down.

Tenzing brewed up a sweet lemonade drink on the stove and then, tired almost beyond understanding, they set off again down towards Camp VII. Their complete exhaustion was hardly surprising, but it hit home when George Lowe and Wilfrid Noyce met them a few hundred feet above Camp VII with hot soup and emergency oxygen. They were simply too tired to acknowledge their team-mates' overwhelming excitement when they told them they had made it. The four staggered back to camp, where Hillary and Tenzing collapsed into their sleeping bags.

Conquering Everest is one thing: scooping the world with the story is quite another. It was not until well into the next day, 30 May, that Hillary and Tenzing arrived back at last at Camp IV, almost 8,000 feet below the summit, where the rest of the party were waiting for them. The celebrations that ensued when the news of the success was relayed were very un-British. 'There were shouts of acclamation and joy. Handshakes – even, I blush to say, hugs – for the triumphant pair,' wrote Hunt. The significance of the achievement is most clearly defined in the image of a 42-year-old British Army colonel hugging a New Zealander and a Nepalese on the slopes of the mountain. However sheepish the hugs might have been, they were hugs nevertheless, and in 1953 that was something unprecedented in British upper-middle-class social circles.

At Camp IV, after all the hugs and handshakes, Hillary and Tenzing were able to relax at last, to eat something more substantial than sardines on dry biscuits (for Hillary it was an omelette) and to tell the group their story. James Morris, *The Times'* special correspondent, took copious notes. When Hillary had finished both his tale and his omelette, Morris, guided by Westmacott, set off for Base Camp to write and publish the account. It was necessary to get the good news to London as quickly as possible, and yet to keep it as secret as possible until it reached there, so that *The Times* would indeed scoop the world. While Morris was writing his despatch at Base Camp for the runners to take to Kathmandu for onward transmission to London, a radio message was sent to the British ambassador in Nepal, in whose garden the party had gathered before setting out for Base camp. The message to Christopher Summerhayes read, 'Bad snow, failed 29th.' This, in their prearranged code, actually meant 'Hillary and Tenzing succeeded 29th', or in Edmund Hillary's more colourful words to his fellow climbers, 'We knocked the bastard off.'

Morris's full despatch was sent by runners who covered the route from Thyangboche Monastery to Kathmandu in two days (it had taken the team 16 days to march out at the beginning of the assault). The report was radioed to London in time for *The Times* of 2 June, Coronation Day, to be published with a special headline in the top right-hand corner of the front page: 'Everest Climbed'. Those were the days when the front page of *The Times* was entirely given over to births and deaths and personal notices – the news was all on the inside, so it had to be a very major story to merit even a mention on the front page. The conquest of Everest was just such a story. Morris, who in those days admitted to being almost too ambitious for success, had succeeded momentously, his brilliant final despatch 'from our special correspondent' breaking the news to the crowds who lined the streets of London in the rain, waiting for the Coronation coach to come past.

The team that had provided this news was meanwhile still up at Base Camp, in the latter stages of bringing down all its equipment. After their supper, they tuned their wireless into All India Radio for the news of the Coronation and were amazed to hear the announcer say, 'The wonderful news broke in London last night that Everest has been climbed by the British expedition.' They had no idea that Morris, now on his way to Kathmandu a few days behind the runners, could have got the full story to London quite so quickly. The reaction of the crowds in London was one of excitement upon excitement: after all the horrors of war, the new Elizabethan age was already putting Britain and its Commonwealth back on top, both literally and figuratively. The reaction of the climbers at Base Camp was one of equal astonishment and excitement as they listened further. The Queen, the Duke of Edinburgh and the Prime Minister had sent telegrams of congratulation (which had not, of course, yet arrived at Base Camp), and crowds in London were cheering the cold, exhausted but triumphant band of men sitting in a large tent almost three and a half miles up the side of a mountain. That cold, exhausted but triumphant band cracked open another bottle of rum and toasted the Queen. Her Majesty's telegram had asked the British ambassador to convey 'to Colonel Hunt and all members of the British expedition my warmest congratulations on their great achievement in reaching the summit of Mount Everest'. The Queen's emphasis on the Britishness of the expedition was not surprising – after all, it was British-funded and organised even if no Briton had actually reached the summit. Sir Winston Churchill was even more nationalistic in his telegram: 'My congratulations on this

The successful team on arrival at London Airport where a large crowd gave them a
heroes' welcome. Left to right: Alf Gregory, Griffith Pugh, Edmund Hillary, John Hunt,
Michael Ward and Tenzing Norgay.

memorable British achievement, in which the whole world has been interested for so many years.' The whole achievement, it was clear, was made greater by virtue of the fact that the whole world had been trying but only a British team had succeeded. The British team called for a runner to carry messages of thanks back to Kathmandu, and thence by telegram to Buckingham Palace and 10 Downing Street. They began to plan their return to England. Only now did they decide that Hillary and Tenzing should come too.

They reached their base at the Buddhist monastery of Thyangboche two days later. When Hunt told the head of the monastery that his team had climbed Mount Everest, the abbot did not believe him, merely contenting himself with congratulating the team on 'nearly reaching the summit of Chomolungma'. But they had reached the summit. They had the photographs to prove it. A far less sceptical recipient of the news was Mrs Percy Hillary, Edmund's mother, who was told in Auckland of her son's success. 'He told me when he was twenty years old that some day he would climb Everest.' It had taken him 14 years, but he had done it.

It is hard to imagine today how great an impact this intrinsically pointless feat had on the psyche of the British people in 1953. The party landed back at Heathrow on 3 July, 'where they received a great welcome', as *The Times* captioned its photograph of the team at the steps of their aircraft, a rather embarrassed-looking Hunt at the front waving a Union Jack. Hunt and Hillary were knighted at once, and Hillary and Tenzing were fêted wherever they went that summer. Their feat was such that their names remain two of the most instantly recognisable of the twentieth century, alongside the likes of Charles Lindbergh, Roger Bannister, Yuri Gagarin and Neil Armstrong.

Fifty years on, Mount Everest is a bit of a pussy cat – or, more accurately, it is a caged tiger that you treat as a pussy cat at your peril. It is still a killer, despite our increasing familiarity with its habits and moods. It is now one of the main sources of foreign income for Nepal and an overused tourist trap. The Nepalese government charges several thousand dollars to every person who sets foot on Everest, and Sherpas can earn as much as $2,500 each season, 10 times the national average income in what is one of the poorest countries in the world. Some six or seven hundred people have reached the top, men and women, young and old, even an American with an artificial leg. At least one Sherpa has climbed it 10 times. In May 2001, no fewer than 40 people went on a package holiday that took them to the top of the mountain. The congestion at the top was so great that one of the party said it was more like a supermarket check-out than wild mountainside. The litter on the mountain is now a major hazard. It is reckoned by some environmentalists that there are up to 100 tons of rubbish littering the sides of Mount Everest, not to mention maybe 100 corpses. The Mother of the Snows is a powerful and unforgiving goddess.

In 1953, however, Everest represented one of the last great physical challenges on the Earth, and reaching the summit was the crowning achievement of Coronation Year. The success of John Hunt and his team may have been prosaically planned and scientifically carried out, but it brought out the poetry in all our souls. It was pure adventure for adventure's sake, and it was wonderful.

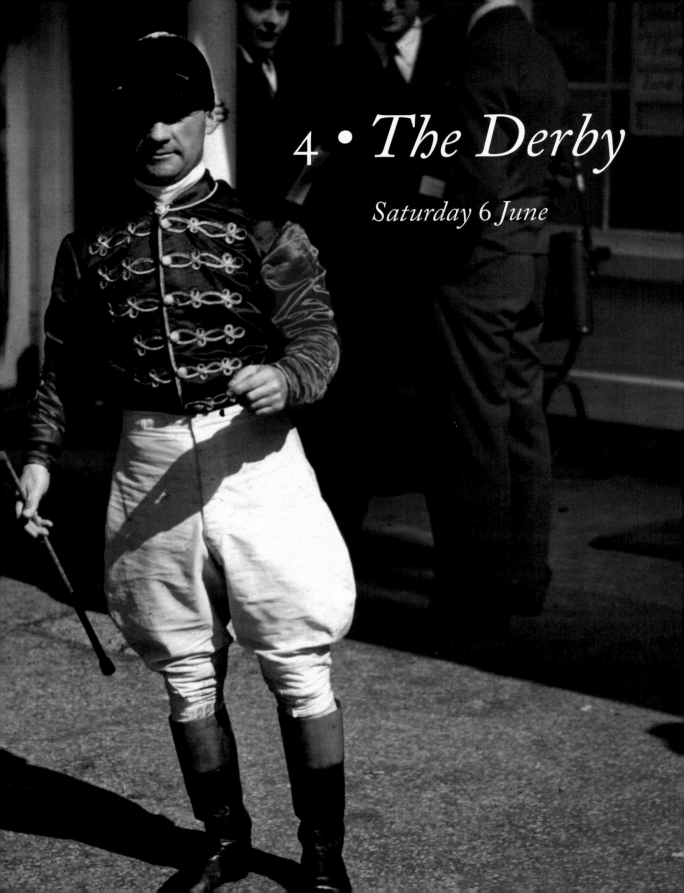

4 • *The Derby*

Saturday 6 June

J ust four days after the Coronation, five days since the news of the conquest of Everest had reached England and barely a week since Gordon Richards' knighthood had been announced, it was time for the great flat race of the year, the Derby. Unlike Coronation Day, which had been wet, cold and uncomfortable for the millions gathered on the streets of London, Derby Day dawned clear and bright. The new Queen was not known to be a great follower of sport unless horses were involved, but when they were her horses her interest was passionate.

For the greatest day of her sporting year, the skies were a deep clear blue. The crowds making their way to Epsom Downs were in a happy mood, the early summer sun promising to dry out the ground on the common land where many of the spectators would spend the afternoon. Derby Day is an accidental mixture of proletarian pleasure and upper-class enthusiasms: top hats and morning suits mixing with fairground hucksters and day-tripping coach parties. Tipsters, pickpockets, noblemen and merchant bankers all have their place in the day's festivities, which is as much a celebration of Britain at play as a world-renowned race meeting.

Preparations for the 1953 Derby were no different from those of any other year. The real work began months ahead of race day, which in Coronation Year was a Saturday rather than the customary Wednesday. For Gordon Richards, Britain's most successful flat jockey of all time, it could be argued that the 1953 Derby began for him in 1924, when he rode for the first time in the great Classic. By June 1953, he had passed his forty-ninth birthday. He had ridden well over 4,500 winners in his career, including 13 Classic winners, but despite having won about 2,000 more races than anybody else in the history of the British turf, he had never won the Derby in 27 attempts. The nearest he had come was second place, three times. This was a man who had been Champion Jockey 25 times, in other words every year from 1925 until 1953 with the only exceptions being in 1926, when he was out with tuberculosis, 1941, when he broke a leg, and 1930, when Freddie Fox became the only jockey ever to deny him the champion jockey title fair and square, beating him by one win. So in the twilight of his career Richards' will to win the Derby burned as brightly as ever as he determined to shake off the unwanted title of the greatest jockey never to have won the world's greatest flat race.

In the Coronation Honours List, published on 1 June, it was announced that Gordon Richards was to receive a knighthood. It was the practice at the time that the title 'Sir' could not be used until the recipient had actually been knighted, so Richards was not yet Sir Gordon. However, it was sufficiently rare for an active sportsman to receive a knighthood that everybody assumed it would not be long before the great man retired from racing. In an interview published to mark his honour, Richards noted, 'I have now been riding for 33 years and cannot continue indefinitely. I shall have to consult the owners who retain me before making a final decision, but I suppose I shall retire at the end of this season, or perhaps next year.' He went on to add, 'You know my Derby luck, but I am hoping the turn is not far off.' If, by his own admission, this was likely to be his final Derby, the turn in his luck had to be very soon.

A day or two after this interview was published, and two days before the Derby, the 1953 Oaks was run over the same course. If the punters were looking for a good omen, this was not one. Richards, who had already won the Oaks twice before, came second on the Aga Khan's Kerkeb, behind Ambiguity with Joe Mercer up. Mercer was then an apprentice, so a win in the Oaks was a bonus in his fledgeling career. He was booked to ride a rank outsider, Gala Performance, in the Derby.

'Sir Gordon was the most competitive rider I ever rode against,' says Jimmy Lindley, who as a young jockey in 1953 was riding in his first Derby. 'Only Lester Piggott and Tony McCoy can even compare with Gordon's will to win.' In 2002, the racing world was agog as Tony McCoy first approached and eventually passed Sir Gordon's 1947 total of 269 winners in a season, but the two men's achievements cannot be compared. Richards was a flat-race jockey, McCoy is not. You might as well compare the record of Ed Moses over hurdles with Michael Johnson on the flat, or Michael

Schumacher in cars with Carl Fogarty on bikes: the comparison is invalid. Is Michael Atherton a better sportsman than Bobby Charlton because he played more times for England? What is more, Richards rode in far fewer races than McCoy to achieve his 269 winners (one of 12 seasons in which he rode over 200 winners). We should not detract from A. P. McCoy's amazing achievement, which has not broken Richards' record but he has set a mark that future jump jockeys will do well to match.

Gordon Richards was an immensely popular man, both with those inside the racing world – the trainers, owners and fellow jockeys – and those on the outside who loved to bet on him. Perhaps only the bookies had reason to be less than affectionate towards him. Over the years they had lost a lot of money as Richards rode home winner after winner, and only in the Derby each year had they had a chance to make a little of it back. Richards had dark hair and beetle eyebrows and looked as though smiling did not come naturally to him. He was always a tiny man (when fully grown he barely reached five feet), but still managed to look authoritative and forbidding. The looks belied the man. He commanded great respect from his fellow jockeys and from the rest of the racing world for his astonishing achievements in over 30 years in the saddle, but he was not unapproachable or difficult. 'He was an absolutely charming man,' says Sir Peter O'Sullevan. 'Whatever he'd done, he would have been a success.'

The public support for Richards was genuine, perhaps because he had achieved his success despite a rather modest background. He had no real trouble with his weight, so the idea of being a jockey came to him at a very young age, though his only riding experience was on pit ponies in his native Shropshire. When he was 15 he saw an advertisement for stable lads, which resulted in him being taken on by the trainer Martin Hartigan. A year later he had his first ride, and the following summer, on 31 March 1921 at Leicester, he rode his first winner, Gay Lord. He was not quite 17 years old. It was said that after this win, during which the horse had meandered all over the course, Gay Lord's owner asked the jockey why he had taken such a circuitous route. Richards' reply was, 'The horse really wanted a mile and a half.'

The Queen and the Duke of Edinburgh talk to Gordon Richards just before the Derby.

His riding style was unusual. As Sir Peter O'Sullevan says, 'He was not a natural. He developed by application. By all precepts of horsemanship, he should not have been successful.' He rode on a long rein, and gripped his mount with his knees, which gave him the exceptional ability to turn in the saddle without unbalancing his horse, but it was his determination that set him apart. Jimmy Lindley put it succinctly: 'They used to say that a cowboy could ride a horse for a hundred miles before resting, but an Apache would get the horse up and ride it for another fifty. Gordon was an Apache. I still feel very honoured to have ridden against an icon of his calibre.' But despite this burning desire to win, he was very popular among his fellow jockeys, a doyen of the weighing room, a natural storyteller and a great stickler for the etiquette of riding.

The horse he had decided to ride in the Coronation Year Derby was Sir Victor Sassoon's Pinza, trained by Norman Bertie. Pinza has proved himself in retrospect to be one of the better Derby winners of the second half of the twentieth century, but to many expert eyes this large bay colt looked more suited for the Cheltenham Gold Cup than the Derby. His breeder, Fred Darling, described him as 'more like a Suffolk Punch than a racehorse'. The measurements of the entire field, as published in The *Sporting Life*, showed that Pinza's girth was far larger than any of his rivals, and he was also the longest from hip to hock. As the *Bloodstock Breeders' Review* noted, 'by any standards he is a substantial horse physically'. In the paddock at every race, he dominated the other runners.

Pinza's development from Suffolk Punch to Derby winner was gradual. Fred Darling, who had bought Pinza's dam, Pasqua, when she was in foal in 1949, put him up for sale at Tattersall's July Sales of 1951, where he was bought by Sir Victor Sassoon for 1,500 guineas. Sir Victor, who had spent hundreds of thousands of pounds on bloodstock over the years, thus acquired his greatest horse of all at a bargain price. Gordon Richards, a close friend of Darling, had seen Pinza as a yearling, but neither man thought at the time that the colt would amount to much. But Sir Victor placed his ungainly new purchase with trainer Norman Bertie, Darling's right-hand man over many years, and it was he who brought out the horse's hidden talents. The two-year-old star of Bertie's stable at the beginning of 1952 was a horse called Fountain, on which Richards came second in the Champagne Stakes at Doncaster that year, and which he considered to be a very fine prospect. However, in a six-furlong trial with several stable companions Fountain, ridden by the champion jockey, was well beaten by Pinza. Richards said afterwards, 'From that moment I knew the big chap was a real racehorse.' At the end of the 1952 season Pinza won the Dewhurst Stakes, and despite an injury in winter training he won the Newmarket Stakes in May 1953, easing up. The injury had meant that Pinza was not in good enough condition to contest the Two Thousand Guineas, so he missed that race, but to Richards things were looking good. 'I liked Pinza when he won the Newmarket Stakes so easily,' he remarked a few days before the Derby, 'and I have liked him even more in subsequent gallops.'

This kind of statement carried a great deal of weight with the punters. Richards never felt that he could have done any more than he did in previous attempts to win the Derby, so when he spoke of fancying the chances of his latest mount people took notice. The reasons he gave for losing in his first 27 attempts were simple: 'Some of the horses were non-stayers, one or two were faint-hearted, others plainly not good enough and a few just second or third best in their years.' A few times he had chosen the wrong horse from the stable, but he had never, in his opinion, ridden the wrong race. The racegoers agreed. The issue of Pinza's size – to quote Jimmy Lindley, 'He was so burly that he might not come down Tattenham Hill' – was not enough to put off the vast majority of punters, especially those who only bet once or twice a year. On the morning of the Derby, Pinza was installed as the favourite.

Pinza's main rival, at least in the press, was Aureole, trained by Captain Cecil Boyd-Rochfort and ridden by Harry Carr. What made the rivalry between Aureole and Pinza so poignant and the day so exciting, however, was that Aureole was owned by the newly crowned Queen herself. The chesnut colt had been bred by the Queen's late father, King George VI, at the Sandringham Stud, and was the first real Derby hope for a royal owner since Edward VII's Minoru won in 1909 and George VI's Big Game had started favourite for the 1942 version of the race, run at Newmarket because of the war. Racegoers certainly wanted Gordon Richards to win after years of trying, but they also wanted a royal winner to mark the start of the second Elizabethan Age. They could not have both.

The Queen's trainer, Captain Boyd-Rochfort, was a tall, handsome and immaculately dressed Irishman whose natural expression was one of haughty disdain. One contemporary report noted that 'he has in full measure the charm and manner for which his countrymen are famous, though he may quite rightly be a little discriminating in its application'. He was a Freemason, a pillar of the racing establishment and a confidant

Sir Gordon Richards in the royal colours – the colours he was wearing in his final race in 1954, but significantly not on Derby Day in 1953.

of the new Queen, but not an easy man to get to know. He was, however, a very good trainer, and had enjoyed considerable success with the royal horses in the past few years. So there was a great deal of money on Aureole as well, because in the public mind the view was that if Richards could not win, then Her Majesty should.

Aureole was no average horse. He was a son of Hyperion, the winner of both the Derby and the St Leger in 1933. Hyperion won the Derby in the very fast time of two minutes 34 seconds, the fastest time recorded to that date and only twice beaten since then, by Mahmoud in 1936 who clipped two tenths of a second off Hyperion's time and Lammtarra in 1995 who set a new record of two minutes 32.31 seconds. Aureole was a very fast horse too, but had a tendency to show his nerves, which often led to him breaking out in a sweat in the paddock. Earlier in 1953, he had been beaten by Nearula in the Two Thousand Guineas, but easily won the Derby Trial Stakes at Lingfield Park, which Tulyar had won in 1952 before going on to take the Derby as well. If his temperament held, his backers' money would not be misplaced.

Captain Boyd-Rochfort also trained another highly fancied horse, Premonition, ridden by Eph Smith. Premonition was one of seven colts in the field who had won that season over the full 12 furlongs, and was highly fancied, having already won the Blue Riband Trial Stakes at Epsom as well as the Great Northern Stakes at York. His appearance in the paddock before the big race only enhanced his backers' view that this was the Boyd-Rochfort horse to go for: he looked the part absolutely, being neither as big as Pinza nor as excited as Aureole. When the tape went up to start the race, Premonition was joint favourite with Pinza, at 5–1. Aureole started at 9–1.

There were many other horses in the race that had serious backing and of the 27 runners, few could be dismissed as also-rans. Nearula, bred in Yorkshire, had looked the pick of the two-year-olds in 1952, and began the 1953 season in dominant form, easily outclassing the rest of the field to win the Thirsk Classic Trial Stakes by the wide margin of six lengths on 18 April, and then the Two Thousand Guineas by four lengths 11 days later. He seemed certain to start the race as a short-priced favourite, but then bruised a foot in training a few weeks before the Derby and, although he recovered in time, his price drifted. He had also not yet been tested over the full Derby distance of one and a half miles: did he have the stamina for the race? He began the race as fourth favourite, at odds of 10–1.

There were three French challengers for the 1953 Derby – Pharel, Pink Horse and Shikampur. Pharel was the only one of the trio to be ridden by a French jockey, Jean Doyasbère. The chesnut Shikampur, owned by the Aga Khan, wore blinkers and was ridden by Charlie Smirke, a great jockey in his own right whose rivalry with Gordon Richards was known to be less than friendly. Smirke had won in 1952, riding the Aga Khan's Tulyar, and he was well backed to repeat the feat in Coronation Year. Pink Horse, owned by Prince Said Toussoun and ridden by Rae Johnstone, left the paddock as the least fancied of the three French horses, quoted at 33–1 compared with starting prices of 100–6 for Shikampur and 22–1 for Pharel.

There were two of Nearula's half brothers taking part too. All were sired by Nasrullah, but while Nearula was out of Respite, Novarullah, starting the race as joint fifth favourite at 100–8, was out of Nova Puppis and Victory Roll was out of Chinese Puzzle. Victory Roll was priced at

50–1 despite having won the mile-and-a-half Dee Stakes at Chester earlier in the year, but there was a bizarre story behind the selection of his jockey. Michael Beary had been in the racing world for 40 years, having begun riding in 1912. By 1953 he had – he thought – retired from riding and had taken out a trainer's licence. However, Atty Persse, the trainer of Victory Roll, found himself without a jockey at short notice so Beary, who had been given his first job in riding two World Wars ago by Persse, relinquished his trainer's licence and became a jockey again in time for the Derby. Unfortunately for him, in the event Victory Roll lived up to the second part of his name more than the first. Although he showed well in the early stages of the race, running second to Shikampur at the top of the hill, he lost his stride on the downhill run to Tattenham Corner, began to pitch and finished at the back of the field. There was not to be a fairytale ending for Beary that afternoon, although he did go on to ride several winners later in his comeback season.

Few jockeys were of the vintage of Beary and Richards. For two young men who would both make their names on the flat, riding in the Derby was a much newer experience. Jimmy Lindley, in his very first Derby, was aboard Lord Londonderry's Scipio, but he was to have a very undistinguished race. Lester Piggott, then 17 years old, was given the ride on Prince Charlemagne at short notice, when Fred Hunter dropped out. At 66–1 he had shorter odds than Scipio, but there was no real possibility of a win this time, even for the boy who already was beginning to be talked about as a potential successor to Richards as Champion Jockey. Despite his extreme youth, this was already Piggott's third Derby. In 1951, at the ridiculously young age of 15, he had ridden Zucchero, and after being left at the start finished thirteenth in a field of 30. The esteem in which Piggott was already held by trainers and owners is shown by the fact that Zucchero was no mean horse: by 1953 he was considered the best middle-distance horse in Britain, when in the mood. His brilliance and unpredictability were already evident as a three-year-old, but that did not stop his connections from putting a 15-year-old boy in the saddle for the biggest race of his life. A year later, when Piggott had finally attained the minimum age that boys must now reach before they can ride in a professional race, he rode Gay Time to finish second, just three-quarters of a length behind Charlie Smirke on Tulyar. As Piggott tried to slow Gay Time after the post, the horse hit the rails, fell over, threw his jockey, got up again and galloped riderless into the town of Epsom. It took almost half an hour to catch him and bring him back for unsaddling so that Piggott could weigh in. Piggott must have been hoping for a less chaotic post-race reception this time. He got it: he and his mount were virtually anonymous.

Piggott's cousin, Bill Rickaby, was also riding in the race, on Lord Milford's Empire Honey, another horse that had won over the distance already. Chatsworth, owned by Major L. B. Holliday, was yet another, having taken the Payne Stakes at Newmarket, and as a result was backed down to 100-6. These were the horses that were in serious contention for the trophy, valued at £250, and the almost £20,000 stake money for the one hundred and seventy-fourth running of the Derby Stakes.

The crowds were as enthusiastic and as colourful as anybody could remember. The presence of the new Queen had given style and excitement to the day, but only she, and perhaps Gordon Richards, looked calm among the jostling crowds. Both would in truth have been very far from calm on the inside. A vast scrum of racegoers began to assemble around the paddock even before the running of the Caterham Stakes, the race before the Derby, and by the time the Derby runners were in the paddock only a fortunate few can have had much of a look at the horses. No wonder that Aureole was playing up a little, sweating and nervous. Pinza, who had already been out early in the morning for a run down Tattenham Hill with Richards, was unruffled by the hubbub. Richards too was outwardly calm, although inwardly he must have been feeling the strain. 'He was a very nervous man,' remembers Jimmy Lindley. 'He was not as laid back as he appeared. He went through a period after the war when he was very highly strung, but it never showed in his riding.' Richards acknowledged this nervousness as well. 'I never believed those

jockeys who claimed to have no nerves at all before riding a fancied horse. It's only human to feel a bit tense.'

Despite the crowds, the horses got up to the post without incident, and there were no problems at the start. The race began pretty well on time, at 3.30, with every horse getting away well, apart from Lindley's mount, Scipio, which was the only one not in line when the tapes were raised. City Scandal made the early running, but after only about two furlongs Charlie Smirke brought the Aga Khan's Shikampur to the front. Jaffa II and Star Of The Forest were also briefly in the leading group, while Michael Beary on Victory Roll was going well. Pinza was tucked in neatly in about seventh place, just behind Nearula. There was the usual jostling and nudging for position in the pack following Shikampur, whose lead at the top of Tattenham Hill had lengthened to four lengths. The familiar green and chocolate hoops of the Aga Khan, already worn five times by Derby winners, looked as though they would be gracing the winner's enclosure for a sixth.

The race down the hill sorted out the winners from the also-rans, as it usually does. Pinza moved into second place behind Shikampur, and Aureole began to move up through the field. Victory Roll fell back, but Star Of The Forest and Mountain King were with the leading pack. Nearula, who had looked so easy on the canter down to the post, had dropped off the pace: his hopes of a Derby crown were finished. Around Tattenham Corner, Shikampur was still a length or so ahead of Pinza, but by this time Richards had put his foot down. 'He'd been getting edgy,' says Lindley. 'He fired him off with about five furlongs still to run. He'd always had a handy position, but when he pulled the trigger, he meant the bullet to come home.' Within a few strides, Pinza drew level with Shikampur, and Smirke's horse seemed disheartened by the sudden appearance of a rival after such a long time unchallenged at the head of the field. In almost no time, Richards and Pinza were four lengths clear

Previous pages: At last! At the twenty-eighth attempt Gordon Richards, riding Pinza wins the 1953 Derby.

3.30 - THE 174th DERBY STAKES (RENEWAL)

For entire colts and fillies foaled in 1950; colts 9st, fillies 8st 9lb

VALUES: WINNER £19,118.10s: SECOND £2,261: THIRD £1,130.10s

	Owner	Name	st	lb	Trainer	Jockey
1.	H.M. The Queen	AUREOLE	9	0	C. Boyd-Rochfort	W.H. Carr
2.	Lord Antrim	CITY SCANDAL	9	0	H. Smyth	A.P. Taylor
3.	M. M. Boussac	PHAREL	9	0	C. Semblat (France)	J. Doyasbère
4.	Lady Bullough	PRINCE CANARINA	9	0	H. Leader	C. Elliott
5.	Mr R.S. Clark	GOOD BRANDY	9	0	H. Peacock	D. Smith
7.	Mr F.W. Dennis	DURHAM CASTLE	9	0	J. Fawcus	A. Roberts
8.	Mr F.W. Dennis	TIMBERLAND	9	0	H. Peacock	G. Littlewood
9.	Mr J.E. Ferguson	MOUNTAIN KING	9	0	J.A. Waugh	T. Gosling
10.	Major L.B. Holliday	CHATSWORTH	9	0	H. Cottrill	S. Clayton
11.	Mr W. Humble	NEARULA	9	0	C. Elsey	E. Britt
12.	H.H. Aga Khan	SHIKAMPUR	9	0	R. Carver (France)	C. Smirke
14.	Mr H. S. Lester	GALA PERFORMANCE	9	0	G. Todd	E. Mercer
15.	Mr Ley On	FE SHAING	9	0	J. Beary	S. Wragg
16.	Mr L. Lipton	PRINCE CHARLEMAGNE	9	0	T. Carey	L. Piggott
17.	Mr J. McGrath	NOVARULLAH	9	0	W. Stephenson	C. Spares
18.	Lord Milford	EMPIRE HONEY	9	0	J. Jarvis	W. Rickaby
19.	Mr J. Olding	VICTORY ROLL	9	0	H. Persse	M. Beary
21.	Mr J.G. Morrison	FELLERMELAD	9	0	N. Cannon	A. Breasley
22.	Mr C. H. Rodwell	PETER-SO-GAY	9	0	T. Griffiths	P. Evans
23.	Sir Victor Sassoon	PINZA	9	0	N. Bertie	G. Richards
24.	Prince Said Toussoun	PINK HORSE	9	0	J. Cunningham (France)	W.R. Johnstone
25.	Mrs G. Alderman	WINDY	9	0	D. Hastings	F. Barlow
26.	Capt. A.S. Wills	STAR OF THE FOREST	9	0	J. Dines	K. Gethin
27.	Brig. W.P. Wyatt	PREMONITION	9	0	C. Boyd-Rochfort	E. Smith
28.	Mr F. H. Bowcher	BARROWBY COURT	9	0	J. Dines	T. Carter
29.	Mr C. Wijesinghe	JAFFA II	9	0	F. Armstrong	J. Egan
30.	Lord Londonderry	SCIPIO	9	0	C. Elsey	J. Lindley

Betting: 5–1 Premonition, Pinza; 9–1 Aureole; 10–1 Nearula; 100–8 Good Brandy, Novarullah; 100–6 Chatsworth, Shikampur; 22–1 Fellermelad, Pharel, Star Of The Forest; 33–1 Mountain King, Pink Horse; 40–1 Empire Honey; 50–1 Prince Canarina, Victory Roll; 66–1 Prince Charlemagne; 100–1 others.

of the field, with only Aureole looking strong enough to make any sort of a challenge. But Pinza and Richards stayed on to win by four lengths in the fast time of two minutes 35 3/5 seconds. After three decades of trying, victory when it came was remarkably easy.

Aureole was second, and third, as if from nowhere, was Pink Horse, one and a half lengths further behind. Shikampur finished fourth, but the real disappointment was the joint favourite, Premonition, who never looked like challenging, and finished last of the 27 runners. No reason was ever found for his poor race, described in the *Bloodstock Breeders' Review* as 'too bad to be taken at its face value', but there was some compensation for the horse, and for his trainer Captain Boyd-Rochfort, when he won the St Leger later in the year. Lester Piggott's ride was undistinguished: Prince Charlemagne never had a chance, finishing well down the field. He did, however, finish one place ahead of Jimmy Lindley on Scipio, and three places ahead of cousin Bill Rickaby on Empire Honey.

However, the also-rans did not concern Pinza or his jockey. The scenes in the unsaddling enclosure were remarkable. You expect hats to be thrown in the air, along with unsuccessful betting tickets, but the outpouring of genuine excitement, happiness and relief was overwhelming as Richards and Pinza were led in with an escort of mounted police. Sir Peter O'Sullevan remembers seeing Richards wiping away a tear. All the doubts about Pinza's potential as a Derby horse had gone and all the racegoers were suddenly able to give their reasons why they had known all along he would win. But then all horses look so different once they are inside the winner's circle.

The owner of the second-placed horse asked to see him (the contemporary reports say that she 'summoned him', along with Sir Victor Sassoon and Norman Bertie), to give him her congratulations. Her horse had proved to be second best on the day, but as The *Sporting Life* noted, 'The Queen voiced the sporting spirit – the satisfaction that the best horse had won, ridden by the greatest jockey of all time.' In truth, her emotions may well have been more mixed than that. Nevertheless, there is no doubt that if her horse had to be beaten, Richards was the man she would have liked to see winning. 'Knowing Her Majesty, she wouldn't have been very pleased,' is Jimmy Lindley's view, 'but she is too much of a lady to show it. She was gracious enough to be pleased for Sir Gordon. Another monarch might have had his head off.'

Delighted owner Sir Victor Sassoon, and trainer, Norman Bertie greet Derby winner
Pinza and Gordon Richards.

When the Queen turned her attention to Norman Bertie, she held
out her hand and said, 'Congratulations, Mr Bertie, on winning the race.'
Bertie replied, 'Congratulations to you, Your Majesty, on winning the
world.' On a glorious Saturday afternoon in the early summer of 1953, in
the week of her coronation, amidst scenes of celebration with people
amongst whom the Queen felt truly at home, it was easy to believe that
she had indeed won the world.

Gordon Richards spoke a few words to the crowds over the loudspeakers after he had been presented to the Queen. 'Pinza is a wonderful horse,'
he said. 'We lay about seventh or eighth at the top of the hill and I was
lucky to get a clear run down the inside. I never had to pull away from the
rails until I went up to challenge Charlie Smirke on Shikampur. The
moment I asked Pinza to go on and win he responded immediately, and I

have seldom had an easier winner. He was going so well at Tattenham Corner that even then I knew I had won. Everything I asked of Pinza he did at once.'

The man who bred Pinza, Fred Darling, was not at Epsom. Described as 'the greatest trainer of his time', he died just three days after the race, aged 69. He had been desperately ill with cancer for some time, and it was perhaps only his determination to see the triumph of Pinza and his great friend Gordon Richards that kept him alive until June. He had trained seven Derby winners and 12 other Classic winners, and even on his deathbed was passing on hints and advice to Norman Bertie in order to make sure that Pinza was in peak condition on 6 June. His obituaries gave full credit to his part in Pinza's triumph, as did both Richards and Bertie on the day and ever afterwards.

Pinza's racing career lasted only one more race. In mid-July he ran in the King George VI and Queen Elizabeth Stakes at Ascot and finished three lengths ahead of Aureole, who again had to be content with second place. But this was the last time that hats were thrown in the air for Pinza. He was being prepared for the St Leger, the last Classic of the season, when he strained a tendon and never raced again. His career finished after seven races, of which he won five and finished second once.

The 1953 Derby proved to be the final peak in Gordon Richards' glorious career as well. Three days after his Derby triumph, he rode a treble in the less glamorous setting of Lewes racecourse, winning three consecutive races at 3.00, 3.30 and 4.00, having already come second in the two o'clock. On Tuesday 30 June, he was knighted at Buckingham Palace, and flew immediately to Newmarket, where in his first race as Sir Gordon he came third on Tintinnabulum. It seemed as though there was considerable life in the old dog yet, but although he had intended to race for perhaps a couple of years more, events overtook him. He had hoped to ride for the Queen in the 1954 Derby, as her horse, Landau, was one of the early favourites. However, he fell at a meeting at Salisbury a few weeks before the big day and had to miss Epsom altogether. Landau, ridden in his place by Willie Snaith, finished eighth behind the 18-year-old Lester Piggott on Never Say Die.

Richards did ride again after recovering from his Salisbury injuries, and his final ride was in the royal colours. On 10 July 1954, he finished third on his intended Derby mount Landau in the Eclipse Stakes at Sandown Park. Half an hour later, once again riding for the Queen, his horse Abergeldie reared up as it left the parade ring and Richards was thrown again. This time his injuries were more serious – a fractured pelvis and four broken ribs. At the age of 50, Sir Gordon decided that enough was enough. After 4,870 winners over 34 years of racing, still an untouchable record 50 years on, he retired as a jockey. His record of 26 Champion Jockey titles is also still unchallenged, as is his 1947 total of 269 winners in one season on the flat. Other jockeys – Lester Piggott, Willie Carson, Frankie Dettori and a handful more – have dominated the sport for a while, but none has been so far ahead of his rivals for so long as Sir Gordon Richards. Only on Derby Day each year did he appear to be a mere mortal – until 1953.

In retrospect it is easy to think of the 1953 Derby as the last triumph of the pre-war generation, and that with Lester Piggott's win in 1954 the baton had been passed to the new generation. But it did not feel like that at the time. After all, horse racing was never a very young man's game, and owners, trainers and even jockeys are rarely callow youths. 'Nobody felt this was the last hurrah of the old guard,' says Sir Peter O'Sullevan. 'Nobody thought that – they just were glad that Gordon Richards had won at last.'

'When you ride in a Derby,' adds Jimmy Lindley, 'it does not matter what horse you ride. Even if you are riding a donkey you think you will win.' Finally, on Saturday 6 June 1953, at a few minutes past 3.30 p.m. on a sunny afternoon at Epsom, Gordon Richards' thoughts and dreams had become reality.

Next pages: An admiring crowd welcome Pinza and Gordon Richards and owner Sir Victor Sassoon into the winner's enclosure after their victory in the Epsom Derby.

5 • *The Motspur Park Mile*

Saturday 27 June

The Everest of athletics in 1953 was the four-minute mile. It was the goal for all middle-distance runners, and had been since before the Second World War. By 1953 it was, like Everest, a target that was at once very close to being beaten and apparently as far away as ever. The world record, four minutes 1.4 seconds, had been set as far back as 1945 and although a gaggle of athletes were closing in on the record, it stayed stubbornly intact.

To coincide with Coronation Year, one newspaper came up with an idea that encapsulated the struggle for this particular holy grail of athletics: it announced the sponsorship of an all-comers one-mile race, to be known as the Emsley Carr Mile. The race, named after Sir Emsley Carr, who edited the *News of the World* for more than 50 years, was to be run at the White City stadium for the first time on 8 August. The trophy for the winner was, and still is, a morocco-bound book telling the story of mile racing, and its foreword begins thus: 'In the Coronation Year of 1953, an outstanding ambition of world track athletes is to achieve the four-minute mile. In order to encourage runners from home and overseas in this quest, the *News of the World* has instituted this annual contest.' The paper was determined that the race should be well supported by runners and fans alike, and publicised it expertly and heavily before the great day. This faith was amply repaid by the big crowd that came to watch the race, and by the quality of the runners who competed for the title. Before the race began, there was a lap of honour (in an open-top Aston Martin rather than in spikes and running vests) by four legendary milers – the Englishman Sydney Wooderson; Paavo Nurmi, the Flying Finn; Joe Binks, then aged 79, who had set a British record of 4:16.8 in 1902; and the world record holder since 1945, Gundar Haegg of Sweden. Haegg and his compatriot Arne Andersson had dominated middle-distance running in the early 1940s. In all, Haegg broke 16 world records during the war years. However, he and Andersson were both suspended from amateur meetings after the war for breaches of the strict amateur codes, so were not able to spearhead the worldwide drive towards the four-minute mile. It was left to others to subtract that tantalising 1.4 seconds from Haegg's world-record time.

The main contenders for the immortality that would surely come with the first sub-four-minute mile were British, American and Australian. The American was Wesley Santee, who had run for his country in the 5,000 metres in the 1952 Olympics in Helsinki without success, but who was now producing a series of very fast times at the shorter distance. The Australian was John Landy, who had run in both the 1,500 metres and the 5,000 metres in Helsinki, without making the final in either event, but who under the guidance of the brilliant Australian trainer Percy Cerruty was making great improvements with every race. The Briton was Roger Bannister, who had finished a disappointing fourth in the Olympic 1,500 metres final. There were other contenders, too, notably Josey Barthel of Luxembourg, Robert MacMillen of the United States, and Werner Lueg of Germany, the three men who had taken the medals in the Helsinki Olympics 1,500-metres race the year before. Rolf Lamers, another German, Patrick El Mabrouk of France and Wim Slijkhuis of the Netherlands, the current European champion at 1,500 metres, were also recording fast times on a regular basis. Sooner or later one of these men would achieve the magic four minutes. Roger Bannister was determined that it would be him.

It was a shock that he did not win the Olympic 1,500-metres title. If he had won he would almost certainly have retired there and then and gone full-time into finishing his medical training and becoming a doctor. But he did not win, and he was not ready to retire without at least one major achievement to his name. Immediately after the Helsinki Olympics, he wrote to Chris Chataway, then still an undergraduate at Magdalen College, Oxford, but already a highly gifted middle-distance runner. Bannister asked if Chataway would be willing to act as his pacemaker in races in 1953. He felt sure that the four-minute mile would be reached at any time, and he knew that the man to do it would be the one who was best prepared, both physically and mentally. Looking back with the experience of hindsight, it is clear that one reason why Bannister was the man to run into the history books was that he was mentally far stronger than his rivals.

In 1953, pacemaking was officially illegal: nobody was supposed to enter a race unless they intended to complete it and to try to win it, but already in middle and long-distance races this rule was being blurred as athletes strove for ever faster times. For Bannister, and for his principal colleagues in his quest, the pacemaking rule was an inconvenience, but one that could be sidestepped easily enough. All the 'rabbits', as they were known, had to do was to say 'yes', when asked if they were all trying their hardest to win, and the authorities tended to turn a blind eye to the tactics actually employed in the race.

Bannister did not even hold the British record for the mile at the start of the year. The record time had been set by Sydney Wooderson, in 1945 when he clocked four minutes 4.2 seconds. In 1953 the bespectacled Wooderson was 39 years old and in retirement, having lost his best years of running to the war and his chance of an Olympic gold medal in 1936 to an ankle injury in the heats. So Bannister's first target was to break the British mile record, and then to take aim at the world record – and the four-minute barrier.

Bannister's season was built around his attempts on this seemingly impenetrable barrier. He intended to attack the world record in several races, using tactics that showed his innovative attitude to his sport. As it turned out, his first real effort proved to be – officially, at least – his best. On 2 May, when most of the country was cheering on Stanley Matthews to his FA Cup triumph, the annual athletics fixture between Oxford University and the Amateur Athletics Association took place at the Iffley Road track in Oxford. The match itself was very one-sided, with the AAA beating the students by 96 points to 46. However, the crowds who had decided that athletics was more interesting than football that afternoon had not come along expecting to see a close contest: they had come to see Oxford graduate Roger Bannister run a fast mile. He did not disappoint them.

Chris Chataway, taking an afternoon off from studying for his finals, agreed to act as Bannister's unofficial pacemaker. He knew what his job was: he had to take the runners off at a fast pace and keep that pace going at least until the three-quarter-mile mark, at which point Bannister would make the run for home on his own.

It all went like clockwork. Everybody knew that Chataway was simply there as a pacemaker (*Athletics Weekly*'s man at the meeting wrote that he had been told that Chataway would make the pace, 'endeavouring to make the first three laps as fast as possible'), but the AAA officials chose not to know this. Chataway paced the first three laps brilliantly, in 61.7 seconds, 62.4 and 61.1. At the bell Bannister strode past his exhausted pacemaker, who dropped out a few yards further on, his job done. Bannister sprinted down the back straight of the cinder track at Iffley Road, killing off the rest of the opposition to win by about 80 yards. His final lap was a brilliantly fast 58.4 seconds, and he breasted the tape in four minutes 3.6 seconds, knocking 0.6 seconds off Wooderson's record. Second was John Disley, bronze medallist in the 3,000 metres steeple-chase at Helsinki, who recorded a time of four minutes 15.4 seconds.

The media were very excited. 'That four-minute mile moves ever nearer with Bannister's great new British record,' enthused *Athletics Weekly*. But they were realists who knew what methods Bannister was using to get within touching distance of immortality. 'If and when it is done, it is likely to be in a race where he has a fast pacemaker such as Chris Chataway, who must take a good deal of the credit for last Saturday's time.' Pacemaking, though still officially illegal, was being talked about openly in the press, and Bannister and his friends were making plans to take things a step further. They needed to be quick. In America on Derby Day, Wes Santee ran the fourth fastest mile ever, 4:02.4, with Denis Johansson of Finland second in 4:04 and the Belgian Gaston Reiff third in 4:05.7. Any one of these men could beat him to the target.

Three weeks after that American superfast mile, and six weeks before the Emsley Carr Mile was due to be run, Bannister tried again, this time at

Chris Brasher, deceptively weedy-looking as an athlete, who was crucial to Bannister's four-minute mile plans and who in 1956 became the first Briton to win an Olympic gold medal in the 3,000 metres steeplechase.

the Surrey Schools' Championships at Motspur Park. This may seem an unlikely setting for an attempt on a world record, but the organisers agreed to hold a special Invitation Mile, which would bring in the crowds to what might otherwise have been a fairly sparsely attended event. It was, after all, the Saturday of the Lord's Test and the middle Saturday of Wimbledon fortnight, giving sports lovers ample reason not to be at Motspur Park to watch the schoolchildren. Those who chose not to be there missed a remarkable footnote to athletics history.

There were only three runners in the Invitation Mile: Bannister, his close friend the bespectacled steeplechaser Chris Brasher and a tall, blond, curly-haired Australian named Don MacMillan (not to be confused with the American Robert McMillen). The purpose of the race was to enable Bannister to break what was now his own English Native, British National and British All-Comers' record for the mile and to get as close as possible to the four-minute mile. The conditions for the race were ideal: Motspur Park's track was a first-class one, and fairly fast. The sun shone and the wind had dropped. The small crowd (for even the promise of a new mile record had not lured many people away from Lord's or Wimbledon) eagerly anticipated something special.

They got it. In planning for this race, Bannister and his colleagues had realised the drawback of using just one pacemaker: as soon as he became exhausted, Bannister would be on his own having to drive himself for the rest of the race, which meant that very fast times would prove difficult. The obvious solution – running with and against other men who were capable of the four-minute mile – held one clear risk. One of these other men might actually prove better on the day, and be the first to break the four-minute barrier. So it had to be pacemakers, and the more the merrier.

That Saturday at Motspur Park, Bannister used both his running companions as pacemakers. The idea was that Don MacMillan would take Bannister through three laps at the best pace he could manage, and then hand over to Brasher for the final lap. Of course, if Brasher were to run three fast laps ready to take over for the final one he would very probably be as exhausted as MacMillan, and of no practical use to Bannister. That was where the simple beauty of their plan kicked in. MacMillan, as arranged, set off at a pace that would take them through three laps in three minutes. The first lap was run in 59.6 seconds and the half mile was reached in 1:59.7. Bannister was still on MacMillan's shoulder.

Had Bannister looked over his own shoulder, he would not have found Brasher. Brasher, despite being a quick enough middle-distance runner to win the 3,000 metres steeplechase gold medal at the Melbourne

Roger Bannister in 1953, a trainee doctor and determined to become the first ever four-minute miler.

Olympics in 1956, was lagging far behind. The crowd began to fear that the record attempt was doomed because the third runner could not keep up. To make matters worse, halfway through the third lap MacMillan tired badly and, with another 600 yards or so still to go, Bannister was forced to go out on his own. He ran unpaced until the bell, reaching it in 3:01.8, at which point he was about to lap the apparently listless Brasher. However, the threat of being overtaken seemed to work like a red-hot poker up the backside of Brasher, who suddenly accelerated into 59-second lap pace to give Bannister the pacemaking he so dearly needed. The plan was so simple it was brilliant, and it almost worked. Brasher, with only half a mile on the clock, was able to give Bannister the lift he needed for 300 yards and then let him overtake and drive for the line. The final result was: first, Roger Bannister in a new track, English

Native, British Empire and UK All-Comers' record time of four minutes and 2 seconds, the third fastest mile in history. Second and third, nobody. Wes Santee, eat your heart out.

The only problem with the Motspur Park Mile was that quite clearly even a blind eye would be able to spot the fact that neither MacMillan nor Brasher was trying to win the race. Even if MacMillan could have convinced the AAA that he was racing in earnest but just got tired, nobody could have believed the same of Chris Brasher. Brasher was in the race purely as a pacemaker for the final lap, with no thought of anything else. The image of the boys' comic character, the Great Wilson, who used to win races in record times against relays of runners comes bounding to the fore. Unfortunately, what happens in boys' comics does not happen in real life, and if it does, there must be a rule against it.

When the British Amateur Athletic Board met a couple of weeks later to ratify several new British record marks, they were faced with the dilemma of what to do about the Motspur Park Mile, which had been put forward for ratification. In the end, they produced the following statement:

> The British Amateur Athletic Board does not accept the 4:02 mile by R.G. Bannister, at Motspur Park on June 27th, as a record. The Board wish to draw attention to the fact that it has unfettered discretion whether to accept or to refuse to recognise a record. The Board has carefully considered all the circumstances and regrets that, while it has no doubt that the time was accomplished, it cannot recognise the performance as a record. It has been compelled to take the view that it was not done in a bona fide competition according to the rules. The Board wishes it to be known that while it appreciates the public enthusiasm for record performances and the natural and commendable desire of athletes to accomplish them, it does not regard individual record attempts as in the best interests of athletics as a whole.

The Board then went on to recognise Bannister's earlier 4:03.6 mile as the new British record, even though that had also been pretty obviously paced. But it had happened during 'bona fide competition', so that was all right then. The decision caused much debate in the press, with equal numbers supporting the BAAB for its stand against record chasing and opposing it for its fuddy-duddy failure to understand the way the sport was going. Bannister accepted the decision without demur, despite the slur on his name implied by the fact that his tactics had been branded as not being 'in the best interests of athletics as a whole'. He had the British record, and neither race had brought him the four-minute mile, so the ratification of the Motspur Park Mile was not an important issue. What was important was that if he were to break the four-minute barrier using the same tactics again it would not count, and the effort would all have been wasted. He did not try those same tactics again.

From our twenty-first-century vantage point, we can see that record-chasing, pacemaking and the mind games that distinguish the great from the merely very good athletes were beginning to infiltrate athletics and turn it into a professional sport. We can also see that the process took much longer than we might have suspected, given the hefty nudge in that direction that Bannister's attitude and tactics represented. The amateur athletics authorities kept their fingers in the dykes longer than the progressive forces in all sport could have expected, though when the tidal wave of professional athletics finally swept in, it brought in its wake many of the worst aspects of human behaviour, which were certainly not 'in the best interests of athletics as a whole'. Bannister, a true amateur in the financial sense if a true professional in his attitude towards achievement, was never guilty of anything except trying to be the best in the world.

There were two sequels to this mile race. The first occurred in mid-December 1953, when another odd mile was run at Motspur Park. Don MacMillan, Bannister's pacemaker, needed to run a qualifying time for the Australian team to go to Canada for the following year's Empire Games (as they were then known), but the conditions of the English winter are against fast times. Still, as MacMillan had helped Bannister,

Bannister was now determined to help MacMillan. They therefore arranged with the Motspur Park management to run what became known as the 'MacMillan Mile', on 19 December, featuring many of the fastest runners of the season, all there to help MacMillan run four minutes 10 seconds and thus secure his ticket to Vancouver. His fellow-countryman John Landy had very recently run an officially approved 4:02 mile, which put him one small step ahead of Bannister, so MacMillan, based in Britain during 1953, knew he had to run a fast time somehow.

A galaxy of stars was announced for the MacMillan Mile. The papers were full of speculation about the prospects of the various runners and, whether intentionally or not, built up the race to something greater than it was ever meant to be. Would Bannister win the mile in a record time? Or would it be Gordon Pirie? Pirie, a wafer-thin long-distance runner who was all elbows and knees, had been even more of an athletics star in 1953 than Bannister. He broke records all the way through the summer, beginning with a new British six-mile record of 28 minutes 47.4 seconds on 18 April, and finishing with a win in the Emsley Carr Mile in August. The mile was not Pirie's preferred distance and he was not expected to win the race. But win it he did, albeit in a time of 4:06.8, nowhere near the four-minute mile that the *News of the World* wanted from the race. Pirie, a Brit, did at least beat the dangerous American Wes Santee into second place, a major upset and a result that generated so many column inches for the race in the next day's papers that the success of the idea of the race was confirmed, as was its continuation as an annual event thereafter. Roger Bannister, incidentally, did not run in the race. Instead, he and three others (Chataway, Seaman and Nankeville) broke the rarely run world 4 x 1 mile relay world record.

Pirie's year went from brilliant to even better. He set a new British three-mile mark in June, and broke the world six-mile record on 10 July, lopping almost half a minute off the British record time he had set three months earlier. This record did not last the year out, being beaten by the great Czech Emil Zatopek in November, but all the same Pirie had been

Britain's one individual world record holder during the year, and finished the season ranked first in Britain at every distance from 3,000 metres to 10,000 metres, as well as being ranked second only to Bannister at one mile. He did not at this stage compete in the marathon, where Britain's third truly world-class runner, Jim Peters, was dominant. In October 1953 Peters broke his own world best time for the marathon (the distance does not have an official world record because every course is different) when he won in Turku in Finland in a time of 2.18:34.8. Peters thus became the first man in history to beat two hours 20 minutes in competition. Middle- and long-distance runners in Britain in 1953 were as strong as they had been in many years.

Gordon Pirie's training methods were revolutionary, involving running huge distances at a time when most athletes saved energy for the events themselves rather than covering hundreds of miles a week in preparation. Pirie's training methods worked, although how much was due to his punishing running schedules and how much to his innate talent is hard to gauge, and thousands of lesser athletes in years to come followed his example. But not even Pirie fancied racing much in December. After a build-up in which the press speculated about the possibility of a record time if the mild winter conditions persisted (they did not), a good-size crowd turned up on a cold windy day at Motspur Park to see the big race. It was a fiasco. The MacMillan Mile proved to be a victory for neither Bannister nor Pirie nor any of the other possible runners: it was won by Don MacMillan himself, who was the only finisher. He was also 50 per cent of the starters.

Despite all the ballyhoo, only MacMillan and Roger Bannister actually made it to the starting line. All the other much-touted runners failed to turn up, pleading a wide variety of entirely reasonable excuses, because no serious athlete wants to run a mile in cold winter conditions just to help another man, and an Australian at that, post a qualifying

Previous pages: Bannister wins the mile at the the AAA Championships on 11 July by a large margin, but still fails to beat the elusive four minutes for the distance.

time. Bannister, returning the favour of June, ran with him for three laps but at the bell, which they reached in 3:11.6, he dropped out and left MacMillan to fend for himself on the last lap. MacMillan did his best, but the conditions and the lack of other opponents counted against him. In the circumstances 4:15.4 was a creditable time, but it was not good enough to qualify him for the Australian team. The media, which had built the race up somewhat irresponsibly, now changed its collective tune and berated the organisers for expecting something special. 'Fortunately it will soon be forgotten,' opined *Athletics Weekly*, 'for the sport cannot afford such bad publicity.' The sport has endured all sorts of worse publicity than this in the ensuing 50 years, but winter time trials in England have not caught on.

The other sequel to the Motspur Park Mile came in 1954. When Bannister finally broke the four-minute barrier, at Iffley Park in Oxford on 6 May of that year, he was running in an official race (AAA versus Oxford University again), but, as is now a part of athletics legend, he could not have achieved his goal without the pacemaking of two of his henchmen of 1953, Chris Brasher and Chris Chataway. As Chataway remembers it, they had learnt their lesson in dealing with officialdom. After the record had been broken and Bannister was gasping for breath as a vast horde of excited well-wishers slapped him on the back, Brasher and Chataway were asked by BAAB officials whether or not they were trying to win the race. Both replied, 'Yes. Of course.' The Motspur Park Mile had not been run entirely in vain.

6 • *The Second Test Match*

Thursday 25 to
Tuesday 30 June

The day after Arsenal won the First Division title, in the week that Frankie Laine's recording of 'I Believe' climbed to the top of the new-fangled Hit Parade, the touring Australian cricket team began their season with a one-day charity match at East Moseley. 'I Believe' was the song of the summer, staying at the top of the charts for 18 of the next 20 weeks, not dropping finally from the number one position until the very last day of the tour, when the Australians were up at Scarborough and Richie Benaud was hitting sixes for fun. Even if the Australians were not tired of England and the English by then, they must surely have been tired of Mr Laine's full-blooded baritone belting out those soupy lyrics every time they tuned their radios into the Light Programme.

The touring party had arrived in Southampton aboard the SS *Orcades* on 13 April, after a four-week voyage from Fremantle, and spent a couple of weeks acclimatising to the bracing English April, a process that was achieved by means of some net practice at Lord's, some sight-seeing, some cricket dinners and a couple of days at the races. It was five years since an Australian touring team had visited England, and five years since Sir Donald Bradman had retired from the game. MCC had most recently toured Australia in 1950/51, under the captaincy of the Northamptonshire all-rounder Freddie Brown, but the result was the same as usual – Australia won the series by four matches to one, thus retaining the Ashes, the most coveted and at the same time intrinsically the most worthless prize in cricket. They had been won in 1934 by Australia, who had held on to them ever since, through four more Test series, two in each country. The Coronation Year series was surely England's big chance to win back the historic trophy. Australia had no Bradman, and they were playing under English conditions.

Many of the Australians, however, had considerable experience of English conditions. The captain was 40-year-old Lindsay Hassett, a small, prolific batsman who was universally popular within the cricket world. Hassett was making his third tour of England, having already played on the 1938 and 1948 tours. 'Dapper' is the adjective that is most often applied to him – he was clean, neat, precise and stylish in all he did, and always with a dry sense of humour. Neil Harvey calls him 'the best captain I played under', and he was on Bradman's 1948 tour as well. As Neville Cardus wrote of the Australian captain in the 1954 edition of *Wisden Cricketers' Almanack*, 'An Australian of Hassett's vintage likes to win, we may be sure, and, moreover, does his darnedest to win. But should the luck go the wrong way, well, there's always the consoling thought that, come to think of it, we've been playing a game; and none of us is the worse for it, and some of us much the better. And there are friends as well as runs to be got out of it.' Hassett, who finished his career with a Test batting average of 46, made friends as readily as he made runs, and he made an awful lot of runs. The great pre-war Australian leg-spinner Bill O'Reilly reckoned that Hassett played him better than anybody, Bradman included, which makes him a formidable batsman by any standards.

'He was a great tactical captain. He took chances,' says Harvey. Hassett was a contrast to the more conservative Bradman, whom he succeeded, and certainly utterly different from his English opposite number. Len Hutton, one of the greatest opening batsmen in the history of the game, was England's first professional captain of the modern era, and as such he was very conscious of his role in the history of the English game. His first thought as a captain was not to take risks. In the words of the Australian vice-captain Arthur Morris, 'He was frightened of being sacked, so didn't do much.'

Morris was one of the greatest of all Australian openers, now enjoying his second tour of England. In 1948 he had topped the Test batting averages with 696 runs at 87 per innings, and this was in a team that also included Bradman, Hassett, Sid Barnes, Neil Harvey, Keith Miller and many other superb batsmen. Five years on, as Australia's vice-captain, he was recognised as the key wicket for England: get Morris early and England could be on top, but let him get past 50 and who knows what he and the rest of the team could do? He worked well with Hassett, and now remembers with a smile

Alec Bedser practises before the start of the First Test. He was to take 39 wickets in the series, a new record, and play a major part in England's regaining the Ashes.

that although Hassett was a first-class captain, 'he was a bit lucky that he had an intelligent and loyal vice-captain in all his Tests'.

The 1953 Australians had an opening bowling attack that worried even the best opposition batsmen. The fast-bowling partnership of Ray Lindwall and Keith Miller, with the metronomic fast-medium accuracy of Bill Johnston to back them up, was so good that no side ever thought they were well set against them. Ray Lindwall is still regarded by all his contemporaries as the very best fast bowler there ever was. Alan Davidson, then a young all-rounder on his first tour to England and destined to become one of Test cricket's great all-rounders, says that Glenn McGrath 'is not as good as Lindwall. Even Dennis Lillee was not in Lindwall's class.' Neil Harvey would agree: 'Nobody rates as high as Lindwall.' His beautiful rhythmic run-up, accelerating smoothly all the way to the wicket, his classic side-on action and the speed, accuracy and unpredictability of every delivery made him an opponent to be feared under any conditions. He was also not a bad batsman, either, capable always of a half-century and on two occasions in Tests a century.

Keith Miller, the Second World War flying ace with the film-star good looks, was the most exciting, flamboyant and talented of the many all-rounders in world cricket in the early 1950s. Even in an Australian touring side that boasted players like Davidson, Ron Archer and Richie Benaud, Miller was the star player. He was a man whose moods might change from moment to moment, but when he felt like it he showed that he was one of the great players in Australian cricketing history. He too had toured in 1948, and had made firm friendships with English players like Bill Edrich, Denis Compton and Godfrey Evans, cavalier cricketers to a man. Edrich had been a pilot in the war, like Miller, and they both understood the relative value of cricketing success in the overall scheme of things. Where Bill Shankly ten years later might believe that 'winning isn't a matter of life and death, it's more important than that', Keith Miller knew that winning a sporting fixture was just part of the pleasure of being able to play. The immediate post-war generation of sportsmen had different values from today. Even the professionals, more often than not, played with the spirit of amateurs. Miller is described by Richie Benaud as the best captain he ever played under, but he never captained Australia. His captaincy of New South Wales was littered with eccentricities: once he forgot to tell one of his squad that he was to be twelfth man, and began the game with all 12 players on the field. His field placings used to consist of checking that one man was wearing pads – he must be the wicketkeeper – then throwing the ball to whoever was to open the bowling and saying to the other nine (or sometimes 10) men, 'Spread yourselves out.' There was something too carefree about his play, even for the Australian selectors.

The other dangerous bowler was Bill Johnston, a tall, balding Victorian who bowled left-arm fast medium and occasional orthodox spin, and who often took on the stock bowling duties when the opening pair were resting. He did this to such effect that it only took him just over four years to reach 100 Test wickets, which in an era when far fewer Tests were played was the shortest time ever taken to reach that milestone. He was no sort of a batsman, but the story of his batting in 1953 has entered cricketing legend.

The backbone of the batting, along with Hassett and Morris, was the little left-hander Neil Harvey. When he had come to England in 1948, Harvey was just 20 years old. Now, five years on, he was an experienced and very successful Test batsman on whom a great deal of responsibility devolved. He was also, by common consent, the best cover fielder in the world, saving runs and making batsmen think twice whenever they hit the ball near him. He does not regret the fact that he did not play one-day cricket to any extent, but does admit that one-day cricket creates opportunities for fieldsmen to become wicket-takers. He would have enjoyed that.

'It was a team with a lot of players who had been through the Second World War, mixed with youngsters. Lindsay was good with the younger players and, as is well documented, had a wonderful, dry, straight-faced, sense of humour,' as one of those younger players, Richie Benaud, recalls. The new generation of Australian cricketers was represented by the young batsmen Ian Craig, Colin McDonald, Graeme Hole and Jim de Courcy, and the all-rounders Benaud, Ron Archer and Alan Davidson. The Australian selectors had decided it was time to go for youth, and so they picked these seven men, who between them had played only 23 Tests. Great players like Stan McCabe and Jack Iverson were left behind for reasons more connected with personality than cricket. The 23-year-old opener Jim Burke and 35-year-old off-spinner Ian Johnson were also overlooked in favour of other players. (Johnson, who had toured England in 1948 with limited success, was to return in 1956, this time as captain, and Jim Burke would be a stalwart of his side.)

The rest of the touring party, 17 men in all, was made up of the two wicketkeepers, Don Tallon and Gil Langley, and the spinners Doug Ring and Jack Hill. 'Lindsay Hassett's problem on the 1953 tour was that the Australian selectors had decided the time had come to blood some young players and we didn't do the job for him,' remembers Richie Benaud. Lindsay's overall record as captain stands up to anyone else in the game, but Davidson, Archer and Benaud were light on success for him though keen to do more. Of the younger group, Benaud, Davidson and McDonald in particular went on to become mainstays of the side for the next decade or so, but in 1953 they did not quite deliver. In Tom Graveney's view, Australia was 'overburdened with all-rounders. Richie was a nothing cricketer in those days, but they'd decided he was the future leg-spinner, so they gave him a chance.' Ian Craig, who turned 18 on the tour but was already established as Australia's youngest ever Test

Willie Watson hooks on his way to his Test century at Lord's.

player, had a tough time of it on the cricket pitch in 1953, and as he now says, 'we were obviously on the down side of a cycle whilst England were on the up'. At the time, it was not obvious. Indeed, nobody noticed at all.

The opening friendly fixture at East Moseley on Sunday 26 April (the same day that England's Tony Rolt won the Le Mans 24 Hour Race driving a Jaguar) proved to be highly significant for the whole tour. Bill Johnston, bowling gentle medium pace against the local club batsmen, badly hurt his right knee, the one that takes the weight when a left-armer bowls. From that moment on he was never the bowling force he had been in 1948, though the Australians did their best to camouflage the extent of his injury. When asked what the difference between the two teams over the summer was, most of the Australians came up with the same answer. 'The injury to Bill Johnston was probably crucial,' said Ian Craig, 'because he was never the force he had been in 1948.' 'He was the key man in the attack as far as Lindsay was concerned,' added Richie Benaud, 'and he had to miss the third and fourth Tests and took only seven wickets in the series.' It was not just Johnston's bowling that was missed. It was also the precious rest he gave to Lindwall and Miller, who without Johnston had to send down far more overs than they would otherwise have done.

The Test series was a focus for sports lovers' attention throughout the summer. Stanley Matthews had his day gaining his Cup Winner's medal, Gordon Richards had his Derby Day and Everest had been climbed in a matter of a week or two, but the fight for the Ashes lasted all summer. The Australians played hard but also took every chance to enjoy themselves. They watched the Queen from a hotel balcony along the processional route, and the memories of that day remained with them for ever. Craig says, 'Having spent a lot of time in London since then, I have to say the atmosphere was more upbeat than at any time since. The Coronation produced a focus for enthusiasm and good humour which I can only equate to the feeling in Sydney during the 2000 Olympics. Everyone wanted to enjoy themselves and I can still recall the good-natured reception we received from the crowds on Coronation Day as we drove in our bus along part of the route – having been directed to do so by the police after getting hopelessly boxed in the maze of closed streets!'

It was a different time then. Australians in general were staunchly monarchist and proud of their British heritage. Lindsay Hassett wrote this Coronation Day message: 'May I take this opportunity to express, on behalf of all cricketers in Australia, not only our undying loyalty to the Crown, but our genuine love for Her Most Gracious Majesty.' He went on to say, in words that seem remarkably humble from the pen of an Aussie cricketer, 'We are proud of the part, however small, that we play in the scheme of the British Empire. This Australian team considers itself

Bailey cuts a ball from Miller between Davidson and Benaud.

particularly fortunate to be present in England during the Coronation celebrations, and we would like to add our sincere wishes that Her Majesty Queen Elizabeth II be long spared to rule her Empire through a period of peace and great prosperity.' Wow! Fifty years on, even the staunchest monarchist would blush a little at those sentiments. Even the Irish–Australian former Test cricketer Jack Fingleton, who was covering the tour as a journalist, waxed lyrical about his day as an invited guest within Westminster Abbey. 'In her presence of youthful beauty and majestic bearing,' he wrote in his book *The Ashes Crown the Year*, 'the doubts and the tribulations of the future seemed to fade away. And so it may be. God save and aid Queen Elizabeth!' Such was the effect the young Queen had on everybody who came into contact with her during 1953.

Well, almost everybody. Another person inside the Abbey for the Coronation was Christopher Brooker, as an eight-and-a-half-year-old treble, perhaps the youngest chorister there. At that age, it is hard to be impressed, and young Brooker's memories of the day are not of the youthful beauty of the Queen, but of having to wear a ruff and losing the stud that held it together. The entire choir was put up on a scaffolding

Lindsay Hassett (left), captain of the Australian touring team, and Ian Craig, still 17 and the baby of the party, arrive at Southampton on 13 April after the voyage from Australia on board SS *Orcades*.

platform above where the Queen was crowned, and had to stay there from 6 a.m until about 3 p.m. 'We were above the choir stalls, which were reserved for visiting dignitaries, and I remember thinking how small the Queen was. They issued us with a bottle of school milk, some Horlicks tablets and a packet of Spangles each. My friend Alastair Sampson dropped one of his Spangles – a red one – and it landed in the crown of the man below, the Maharajah of Baroda or somebody. It glistened throughout the service, much more brightly than the other jewels in his crown.' The trumpeters had little to do between fanfares, so they played cards on the kettle drums. After the service everyone, including Christopher, was given a Coronation Medal.

Eight days after the Coronation, another symbolic ceremony took place, this time at Lord's. The Duke of Beaufort, as President of MCC, unveiled a new inn sign on the Tavern. Until then, the tavern at Lord's was officially called 'Lord's Hotel', and it was only on 10 June 1953 that it became known as the Tavern, boasting an inn sign that showed Thomas Lord on one side and a cricketer of the 1850s on the other. Thus an anomaly was removed: the charitable cricket club, the Lord's Taverners, had been formed in 1950, three years before the edifice from which it took its name officially existed.

The First Test began on 11 June, at Trent Bridge. England were still so frightened of the Australian bowling attack that they packed the side with batting and only selected four bowlers. In the event, both sides showed rather too much respect for each other, and Miller, who had injured his ribs, did not even bowl. England dropped Statham from their 12, leaving the bowling to Alec Bedser, who had to shoulder the main responsibility for England's attack all summer, Trevor Bailey and the two spinners Roy Tattersall and Johnny Wardle. Denis Compton, Tom Graveney and Len Hutton had all bowled at Test level in the past, so they could in theory have been used as gap-fillers, but in 1953 they were not of Test class. In the event, Hutton did not use any of them.

Hassett won the toss and elected to bat. By the end of the first day, which was slightly shortened by rain, the score was 157 for 1 from 92 overs. The pattern for the series had been set: attritional cricket interspersed with rain showers. By the end of the match that pattern, slightly embellished, was set in stone. The match was drawn, with England on 120 for 1 chasing a target of 229, thanks largely to the fourth day being entirely washed out. Alec Bedser had bowled more overs than anybody else on either side, and had taken 14 wickets. Hassett scored a hundred and Morris made two fifties, but England's long batting line-up failed first time round. Only Hutton made more than 30. Second top scorer was Johnny Wardle, whose lusty hitting at the end took him to 29 not out.

The match also proved to be the final Test match for Don Bradman's favourite wicketkeeper, Don Tallon. Before Tallon was due to bat in the second innings, the Australians were discussing the poor light, and wondering how to persuade the umpires to offer it to them. Tallon was obviously locked in his own cocoon of concentration before going out to bat, but when the wicket fell and he set off out of the dressing room, Hassett called to him, 'Give it a go, Don.' Hassett meant, 'Try to persuade the umpires to let you come off for bad light,' but Tallon misunderstood and thought his captain was asking him to score a few quick runs. So in the murk he swung his bat mightily at every delivery. 'An attempt by the later batsmen to hit their way out of trouble failed,' was the laconic report of one journalist. Tallon made a quickfire 15 in this, his final Test innings.

After the frankly dull Trent Bridge match it was the Second Test, at Lord's, that reignited interest in the series. It was one of the most exciting Tests in the long history of Ashes cricket and it made two Englishmen the most famous sportsmen in the land, for a week or two at least. Half a century on, their names are still inextricably linked with Lord's and with each other: Watson and Bailey, the two halves of a match-saving partnership. Without them, the Ashes might have gone back to Australia.

Willie Watson, the Yorkshire left-hand bat and Sunderland wing half, was almost the last double international at football and cricket, with only Arthur Milton of Arsenal and Gloucestershire achieving the feat more recently. Watson played four games for England's football side between 1949 and 1951, and was a member of the 1950 World Cup squad in Brazil, although he did not play in any of the matches in that ill-fated campaign. He was recalled to the England cricket side for the Second Test, in place of Peter May (what riches in the batting order that we could drop Peter May!), along with Brian Statham and Freddie Brown who took over from Reg Simpson and Roy Tattersall. This at least gave England five regular bowlers, although one of them, Brown, was already 43 years old. Such was his vintage that he had been a member of the victorious but controversial Bodyline touring side to Australia just over 20 years earlier.

Trevor Bailey, the Essex all-rounder, was also a footballer, having won an Amateur Cup Winner's medal in 1952 with Walthamstow Avenue. In those days the Amateur Cup Final drew 100,000 spectators to Wembley just as the professional teams did: clubs like Pegasus and Bishop Auckland were as famous in their fifties heyday as any Football League team. For Bailey, however, cricket was his first love, and 1953 was his apotheosis. While most Australians judged that the difference between the two sides in 1953 was Alec Bedser and the weather, at least one opted for Trevor Bailey. 'If I had to pick a man of the series, it would be Trevor Bailey,' says Ian Craig. He then adds the rider that was so

Len Hutton (left), the England captain, with Sir Donald Bradman, chairman of the Australian selectors.

often true of Bailey's cricket: 'It would be nice to make a choice of someone who positively won the series, but his batting at Lord's, and his batting and bowling at Leeds, saved England from defeat on both occasions.' Tom Graveney, Bailey's England team-mate, was more succinct. 'Trevor was terrific.' Bailey's efforts at Lord's earned him the nickname 'Barnacle', which stuck with him throughout his career. Bailey was a fighter, not a glamorous attacking all-rounder like Keith Miller, but in 1953 those fighting qualities made a major contribution to England's ultimate triumph.

The Second Test match started much as the First had done. Hassett won the toss, and decided to bat. He then scored another century, even though he was batting as a makeshift opener, having swapped places in the order with Graeme Hole. Neil Harvey made a fifty and Alan Davidson made 76, batting at number 7, but nobody else made a good score. Still, 346 was a formidable total for England to chase. Despite the early loss of Don Kenyon, the Worcestershire opener, England looked to be in a safe position as the second day came to a close. Hutton and Graveney were batting, and the score was 177 for 1. The newspapers noted that the England batsmen stopped taking any chances – and stopped scoring runs – with still plenty of overs to go before the close of play. Tom Graveney remembers, 'We were going like trains. Then with twenty-five minutes to go, Len said to me, "Don't do anything silly," so I shut up shop. I got bowled fourth ball the next day. I should have got my hundred the night before.' To add insult to injury, when the teams were presented to the Queen, who was making what was to become her traditional visit to the Lord's Test, Len Hutton forgot Graveney's name. 'And we had a stand of a hundred and sixty-eight together!' There was a lot on Hutton's mind that summer and it seemed to come to a head in the Lord's Test. He not only forgot his batting partner's name, but also dropped no fewer than four catches during the match, including one off the chairman of selectors, Freddie Brown. Was he worried that he might be replaced as England captain?

Compton replaced Whatsisname at the wicket and for a while the England progress was serene. Hutton reached his century – the first of only two Test hundreds scored by an Englishman all summer – and Compton moved quickly to his half-century. At 279 for 2 a large first-innings lead seemed probable. But then the usual England collapse set in. Two good catches by Hole accounted for Compton and Hutton, and Watson and Bailey both went cheaply. Brown hit lustily but briefly and Godfrey Evans was bowled first ball, by which time 279 for 2 had become 332 for 8. It was the unlikely pairing of Johnny Wardle, who was only playing because Tony Lock was injured, and Brian Statham, an archetypal number eleven batsman, who put on 31 for the tenth wicket and gave England a first-innings lead of 26.

When Australia batted again, Hassett was dismissed cheaply, but Morris and Miller, batting ahead of Harvey, put on 165 for the second wicket. The balance had swung very firmly back to Australia. Arthur Morris was regarded by many as Alec Bedser's rabbit. In 1953, Bedser took his wicket five out of the 10 times he was dismissed. It is an odd statistic that Bedser got him in the first innings of every Test, and somebody else got him in the second innings. But in reality Morris was nobody's rabbit. 'Alec Bedser was a great bowler,' says Morris, 'but for one batsman against one bowler, I probably batted more against him in Tests than anybody in the history of the game.' He had also scored more hundreds against England than anybody apart from Bradman by the time he retired, so his batting average did not suffer unduly from facing Bedser so often. In the next Test, at Old Trafford, Morris bowled one over during which he had the pleasure of bowling Alec Bedser, one of only two Test wickets he took in his entire career. It was a small piece of retribution from batsman to bowler.

It took the wiles of Compton's occasional unorthodox left-arm spin to dispose of Morris in the end, for 89, but with Miller making a fine century and Graeme Hole knocking up a bright 47 Australia already looked to have a solid and possibly match-winning lead when they reached 308 for 8. At this stage Ray Lindwall, having seen what his opening bowling partner had done with the bat, decided to give it a go himself. In an onslaught that brought him a half-century in very quick time, he made 50 out of 63 in 45 minutes, hitting two sixes and five fours. It took only 25 minutes for Lindwall and Langley to add 54 for the ninth wicket. Australia were finally all out for 368, leaving England to score 343 for victory and with one hour left on the fourth day to negotiate.

England are never at their best when there is a little part of a day to get through, and at Lord's they played to type. Lindwall was the main executioner, taking the wickets of Kenyon, caught by Hassett at mid-on, and Hutton, caught by Hole in the slips, by the time the score had reached double figures. When Graveney followed, brilliantly caught by Langley diving down the leg side, England were 12 for 3 and the match looked to have slipped from their grasp. Compton and Watson saw out the day, but the overnight score was 20 for 3, and it would have been 20 for 4 if Watson had been caught off Ring in the final over of the day. It was a sharp chance to short leg, and these chances either stick or they don't, but the true significance of the miss was not appreciated until the following day.

The last day of the Test, Tuesday 30 June, the day on which Gordon Richards received his knighthood from the Queen, dawned as bright and as warm as every other day of the Lord's Test – a comparative rarity in the dank English summer of 1953. Only about 14,000 people turned up for the final day's play, probably expecting that England would be beaten some time during the afternoon session. All the same, total attendance for the match was 137,915 and the receipts, £57,716.15.0, established a new record for any cricket match. The pundits who were already picking their teams for the Third Test were almost unanimous in dropping both Watson and Bailey for that game. In the England dressing room, things were hardly any brighter. The general view of the England team was, 'We've had it.' Fortunately, this assessment was not shared by those who still had some influence on the outcome of the game, especially the not-out batsmen and the next man in.

Compton (another footballer: he won a Cup Winner's medal with Arsenal in 1950) and Watson played carefully but correctly and with increasing confidence for an hour and a half, until Compton, on 33, was adjudged lbw to a ball from Bill Johnston that kept low. The score was 73 for 4, and there was still the best part of five hours to play. The last six wickets in the first innings had been worth 83 runs: what chance was there of any improvement this time around? Clearly, neither Watson nor Bailey had read the script. What followed was not particularly pretty, but from England's point of view it was one of the great cricketing rearguard actions of all time and the Australians could do nothing about it.

Watson and Bailey, left-hander and right-hander, survived first to lunch, and then well into the afternoon. Bailey played every ball he could with a broad and very straight bat, so that the sight of the Essex man leaning well forward, nose down almost to the bat as he played yet another forward defensive shot, became the defining image of the match. Cartoonists loved him, and the 'Barnacle' was born. Watson, too, played much more dourly than his usual more carefree style and he too kept everything out. Slowly the score mounted, to the point that optimists among the small crowd could even begin to imagine an England victory. But for that to have been achievable, at the rate the English batsmen were scoring, the match would have had to run on for another fortnight or so. An English victory was never likely, but an Australian victory began to slip from the visitors' grasp during the afternoon. Mid-way through that session Australia were able to take the new ball, and Lindwall and Miller bowled magnificently, with speed, swing and fire, in an attempt to remove these two wavy-haired and annoyingly persistent batsmen from their presence. Bailey was hit three times on the hand by bouncers, but he just wrung his hands briefly each time and got on with his job. In 40 minutes of all-out new ball attack England only added 12 runs to their total, but no wicket fell. Miller's analysis at the end of the innings was 0 for 17 in 17 overs; Lindwall's was 2 for 26 in 19 overs. It was not beautiful cricket, but it worked. By the time it was clear that England could well save the Test, the spectators had become so engrossed in the play that they were applauding the forward defensives as much as the few run-scoring strokes.

Bailey reached his half-century and Watson eventually reached his century, his only Test hundred against Australia. Still the pair ground on. The Australian spinners, Doug Ring, Richie Benaud and Bill Johnston in his slower style, kept wheeling away, but Bailey and Watson were not to be disturbed. It was almost a shock when finally, at 10 minutes to six, Watson edged a googly from Ring to Hole at slip, and he was out. His 109 had occupied 346 minutes, during which time England's total had grown from 12 for 3 to 236 for 5. He and Bailey had added 163 for the fifth wicket in 245 minutes, which is actually a fast rate by today's standards. The difference is, of course, that they faced around 90 overs. Nowadays, Test bowlers would expect to bowl no more than about 60 overs in the same time.

England were not yet entirely safe. They were still over 100 runs short of the total required, and who would bet against Australia taking the last five wickets in 40 minutes? Freddie Brown joined Bailey, and almost immediately the Barnacle was prised off the English hull. He played a tired cover drive, also off Ring, and Benaud took an easy catch. Bailey was visibly annoyed with himself, but England's supporters did not share this critical approach. One or two of his team-mates may have felt a little uneasy, because the fall of Bailey's wicket, out for 71 after a stay of 257 minutes, meant that Godfrey Evans joined Brown in the middle with the total at 246 for 6. As Tom Graveney says, 'Fred Brown and Godfrey couldn't block. So there were a few oohs and ahs in the dressing room.'

Brown in particular decided that attack was the best form of defence, as he heaved at almost every ball and made a quick 28. He and Evans put on a further 36 runs in quick time (remember there were only about 40 minutes left when Bailey was out), but when Brown was out in the last over of the day there was still time for English hearts to find their way to English mouths. Benaud still had four balls left with which to take the final three wickets, and Johnny Wardle, another batsman who had no defensive shots in his known repertoire, had to face at least the first of them.

He faced all four, and was cheered off the pitch for his nought not out as he and Godfrey Evans made their happy way back to the pavilion. A match which Australia should have won had been saved, and saved quite easily, and the balance of power in the series moved towards England. In truth, England should never have found themselves in a position where defeat was possible, but in the first innings the lower-order batsmen had failed to establish a good lead, and in the second innings the first three men were back in the pavilion with only 12 runs on the board. Australia's failure to capitalise on the formidable position they had established by the end of the fourth day certainly played on their minds for the rest of the summer, but if there was a failure it was in their spin bowling. They had gone into the Test with Doug Ring and Richie Benaud, and neither of them had bowled well enough. There was much surprise when Ring replaced Jack Hill for the Lord's Test, as Hill had taken four wickets for 61 runs at Trent Bridge. Ring's figures at Lord's were 2 for 127 in 43 overs. Benaud, who had bowled only five overs in the First Test, now bowled 36, taking two wickets for 121 runs. Even in the second innings, when Watson and Bailey were defending the honour of England, both spinners went for three runs an over.

Australia's spin bowling was weak in 1953. For the previous few seasons, their leading spinner had been Jack Iverson, a strange but brilliant man who had developed his own peculiar style of spinning the ball with a powerful flick of his middle finger. 'We'd have won the series with Iverson,' believes Alan Davidson. 'He couldn't bat, couldn't field and didn't have a cricket brain, but batsmen were always at sea to him.' But the completely unorthodox spinner had decided to give up Test cricket, and the England batsmen, who had failed conclusively against him in 1950/51, sighed with relief. The gap he left in the Australian side could not be filled in a hurry. Hill, Ring, Benaud and the others did their best, but it was not enough. With Bill Johnston carrying an injury all summer and Benaud not yet the great leg-spinner he was to become, the English batsmen knew they would have a breathing space in the not always certain event that they were able to survive the initial onslaughts of Lindwall and Miller. Poor Keith Miller, who had to open the bowling and bat at number 3 or 4, was also asked to try some off-spin from time to time, and took at least one wicket, that of Tom Graveney in the Third Test, in his slower mode. The English bowling may have been carried by Alec Bedser, but it was the spinners, Wardle, Lock and Laker, who provided the final twists of the knife.

The English bowling that summer has been underrated over the years, partly because the selectors were so determined to pack the batting that for most of the summer they only picked three front-line bowlers in the Test sides. We must also remember that not all the Australian batsmen had experience of English conditions. 'Hutton showed clearly that good technique is necessary on English pitches and there is no doubt we lacked in this,' says Ian Craig. 'Most of us had never played on anything but true pitches and had become accustomed to hitting across the line with little risk. This proved fatal against good seamers and spinners in a season where the conditions favoured them.' The bowling of Alec Bedser all summer was of the very highest order. In Neil Harvey's opinion, 'He was the best bowler I played against. If he bowled you six balls, you had to play the lot.' Even his own team were slightly in awe. 'Alec was absolutely phenomenal,' says Tom Graveney. 'He bowled fast leg spinners. If he'd ever played on coconut matting, nobody would ever have got a run.' Bedser took 39 wickets in the series, a record, and in dismissing Gil Langley at Lord's in the first innings, he took his two hundredth Test wicket, the first Englishman to reach that mark. 'I held that record for nine years,' remembers Sir Alec. An even more satisfying milestone was his hundredth wicket in Tests against Australia. When he

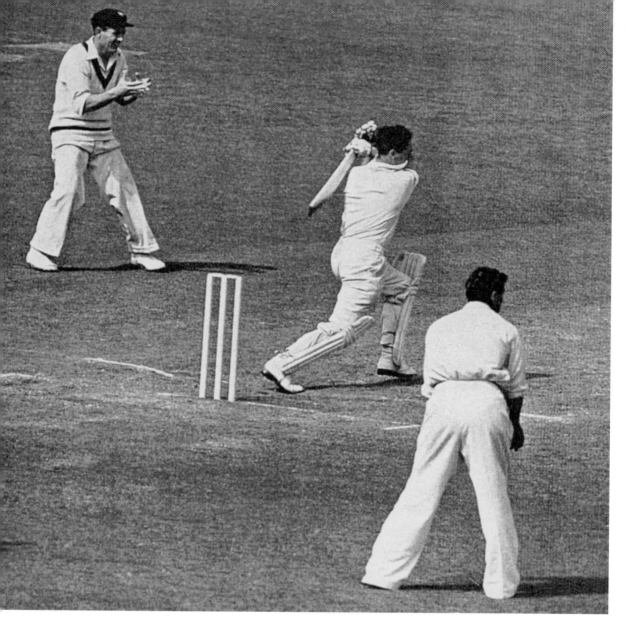

Trevor Bailey, showing a rare aggression, drives during his innings of 71.

achieved this total he became the first man since before the First World War to do so, matching the records of Wilfred Rhodes, Sydney Barnes and Bobby Peel, and in the process bowling more balls against Australia than anybody except his great fast-medium predecessor, Maurice Tate.

The spinners, Johnny Wardle, Tony Lock and Jim Laker, were on the verge of greatness. Wardle and Lock were both left-arm spinners, Lock quicker through the air and Wardle more likely to bowl wrist spin as well as finger spin. Lock, the Surrey man, was considered to be the first-choice left-arm spinner, but Wardle, a Yorkshireman through and through, had his advocates. When Lock was injured for the first three Tests of the summer, Wardle took his place and bowled very well. When Lock came back for the fourth test to bowl in tandem with his Surrey team-mate, the Yorkshire-born Laker (who had missed the two tests himself), there were cries of protest from all true Yorkshiremen, especially as Wardle's analysis in the Australian second innings had been four wickets for seven runs in five overs. There could have been justifiable cries of protest from the Australians, as it was a widely held belief that Tony Lock threw his quicker ball. Arthur Morris describes batting with Hassett against Lock: 'It was difficult to bat with Hassett sometimes as you'd be laughing so much. He'd yell out, "Strike one!" when Lock bowled his quicker ball.' To be fair to Tony Lock, as soon as he saw a film of his bowling action (which was not until several years after the Coronation Ashes series), he completely remodelled it, and still played with great effect for England. Perhaps he was just the Muralitharan of his day.

And then there was Jim Laker. The greatest off-spinner of his generation, perhaps the greatest off-spinner ever, had a fairly quiet summer in 1953, in contrast to his mind-boggling feats when the Australians next toured in 1956. He did not play in the series until the Third Test, but immediately England looked stronger for his inclusion. The England side in the Fifth Test at the Oval was as strong a line-up as they can ever have put out since the war: Hutton, Edrich, May, Compton, Graveney, Bailey, Evans, Laker, Lock, Trueman and Bedser. At the end of their careers none of them had played fewer Tests than Edrich's 39. Two of the team were subsequently knighted for their services to cricket. All five of the bowlers finished with over 100 Test wickets, with a combined total of 1,042. The top five batsmen all finished with Test career averages above 40, and between them scored 66 Test hundreds. Trevor Bailey scored over 2,000 Test runs as well, and as a true all-rounder ended with a Test batting average higher than his bowling average. Wicketkeeper Godfrey Evans made 219 Test dismissals and scored two hundreds in his 91 Tests. 'Godfrey was the best of all the wicketkeepers I saw, better even than

Alan Knott,' is the opinion of Tom Graveney, who played Test cricket
with both men.

Looking back across five decades, it's surprising that Australia ran
Hutton's team so close. We can only suspect that English self-belief was
the missing element after so many years of being second best. All that
would change in August, at the Oval.

The crowds around Lord's queuing to get into the ground for the first day's play in the
Second Test.

1953 : ENGLAND V AUSTRALIA

(2nd Test) June 25, 26, 27, 29, 30.

Australia	1st innings		2nd innings	
A L Hassett †	c Bailey b Bedser	104	c Evans b Statham	3
A R Morris	st Evans b Bedser	30	c Statham b Compton	89
R N Harvey	lbw b Bedser	59	(4) b Bedser	21
K R Miller	b Wardle	25	(3) b Wardle	109
G B Hole	c Compton b Wardle	13	lbw b Brown	47
R Benaud	lbw b Wardle	0	c Graveney b Bedser	5
A K Davidson	c Statham b Bedser	76	c and b Brown	15
D T Ring	lbw b Wardle	18	lbw b Brown	7
R R Lindwall	b Statham	9	b Bedser	50
G R Langley *	c Watson b Bedser	1	b Brown	9
W A Johnston	not out	3	not out	0
	B 4, LB 4	8	B 8, LB 5	13
		346		368

Fall of wickets
1/65 2/190 3/225 4/229 5/240
6/280 7/291 8/330 9/331

1/3 2/168 3/227 4/235 5/248
6/296 7/305 8/308 9/362

England	1st innings		2nd innings	
L Hutton †	c Hole b Johnston	145	c Hole b Lindwall	5
D Kenyon	c Davidson b Lindwall	3	c Hassett b Lindwall	2
T W Graveney	b Lindwall	78	c Langley b Johnston	2
D C S Compton	c Hole b Benaud	57	lbw b Johnston	33
W Watson	st Langley b Johnston	4	c Hole b Ring	109
T E Bailey	c and b Miller	2	c Benaud b Ring	71
F R Brown	c Langley b Lindwall	22	c Hole b Benaud	28
T G Evans *	b Lindwall	0	not out	11
J H Wardle	b Davidson	23	not out	0
A V Bedser	b Lindwall	1		
J B Statham	not out	17		
	B 11, LB 1, W 1, NB 7	20	B 7, LB 6, W 2, NB 6	21
		372	(7 wkts)	282

Fall of wickets
1/9 2/177 3/279 4/291 5/301
6/328 7/328 8/332 9/341

1/6 2/10 3/12 4/73 5/236
6/246 7/282

† Captain *Wicket-keeper

BOWLING

England	1st innings				2nd innings			
	O	M	R	W	O	M	R	W
Bedser	42.4	8	105	5	31.5	8	77	3
Statham	28	7	48	1	15	3	40	1
Brown	25	7	53	0	27	4	82	4
Bailey	16	2	55	0	10	4	24	0
Wardle	29	8	77	4	46	18	111	1
Compton					3	0	21	1

Australia	1st innings				2nd innings			
	O	M	R	W	O	M	R	W
Lindwall	23	4	66	5	19	3	26	2
Miller	25	6	57	1	17	8	17	0
Johnston	35	11	91	2	29	10	70	2
Ring	14	2	43	0	29	5	84	2
Benaud	19	4	70	1	17	6	51	1
Davidson	10.5	2	25	1	14	5	13	0
Hole					1	1	0	0

Australia won the toss   Match Drawn   Umpires: F. S. Lee and H. G. Baldwin

7 • *The Wimbledon Championships*

Monday 22 June to Saturday 4 July

I f June was the month of British invincibility in sport – cricket, horse racing, Le Mans and Roger Bannister's unorthodox mile – July was the month when American dominance returned. The two major sporting championships of the month, the Open Golf Championship at Carnoustie and the Wimbledon Championships, were entirely given over to the Americans. The Brits could only look on in awe and from a distance.

Wimbledon was still, in 1953, the tournament that every tennis player in the world wanted to win. It was the home of tennis championships, the place where it all began and where the local population went spectacularly tennis-mad for a fortnight while the world's leading players served and volleyed on the sw19 grass. Not that the local population had much hope of a local champion to add to the list of sporting heroes in Coronation Year. Among the men, our leading players included John Barrett, later to become a successful coach, and the bespectacled Geoff Paish, who did not look like much of an athlete but still could be expected to advance a couple of rounds. The younger generation, of whom much was expected, was represented by Bobby Wilson, Tony Pickard, Michael Davies and Roger Becker (no relation to Boris, of course), but none of these men was a contender for the title. Fifty years on, we are still looking for a successor to Fred Perry as the most recent British winner of what was then the Gentlemen's Singles Championships, but in 1953 at least it was only 17 years, not 67, since the last British triumph.

The tournament was still an amateur one, as was every major national lawn tennis championship around the globe. With the exception of a few players who had deserted to Jack Kramer's professional tennis 'circus', all the best players were aiming to be on Centre Court at the end of that first week in July to lift the trophy. The first prize for the Gentlemen was 'a piece of silver, known as "The Renshaw Cup", annually presented to the Club by the surviving members of the family of the late Ernest and William Renshaw', the brothers who dominated tennis in its early years and who were largely responsible for making it into a sport rather than a pastime for sunny afternoons on vicarage lawns. No value was placed on this piece of silver, but the second prize was 'of the value of £15 and two third prizes of the value of £8 each' so we can assume that the Renshaw Cup was worth at least £30. In 1953, tennis was not a game for people who needed to earn a living.

The American star Jack Kramer, Wimbledon champion in 1947, had decided early on that tennis was to be his living, and he established a professional circuit in the late 1940s. He persuaded a few of his fellow tennis players to join him, but in the early years it was a hard struggle. Few players wanted to devote their entire lives to tennis, and few players wanted to forgo the chance of winning one of the major championships, which were united in their stance against professional tennis. Even Fred Perry had had to stop competing at Wimbledon and elsewhere when he took up coaching tennis professionally in the 1930s. Kramer remained marginalised for many years, even though by 1953 he had recruited one of the greatest stars of men's post-war tennis, Pancho Gonzalez, who was by common consent the best player of the time, amateur or professional. The pro tour did not attract the crowds, because their tournaments did not mean anything. The big names were all expected to stay amateur, and to come loyally to Wimbledon.

At the beginning of 1953, there appeared the biggest crack in amateur solidarity that had so far been seen. Whether it was the turning point, the defection that gave professionalism the momentum that was to make it irresistible 15 years later, is more difficult to decide, but it certainly hit the headlines at the time. The winner of Wimbledon's Gentlemen's Singles tournament in 1952, the 25-year-old Australian Frank Sedgman, signed up with Jack Kramer and began life as a tennis professional. It was a big blow to the amateur game and to the marketability of the major tournaments (which were making substantial profits while the players, their star performers, were being rewarded with modest silver trophies), but Sedgman's change of status was not followed by a stampede of others in his wake, and the authorities at the time merely considered his action

Bill Tilden, three times Wimbledon singles champion, who died on 5 June 1953, aged 60.

to be a minor inconvenience. But the man was an Australian, after all, so what else could be expected? Sedgman was therefore not invited to defend his title.

Three weeks before the tournament was due to begin, one of the greatest of Wimbledon champions died. Bill Tilden, the first American ever to win the Wimbledon title when he beat Gerald Patterson of Australia in 1920, died of a heart attack at the age of 60 on 5 June. Tilden had won again in 1921 but had not then returned until 1927. He lost in the semi-finals in 1927, 1928 and 1929, but then in 1930, at the age of 37, 'Big Bill' Tilden won the title for the third and final time. He also won the US Open seven times between 1920 and 1929, dominating the game in America, and by extension in the rest of the world, in the process. He was virtually unbeatable when he put his mind to it. In December 1930, after years of earning money writing about amateur tournaments he was competing in and falling foul of the authorities for doing so, he gave up any pretence of amateurism and became a paid tennis player, continuing with some success until after the Second World War. In his obituary in *The Times*, it was noted that 'one of the reasons that Wimbledon moved from Worple Road to its present vast site after 1921 may be said to have been that the singles champions were Tilden and Suzanne Lenglen'. The obituary also pointed out that 'in recent years he fell upon adversity, but it is as the man who bestrode Centre Court like a colossus that he will be remembered'. His adversity included failure to establish himself as an actor and two spells in prison as a result of his living in an age when homosexuality was not tolerated. As *The Times* noted, 'As a player and a character, he was unique.'

The favourites for the Gentlemen's Singles in 1953 were two Australians, Ken Rosewall and Lew Hoad, and two Americans, Gardner Mulloy and Vic Seixas. The displaced Czech, Jaroslav Drobny now playing as an Egyptian, was also highly regarded, but most commentators thought the title would go to Australia or the United States, the two pre-eminent tennis nations. Ken Rosewall, the number one seed, was only 18 in 1953, and was at the start of a remarkable tennis career in which he won eight Grand Slam singles titles and nine men's doubles titles despite moving to the paid ranks in 1957. He reached the Wimbledon finals four times over a 20-year period, but never won there. Lew Hoad, like Rosewall a New South Welshman but 21 days younger than his compatriot, is generally regarded as one of the great tennis players of all time. In 1952, at the age of 17, he had reached the last 32 at Wimbledon and all the pundits were agreed that it was just a matter of time before he started to win this and all the other majors on a regular basis. The pundits were proved right, but only until Hoad turned professional in 1957, immediately after winning that year's Wimbledon with one of the most effective tennis performances ever seen there, crushing his fellow Australian Ashley Cooper, a very fine player in his own right, with the lopsided score of 6–2 6–1 6–2.

The two Americans seen as most likely to succeed were better known as doubles players than singles champions. Elias Victor Seixas Junior, to give him his full name, was coming up to 30 years old but was now at his peak. He, like Rosewall, enjoyed a very long career, playing tennis at the highest levels for almost a quarter of a century. He ranked in the American top 10 in both 1942 and 1966 and many years in between, and played more Davis Cup matches – 55 – for his country than anybody until John McEnroe. In 1966, at the age of 42, he beat a 22-year-old Australian Davis Cup player, Bill Bowrey, in a Philadelphia tournament after a match that lasted almost four hours and finished with the remarkable scoreline 32–34 6–4 10–8. What a pity that tie-breaks were introduced just too late to help him out. At Wimbledon in 1953 he was the number two seed.

Gardner Mulloy was never the singles force that Seixas was, and in 1953 he was already a veteran, approaching 40 years of age. Little did anybody realise that, fit though he was, he was not even half-way through a tennis career that would see him ranked number one in the Over 80s class singles and doubles in the mid 1990s. In 1952, he had been America's number one ranked player, so despite his age, he was clearly seen as a contender. He actually won the Wimbledon doubles, with Budge Patty, four years later at the age of 43.

Seixas and Mulloy played together in the doubles, as did Hoad and Rosewall, and were expected to make more of a mark in that tournament than in the singles. As it turned out, the papers got it slightly wrong. Hoad and Seixas made good progress through the early rounds, and neither man dropped a set on their way to a meeting in the quarter-finals. Hoad had been taken to 7–5 in one set by his first-round opponent, but thereafter swept everybody aside. In four rounds he won 12 sets and lost

It was hot at Wimbledon in 1953. These girls from Gravesend Grammar School made sunhats from newspapers to watch the tennis.

only 26 games in the process. Rosewall, on the other hand, struggled to get past the unrated Frenchman R. Abdesselam in the second round and then was taken to five sets in the fourth round. Mulloy was not making very confident progress either, dropping three sets on his way to the fourth round, where he met an unseeded and unheralded Dane called Kurt Nielsen.

In 1953 there were only eight seeds in each of the singles championships, and yet no unseeded player had ever won the title. More recently, even with 32 seeds in each competition, the men's title has gone twice to unseeded players, Boris Becker and Goran Ivanisevic. However, the way Nielsen was playing anything was possible. The crowd took to the plucky Danish underdog. His first three opponents were two South Africans and an Australian, all of whom he beat well but not without alarms, and this brought him up against Mulloy, the seed in his part of the draw. Mulloy had just survived a five-setter against the Swede S. Stockenburg and perhaps his age was beginning to tell on him. The first set of his match against Nielsen was an epic, but when the Dane finally broke serve to take it, 10–8, you could almost sense the wind coming out of Mulloy's sails. The next set was much more quickly wrapped up, 6–3 to Nielsen, and although Mulloy played strongly in the third set, Nielsen was not to be denied. He finally clinched it 7–5, and went on to meet Ken Rosewall in the next round. All the sensible money was on Rosewall, but the sensible money was lost, as was he. Nielsen took the first set 7–5, but when Rosewall came back to take the next two 6–4 8–6 everybody assumed that the Dane's brave challenge was over. Everybody except Nielsen, that is. Playing remarkable tennis against an opponent who may well have been suffering from an injury or cramp, he took the final two sets for the loss of only two games. Rosewall's Wimbledon singles were over, although the doubles were still there to be won.

The Seixas–Hoad quarter-final was a much closer call. Seixas was seeded higher, and Hoad was still considered too young to have a realistic chance of success this year, though the way he had played in the first four rounds was of championship-winning quality. One thing was for sure, somebody had to lose a set for the first time, and before the end of the day both men did. The match turned out to be an epic: five sets in which the match swung first to Hoad, then to Seixas, then back again and into the final set, which Seixas edged 9–7. The young pretender was eliminated, but Seixas was drained by the challenge.

In the semi-finals Seixas was up against another Australian, Mervyn Rose, a 23-year-old from New South Wales who had partnered Seixas to the US doubles title in 1952, so the pair knew each other's game very well. Nielsen, the surprise packet of the tournament, faced the other European left in the competition, 31-year-old Jaroslav Drobny. A beaten finalist the year before, Drobny was a remarkable sportsman who had won a silver

Maureen Connolly, winner of the 1953 Ladies' Singles at Wimbledon.

medal at the 1948 Olympics as a member of the Czech ice hockey team. By now he had defected from Czechoslovakia and had devoted himself to tennis. He was destined to win the Wimbledon title in 1954, but not this year. Drobny's 1953 Wimbledon had so far been notable for one of the epic struggles in singles history, against Budge Patty in the third

Vic Seixas (right) and Kurt Nielsen before the Men's Singles Final on Friday 3 July.

round, which had seen him edge past Patty 8–6 16–18 3–6 8–6 12–10. That was 93 games in five sets, of which Drobny won 47 to Patty's 46 – about as close and as exhausting as tennis can get. By the time he faced Nielsen in the semi-final, he looked jaded, and his tennis showed it: Nielsen won easily, 6–4 6–3 6–2. The unseeded player was in the final.

His opponent proved to be Vic Seixas, who played another gruelling five-setter to beat Rose 6–4 10–12 9–11 6–4 6–3. After the American had lost the long second and third sets so narrowly, the odds were on the younger Australian, but Seixas was not willing to let him get past. All the same, Nielsen was much the fresher man when the final was played on Friday, 3 July. The final, however, proved to be a far less tiring affair for the second seed Seixas than his semi-final had been, although the newspaper headlines the next morning shouted, 'Seixas Inexhaustible!' He won 9–7 6–3 6–4, and had the match in his grasp all the way. Nielsen, the unseeded underdog, did not let himself down, playing the sort of tennis that had swept Mulloy, Rosewall and Drobny aside, but against the precise, powerful and ruthless Seixas, his athleticism and skill were not enough. His play was described as 'gallant', an adjective applied generally to losers, and despite the backing of the crowd for the Dane, at 5–4 in the third set Seixas was serving for the match. His nerve held so completely that he needed just the four serves to win: as *The Times* put it, 'without a rally Seixas was the champion'. It was the first time that Seixas had won a major singles title, but the general view was that he deserved a championship on his CV, as he had been one of the main contenders at every one for some years, and without Sedgman or a realistic British challenger, who better to take the title? Seixas went on to take the US Open title in 1954, but that was to prove the last of his Grand Slam singles.

By the time he served out that final game, Seixas could have guessed the identity of his dancing partner at the Wimbledon Ball. The Ladies' Singles title was won by the same 'little girl' who had won it the year before, Maureen Connolly, the number one seed. Connolly's domination of women's tennis between 1951 and 1954 was total. She won nine Grand

Slam titles in those years, with only Doris Hart and Shirley Fry presenting a realistic challenge to her brilliance. The only titles she did not win were the tournaments she did not enter. Yet British hopes of a good Wimbledon for the ladies had been high. Three of the eight seeded players were British – Angela Mortimer, Susan Chatrier and Helen Fletcher – and no fewer than 58 of the 96 entrants were home-grown. Several of these were young hopefuls, like Shirley Bloomer, Angela Buxton, Pat Hird, Jennifer Middleton, Valerie Pitt and Joan McLeod, who were all under 21. By the time they were down to the last 32, only 13 British girls were left, an attrition rate far greater than that of other nationalities, but of those 13 six survived to the last 16, which represented a far greater depth in the women's game than we could hope for in our wildest dreams today. It was the beginning of an era in which many British women won Grand Slam titles around the world – Angela Mortimer, Shirley Bloomer, Christine Truman, Ann Jones, Virginia Wade and Sue Barker would all have their names inscribed on Grand Slam cups over the next quarter of a century, but 1953 was just a little too early for the Brits.

Maureen Connolly was not yet 19 years old in June 1953, and just five feet four inches tall, but her youth and her size were no handicap when it came to playing unbeatable tennis. She was known as 'Little Mo' in contrast to 'Big Mo', the USS *Missouri*, but to her opponents her ground strokes were just as devastating as a barrage from a battleship. In setting her record of nine consecutive victories in Grand Slam tournaments she established a mark that is unchallenged half a century later, and it is hard to imagine anybody, male or female, approaching it. 1953 was her best year. She played in all four Grand Slam tournaments (Australia, United States, France, Wimbledon) and won them all, emulating the feat of Don Budge in 1938. What is more, she lost only one set in achieving this feat. Nobody could get near her.

Little Mo was born and raised in San Diego, California, and by the time she was 17 had won the US Open, thanks to the guidance of Eleanor Tennant, who had also coached Alice Marble to a Wimbledon

'Little Mo' on her way to a second consecutive Wimbledon Singles title.

crown in 1939. In 1952 she came to England to compete at Wimbledon for the first time, and caused a stir just before the tournament started by sacking Tennant. At a press conference, she simply announced that 'Miss Tennant is no longer my coach,' and then got on with the process of winning Wimbledon. In those days, her strength was her formidable range of ground strokes. She was not yet a serve-and-volley player at all, but she did not need to be. Her baseline skills were enough to confound her opponents. In 1952 she had a couple of difficult matches on her way to the title, but never looked like losing. She dropped a set against Susan Partridge, a former British junior champion, who persisted in playing down the centre of the court to Connolly's forehand, a tactic that had not been tried before. Little Mo came through 6–3 5–7 7–5 and then had to face the Australian Thelma Long, who employed similar tactics and took another set off her. These turned out to be the only two sets she ever lost at Wimbledon. She beat two Americans after that, Shirley Fry in the semi-final and Louise Brough, the three times champion between 1948 and 1950, in the final. It seemed likely that Little Mo could and would win the title for at least another 10 years.

By the time she reached Wimbledon in 1953, she had already won the Australian and French titles, and was being hailed as one of the all-time greats. She was the Ben Hogan of tennis, and just as unstoppable. Doris Hart was seeded second, but after that there was no competition. Both ladies came through to the fifth round without dropping a set and also without losing more than three games in any set. The rest of the players could only await their turn at the execution block. The British contingent fared reasonably well. Angela Buxton came through three rounds (one with the aid of a bye) before falling to Doris Hart 6–3 6–1. These were the first games Hart had lost all tournament. Helen Fletcher, seeded sixth, also got to the last 16 before coming up against the Hungarian Zsuzsi Kormoczy, and for the first time in 1953, but not the last, Hungary beat Britain in a major sporting contest. Kormoczy was developing into a good enough player to win the French Open, which she did in 1958, so defeat was not a disgrace. Susan Partridge, now Mrs Philippe Chatrier since her marriage to the French player, was seeded number seven after her feat in taking a set off Connolly in 1952, but this time she did not distinguish herself. She only won one match and never got close to the rematch with Little Mo that should have happened in the quarter-finals. Elizabeth Dawson Scott was another Brit to reach the last 16, thanks to three wins over fellow Britons. The first time she met a foreigner, the American seed Dorothy Knode, she made her excuses and left. Knode also beat another English girl, Angela Mortimer, in the next round. Mortimer, who later won Wimbledon before getting married to John Barrett, had beaten three British competitors in straight sets and a French opponent by two sets to one before briefly impeding Knode, who

Vic Seixas leaping the net in the traditional style.

progressed to the semi-final by a score of 6–4 6–3. And that was the end of the British interest in the Ladies' Singles.

Doris Hart, Dorothy Knode, Shirley Fry and Maureen Connolly were the four semi-finalists. All four were American, the last survivors of the nine Americans who had entered the competition. Of those nine entrants one won the title, seven were beaten by other Americans and only one was beaten by a non-American: that was a Mrs Gray, beaten in the first round by a Mlle Bourbonnais of France. Hart had beaten Helen Fletcher's conqueror Zsuzsi Kormoczy in a close straight sets victory, 7–5 7–5, to meet Dorothy Knode. Shirley Fry came up against Little Mo's doubles partner Julie Sampson in the quarter-finals, and eased past 6–4 6–2. Connolly herself had reached the semi-final by winning 48 games and losing just six. All in all, Fry did well to take her to 6–1 6–1. In the other half of the draw, Hart booked her place in the final by beating Knode with slightly more difficulty, 6–2 6–2.

The final, played as tradition then had it on the Saturday, was a brilliant display of women's tennis. Neither finalist having so far lost a set,

1953 Wimbledon Men's Singles Champion.

something had to give. In the end it was Hart who gave way, but both women gave their all in the process. 'An unforgettable singles final' is how it was described in *The Times*. The 28-year-old Hart, who took up tennis as therapy after a serious childhood knee infection that might otherwise have crippled her, was at the peak of her form, but, unfortunately for her if not for the packed Centre Court crowd, so was her opponent. 'Spectators were lost in admiration of a display of strokes of beauty and power, with each player at the height of her skill at the same time, which can surely never have been surpassed,' said *The Times*. Each player knew she had met her match, and the final score, 8–6 7–5 to Little Mo, showed how close it had been. So Maureen Connolly went through Wimbledon 1953 without dropping a set, although she did lose five more games in the final than in all of her previous rounds combined.

The Americans came to win everything at Wimbledon, and they very nearly did. Only in men's doubles did they miss out and in an all-Australian final the top seeds Lew Hoad and Ken Rosewall beat Rex Hartwig and Mervyn Rose. The mixed doubles went to Vic Seixas and Doris Hart, and the women's doubles to Hart and Shirley Fry. The ladies' doubles final showed how far Connolly still had to develop as a serve-and-volley doubles player, because she and her partner Julie Sampson went down to the maximum defeat, 6–0 6–0. In the Junior Tournament there was joy for Britain, as 17-year-old Billy Knight from Northampton won the Boys' Singles. Knight went on to a distinguished senior career, but never managed to win another singles title at Wimbledon.

Maureen Connolly's career as a Wimbledon champion was already more than half over, although nobody knew it. She began the next year as she had finished 1953: she won the French singles title (and the doubles and the mixed doubles for good measure) and she won Wimbledon again, to complete her hat-trick. She went back to the United States and won the US Clay Court title, but days after that victory in July 1954 she was riding a horse (her husband-to-be was Norman Brinker, an Olympic horseman) near her San Diego home when she was hit by a truck and thrown heavily. Her leg was broken, and as she said, 'I knew immediately I'd never play again.' She was still two months short of her twentieth birthday. She became a tennis coach, even working with the British Wightman Cup team in the mid-sixties, but towards the end of that decade she contracted cancer, and died at the beginning of Wimbledon fortnight on 21 June 1969, aged only 34. Lance Tingay, the long-serving tennis correspondent of the *Daily Telegraph*, has written, 'Whenever a great player comes along you have to ask, "Could she have beaten Maureen?" In every case the answer is, "I think not." ' Wimbledon in 1953 saw this brilliant performer at her brief zenith.

8 • *The French Grand Prix*

Sunday 5 July

Sporting contests were different fifty years ago, but perhaps none was quite as different as motor racing. Few would doubt that Michael Schumacher, for example, is a great driver, and that he would have been a winner in any era, but in 1953 the drivers were of a different breed. Racing was not a money-maker, except where the technological advances made in the design and development of racing and rallying cars could be applied to the mass market. There was comparatively little financial spin-off for anybody, because, then as now, the racing-car manufacturers were in the main not also saloon car manufacturers. The saloon car market was growing fast: 'It is believed that about 200,000 new cars may go on to the home market this year,' reported the *Sunday Express* on 18 January. This would represent an increase of about 10 per cent on 1952, with the result that the idea of every home having a motor car was no longer mere wishful thinking. The Motor Show was already a thriving institution, but the British passion for the motor car still had a long way to go. In 2002, the number of new cars registered was more than 10 times greater than in 1953.

World motor racing was dominated by Italian manufacturers and Italian and South American drivers. The languages of the sport were Italian and French. The great Fangio, still racing actively in 1953 at the age of 42, spoke virtually no English, and had no need to. Today there are Grands Prix in Australia, Japan, South Africa, Malaysia and Canada, all countries where English is necessary even if not the native tongue. In 1953, all the Grands Prix were in Europe, with the one exception of the Argentine race, and the great manufacturers were Italian – Ferrari, Alfa Romeo and Maserati. Britain had a couple of star drivers and a number of great rally drivers, but the racing-car industry in Britain was barely in its infancy. Britain was definitely on the fringe of motor racing in the early fifties, not at its centre as it is today.

Racing drivers in those days were not signed up for millions of pounds, euros or dollars to one manufacturer and asked to whiz round specially made circuits at ever-increasing speeds. They were more often than not self-employed motoring enthusiasts who would drive any vehicle anywhere in order to earn a little money and indulge their passion for cars and speed. Their versatility, switching from rallying to sports-car racing to Grands Prix with little more than a check in the rear-view mirror, was extraordinary. They raced and rallied anything, and were among the leaders in every event. As a typical example, the lethally dangerous Mille Miglia, a thousand miles of racing on open roads across Italy ('So what else is new?' I hear survivors of taxi rides to and from Italian airports cry), was won in April 1953 by the Italian Giannino Marzotto, but second, in an Alfa Romeo, was Juan Manuel Fangio. He no doubt thought the race was a good warm-up for the European Grand Prix season just about to begin. Stirling Moss was forced to retire from the race, as was film director and amateur motor enthusiast Roberto Rossellini, who was watched by his wife, the film star Ingrid Bergman.

Moss, the best known British driver of the time and a man who would win the Mille Miglia himself a few years later, was a youthful prodigy, the Jenson Button of his era, just 23 in 1953. He began his year driving a Humber Super Snipe, registration number MRW 671, from Oslo to Lisbon across 15 countries in four days – just to test out the car for the manufacturer rather than to race the 3,352 miles involved. Moss was paid £50 for his trouble. 'I think I grossed about £32,000 in 1953,' says Stirling now. 'That was the equivalent of about £500,000 today. But you had to meet all your expenses out of that. We were not particularly well off.'

The world of motor sport was spiritually an amateur enclave, where people with money and enthusiasm could still compete against people with money, enthusiasm and talent. The Monte Carlo Rally was a typical example. This began as an event in which people could prove the worth of their motor car in extreme weather conditions, and to a certain extent this still applies, even in an era dominated by professionals like Colin MacRae and Carlos Sainz. But it is doubtful that today we would expect to see among the leaders an entry such as the car that came eighth in 1953:

The start of the Le Mans 24 Hour Race. Sixty cars competed, but only 26 finished, led home by Tony Rolt of Britain in a Jaguar.

Air Vice Marshal Donald Bennett and Mrs Bennett in a 3,442cc Jaguar.

Motor racing was also much more dangerous in 1953 than it is now. 'Three or four drivers died each year,' remembers Moss. 'But you always thought, I wouldn't have done that.' The three main causes of a crash, then as now, were oil on the track, mechanical failure and driver error. Mechanical failure was still fairly common, but in general not usually fatal. Driver error was usually triggered by fear, and fear could be eliminated by practice and concentration. Oil on the track was the real danger, deadly and unpredictable. The tracks in those days, with the major exception of the British ones, were not purpose-built. The only surviving road track in Europe 50 years on is in Monte Carlo, where the Monaco Grand Prix is still held around the roads of the principality, but in 1953 most races were on the roads. They were cordoned off for the races, of course, but they were still just roads, without all the safety precautions that are built into the Grand Prix circuits of today. An oil spill from the car ahead or a patch left uncleaned from a little earlier in the race could be lethal. So why on earth did men want to become racing drivers, and risk their lives for little reward?

'I wanted to be a dentist like Dad,' says Moss ingenuously, 'but I hadn't the brains, so I took up motor racing.' The racing world was not populated entirely by people too dim to be dentists: it was full of people who were remarkable athletes first and foremost but who also liked the excitement and glamour that went with the motor-racing world. In that way, the sport has not changed. Motor racing attracted the type of young man who was at ease with the glamour, the danger and the girls who came flocking round the drivers. The image of fighter pilots in the war comes immediately to mind.

There was no sense of fatalism in motor racing. Yes, the drivers knew that what they were doing had its dangers, but they all felt confident they could beat the odds. 'I valued life, and very much so,' says Moss. 'I enjoyed the places we went, the girls, being the driver in his uniform. It was a time when those who could afford to do it enjoyed it.'

One of the biggest and most glamorous events of the motor sport season was, as it had been for 30 years, the Le Mans 24 Hour Race. On the weekend between the Dutch Grand Prix at Zandvoort and the Belgian Grand Prix at Spa, both won by Ascari for Ferrari, the big sports cars were put through their paces in 24 hours of continuous racing. Stirling Moss took part, of course. His was one of four teams driving the new Jaguar XK 120 C-type around the 13.5-kilometre course at speeds that averaged over 100 miles per hour. The C-types took first, second, fourth and ninth places, but it was not Moss who wore the winner's laurels. He and co-driver P. D. Walker came second, three and a half laps behind the winners, Tony Rolt and Duncan Hamilton, another British pairing. Rolt, who was 34 at the time, was enjoying a magnificent year, winning half a dozen major British sports-car titles as well as the world's biggest prize, the Le Mans race. Major Rolt had been a prisoner in Colditz Castle during the war, so going round and round the same piece of ground more than 300 times in a day must have seemed like old times. He raced in several Formula Two events (which is what all the world championship Grands Prix were in 1953), including the British Grand Prix, as he had done in 1950 and would again in 1955, but he failed to finish. At Le Mans, he finished ahead of the entire pack of 60 cars. Runner-up Stirling Moss did at least have the satisfaction of setting the lap record, at something over 105 miles per hour, but second place had not been his intention.

Moss had one great rival among British drivers at this time – the golden-haired, ever smiling 24-year-old Mike Hawthorn. Hawthorn habitually wore a bow tie, which led the French racing fans to nickname him 'Le Papillon'. Moss and the five-months-older Hawthorn were not close friends, but the rivalry between them was overblown by the press. Nevertheless, there was certainly a very competitive edge between them. 'I reckoned I could beat him without much trouble,' says Moss, 'and I'm sure he felt the same about me.' Yet this was a peculiarly British rivalry. Neither Hawthorn nor Moss was thought to be in the same class as the foreign drivers. Juan Manuel Fangio, the introverted Argentinian genius; Alberto Ascari, the charming Ferrari driver; Froilan Gonzales, 'the Pampas Bull' and Giuseppe Farina – these were the men who set the standards for motor racing. No Briton had won a Grand Prix outside Britain for almost 30 years, which was another way of saying almost since the sport began. However, at Rheims on Sunday 5 July, Mike Hawthorn showed the world that once again British drivers had to be taken seriously.

The French Grand Prix was the fifth of the races that year which counted towards the Drivers' Championship, and the first four had all been won by Alberto Ascari. Reigning world champion Ascari was 'a

Stirling Moss at Silverstone. Along with Mike Hawthorn, Peter Collins and Roy
Salvadori, he was part of the influx of brilliant British drivers who within a decade would
dominate the sport.

very nice man', according to Moss, 'and very nearly as good as Fangio. I'd
put him close but not quite there. Fangio had the stamina.' The difference in 1953 was the car: Ascari's Ferrari was just too good for Fangio's
Maserati, as it had been the previous year. At Rheims, the smart money
was on a fifth consecutive Ascari victory. In each race a different driver
had been second to Ascari – Hawthorn, Farina, Villoresi and Fangio had
all come close – but nobody seemed to have the skill, the wit or the luck
to get past him. But that day all three elements came together for
Hawthorn, and in what some papers afterwards described as 'the greatest
motor race of all time' he became the first Briton since Henry Segrave in
1924 to win a Grand Prix. Segrave had also won the French Grand Prix
in 1923, so 30 years on Hawthorn was able to repeat that British triumph.

The British Grand Prix at Silverstone. Alberto Ascari (Ferrari, 5) started among the leaders and finished in first place on his way to the Drivers' Championship.

The race itself, 60 laps of the Rheims circuit of just over five miles, was run at remarkable speeds of well over 100 miles per hour. For the best part of three hours the leading cars battled neck and neck around the track. It was not just a couple or even three, but five cars that contested the lead throughout the race. No boring procession, this. As they entered the final lap, still any one of the front five cars could have won. Ascari, Fangio, Gonzales, Farina and Hawthorn all knew they might still come out in front. Fangio held the narrowest of leads, but Hawthorn, in second place, was using his slipstream brilliantly. Gonzales was right up there with the leading pair, but the other two cars lost touch slightly and fell back. It might have been impossible to pick a winner from the three front runners, but with barely a couple of miles to go it was clear that Ascari was not going to win unless all three leading cars suddenly blew up. They did not. At the crucial moment, Hawthorn came out of Fangio's slipstream and accelerated past him to the chequered flag. He finished one second ahead of Fangio, who had made no move to block the young pretender as he surged through. Fangio in turn was 0.4 seconds ahead of Gonzales. Three seconds later Ascari flashed across the line, and a further three seconds after Ascari, Farina was home. Five cars finished within nine seconds of each other after 165 minutes of racing, which in those days of unreliable cars was an amazing tribute to their engineers. Hawthorn's average speed was 182.885 kph (113.65 mph), his winning time for the 500 kilometres being two hours 44 minutes and 18.6 seconds. A new hero had arrived for the British public to adore and for the rest of the motor racing world to take notice of.

The rest of the sporting world seemed to take little notice, in Britain at least. *The Times* was dismissive, using just three sentences totalling 60 words to tell their readers of Le Papillon's triumph. 'Mike Hawthorn, a British member of the Ferrari works team, won the Rheims Grand Prix here today from Maseratis driven by the Argentinians J. M. Fangio and F. Gonzales,' was the terse opening sentence.

Mike Hawthorn failed to win any more Grands Prix that year, and Alberto Ascari duly went on to his second consecutive world title. Fangio and Farina both won races during the summer, but Ascari's consistency proved unbeatable. Hawthorn did, of course, go on to become the first Briton to win the world Drivers' Championship, in 1958, beating Stirling Moss by one point for the title. That would be the fourth consecutive year that Moss had been runner-up in the title race, and he was destined never to become world champion. Instead, he now has to bear the unwelcome honour of being the greatest driver never to have won the drivers' championship. Hawthorn, sadly, did not have much time to enjoy his world title. He announced his retirement at the end of his victorious 1958 season, but then was killed driving his Jaguar along the Hog's Back in Surrey in January 1959. Ascari was also to die at the wheel, in his case testing a Ferrari at Monza in 1955.

Mike Hawthorn relaxes before the Italian Grand Prix. At Rheims he became the first Briton to win a Grand Prix since the 1920s.

Death kept careful watch over the motor racing fraternity. In August 1953 it claimed perhaps the greatest of them all, the Italian Tazio Nuvolari. His obituary in *The Times* was unequivocal: 'Tazio Nuvolari, in the opinion of many the greatest racing driver the world has yet seen, died at Mantua on 10 August.' Il Campionissimo, as he was known, began by racing motorcycles (as Surtees and Hailwood would do 40 years on), and did not become a major competitor on four wheels until 1928, when he was already 35 years old. However, he carried on at the top until after the war, competing in his final race in 1950, at the age of 57. Driving in his own particular style, mainly in Alfa Romeos, he won many Grand Prix races across Europe in the 1930s, but in the fashion of the era he also competed with huge success in sports-car races, doing the remarkable double of Le Mans and Mille Miglia in 1933, the same year he also won the Belgian Grand Prix. And, to show these achievements were no fluke, he also enjoyed sprints and hill climbs, mainly because he usually won

Alberto Ascari, 1953 world champion, after winning the British Grand Prix. Levels of fitness among racing drivers were apparently lower than they have to be today.

Mike Hawthorn fêted after his victory in the French Grand Prix.

them. His last big race was the 1947 Mille Miglia, in which he came second. His death at the age of only 60 was no less shocking simply because it was from illness rather than at the wheel of a vehicle. The world of motor racing mourned a true great, and then moved on to Bremgarten, where Ascari won the Swiss Grand Prix 13 days later.

Hawthorn's win in the French Grand Prix can certainly be seen as the start of a golden age of British motor racing, what we now call Formula One, although the drivers were all in Formula Two cars in 1953. After his success, and the many near misses of Stirling Moss, British drivers were firmly established at the heart of motor racing. The way was clear for men like Jim Clark, Jackie Stewart, John Surtees and Graham Hill to dominate the sport for a couple of decades to come. Did the drivers see it that way at the time? 'For me, yes, it was the end of an era,' says Moss now. 'The war had made a big gap among drivers, and the old ones were retiring.' Yet in spirit the sport was still in the past. Moss remembers Fangio's sportsmanship in the French Grand Prix as much as the brilliance of the driving or the technically advanced engineering of the cars. In their versatility and willingness just to drive anything anywhere, Moss and Hawthorn seem today to be much closer to the early years of motor racing than the high-tech, ultra-rich sport it has become. This is greatly to their credit.

Hawthorn's year continued well, with fifth place in the British Grand Prix, third in Germany and fourth in Italy, but he was not to repeat his victory that year. Moss had more mixed fortunes: a year which at the outset had seen him as without doubt Britain's pre-eminent motor racing star now saw him with a close rival. To make matters worse, he had picked up a tally of injuries that would soon be considered quite the norm for Moss – a damaged wrist in May and a fractured collarbone and broken kneecap in the Joe Fry Memorial meeting at Castle Combe in October. But at least British motor sport had made significant progress during the year, both in the minds of the sporting public at home and in Europe and, more importantly, in the minds of the team managers and engineers at the heart of racing. Soon, rather than Britain always having to go to Europe for talent and help, Europe would be coming to Britain.

9 · *The Open Golf Championship*

Wednesday 8 to Friday 10 July

Ben Hogan was different from all the other golfers of his era. For a start, he was better than all the other golfers of his era. Then he was older than most of his main rivals, being already almost 41, and he had had to overcome physical challenges that would have broken a lesser athlete. The little man from Dublin, Texas, had a very slow start to his career, playing for seven years – and reputedly going bust a couple of times – before he won his first tournament, in 1938. Even that victory was in a four-ball tournament; his first individual title did not come until 1940, with a win in the North and South tournament at Pinehurst, North Carolina. In those pre-war years it was said that his backswing was far too long, he tended to hook his shots and his putting was not up to much. All in all, he sounds more like a 24-handicapper than a professional, but one thing that Hogan always had was determination and the ability to put in the necessary effort. As Jack Nicklaus said of him, 'I don't think anybody worked as hard as Hogan did. Hogan excelled in hard work, perseverance, determination and the will to succeed.' It is worth remembering that Hogan was naturally left-handed, but on discovering that left-handed clubs were rather more expensive than right-handed ones, he learnt the game right-handed. Golf is not a game for left-handers. Apart from a few successful men like Phil Mickleson and the New Zealander Bob Charles, Open champion in 1963, it is hard to think of left-handed players who have consistently succeeded at golf. So perhaps Hogan was doing himself a technical as well as a financial favour when he began playing right-handed.

Just as his career was getting into its stride the war came between him and the fairways, but when he returned from the army he was suddenly a major competitor. His war had obviously given him time to practise his swing and his putting, although he still feared the unpredictable appearance of his hook until he remodelled his swing in the winter of 1947. He never really took to putting, although his nerves were steady enough. He won his first major, the US PGA title, in 1946 at the

The car-park at Carnoustie during the Open Championship, 1953 when British car manufacturers still enjoyed a monopoly.

age of 34, and from that moment on was always in contention and often a winner. In 1948 he won 11 titles, including his first US Open title, and there was no reason to suppose he would not go on beating the world as often as the fancy took him. Then in February 1949, he was involved in a car accident that nearly cost him his life. He was driving along a foggy road in Texas with his wife Valerie when he collided with a Greyhound bus, which was travelling on the wrong side of the road. He threw himself across his wife just before impact, an action that probably saved both of their lives. However, when they pulled him from the wreck, his pelvis was broken and his legs were very badly injured. For a while, even after his life had been saved, there were serious doubts about whether he would ever walk again. Playing golf seemed to be entirely out of the question.

The doctors made no allowance for Hogan's determination. Within a year he was back playing in tournaments. He captained the American Ryder Cup team in Scarborough at the end of 1949, although he was non-playing captain and it was said that he could only walk as far as the first tee. The pain from his injuries never left him, and this was no doubt part of the reason why, towards the end of his life, he sought solace in a regular diet of martinis. In early 1950 he returned to tournament golf,

although he played far fewer tournaments each year than he had done in his 1940s heyday. To show that he was very quickly back to his best, he won the 1950 US Open, despite having to play 36 holes on the final day of regular play, and an 18-hole playoff the next day. Nobody who had watched him limp home, completely shattered, the night before gave him much chance of victory in the playoff, against George Fazio and Lloyd Mangrum, but he won comfortably, shooting a 69 to Mangrum's 73 and Fazio's 75.

The next year, 1951, he won his first Masters, and those who watched his final round of 68 felt they were watching golf being played at the highest level possible. It was not until later in the year, when many of those same people saw his final round of 67 to win the US Open yet again, that it became clear Hogan seemed entirely capable of taking his golf to another level denied to mere mortals. The Open was played that year at Oakland Hills in Birmingham, Michigan, on a course deliberately designed by the legendary golf course architect Robert Trent Jones to be a brute. Nobody was expected to break 70 on it. 'I'm glad I've brought this course, this monster, to its knees,' Hogan said after that fourth round. Golf was never 'a good walk spoiled' to him. It was always a battle.

1953 was Hogan's year. After a slightly less brilliant 1952, many were saying that a 40-year-old in permanent pain could not come back once again. Yet 1953 for Hogan was as good a year as any golfer has ever enjoyed in the history of the game, Tiger Woods' recent exploits notwithstanding. He entered six tournaments and won five of them, three of which were Majors. But Hogan was not in contention for the 'Grand Slam' because he did not play in the US PGA tournament. There were two reasons for that: first in those days the PGA was a matchplay tournament and Hogan considered that too demanding for him, and second it clashed with the qualifying rounds for the Open at Carnoustie. Hogan very much wanted to win the Open. He had never even entered

Hogan drives from the second tee at Carnoustie on the first day of the Open.

the event before, but he wanted to see his name added to the list of great golfers on the claret jug.

Ben Hogan was not a warm man. The Scots came to know him as the 'Wee Ice Man'. Emotions were not necessary for a great golfer, so he did not show them. 'He had no formal education, but a tremendous presence and a resonant voice,' remembers Peter Alliss, then a newcomer to professional golf, but already a threat to the leading tournament players. 'He was misquoted a lot because he was so uncommunicative.' It soon became clear that Hogan did not like Scotland and Scotland did not like him: it respected him, certainly, admired his golf without a doubt, but like him? That was a different matter.

Hogan was not good at public relations. Although he wanted to win the Open in 1953, which he was pretty sure would be his one chance of glory, he concealed his desire behind a grumpy exterior and brief sentences to the reporters who dogged his footsteps during qualifying and practice rounds. He did little to fit in with local customs and manners, which was perhaps not surprising for a man whose knowledge of Britain was limited to Scarborough during the 1949 Ryder Cup and now Carnoustie. Britain was a bare and desolate place compared with the United States in 1953, and the American professionals all had to make the adjustment to life under rationing and shortages if they were to be successful. Hogan insisted on a room with a bath in his hotel − a comparative rarity 50 years ago but a necessity for a man who had to soak himself in a long hot bath every night if he was to be fit to play the following day.

His caddie was a character, too. Cecil Timms was his name, and he was described by Peter Alliss as 'a blond haired Adonis, better dressed than most of the golfers'. But Hogan hardly noticed this peacock carrying his clubs, and he rarely spoke to him. Hogan even learned to ask him for a cigarette − a very regular occurrence − by mime. When Hogan patted his trouser pockets and struck an imaginary match, Timms handed him a cigarette. Hogan did send his caddie out to buy three dozen of the smaller British golf balls when he first arrived, a quest that must have involved some words of explanation before it

Ben Hogan accepts the claret jug after his brilliant golf on the final day to take
the Open title.

Ben Hogan with American millionaire amateur Frank Stranahan during the Open.

began, and possibly some words of thanks at its conclusion, but beyond that the pair seemed to exchange very few words. We can assume that, even playing four rounds at Carnoustie, 36 balls would have lasted him with plenty to spare.

The course itself has not changed a great deal since 1953. It is still very difficult, with rough that punishes most wayward shots. At 7,200 yards it is a long course and the bunkers in the middle of many of the fairways, so wickedly put there by James Braid, force every golfer to think about his tee shots rather than just blasting straight ahead. The Barry Burn is still there to complicate matters on the final holes, as Jean van der Velde found out in 1999, and the whole course is set alongside the North Sea, which ushers in the mists, the drizzle and the cold northerly winds that make Scottish links golf so testing, and so different from the conditions that Hogan was used to in America. It is, however, hard to compare the feats of, say Tiger Woods or Paul Lawrie, the most recent Open champion at Carnoustie, with those of Hogan because the equipment has changed so totally. In 1953 the golf balls (even the best

British ones) were rarely perfectly round; the clubs had wooden shafts; the woods were made of wood, not titanium or other space age materials; the fairways were less perfectly tended and the bunkers were unraked. As Bob Harlow, editor of *Golf World*, pointed out at the time, 'Vardon was the most accurate I ever saw until Hogan, and Hogan had better tools perhaps. But Vardon played along sort of casual-like whereas Ben acts as if his very life depended on it.'

'In a way,' says Peter Alliss, 'golf is simpler today. The ball goes farther and the greens are ridiculously fast. I'm a great admirer of Tiger Woods – he's brilliant – but Hogan, Snead and company had a greater variety of shots because they had to. Nowadays a lot of the touch and feel and cunning has been eliminated.' For the physically frail Hogan, this was to his advantage. The victory would not go to the longest hitter or the man with the most powerful forearms. It would go to the man with the most touch, feel and cunning.

Hogan gave himself plenty of time to prepare for the Open. He spent two weeks practising with the British balls, learning the course, studying each hole in minute detail, noting the yardages and making some of the preparatory notes that every professional compiles now, but that in 1953 was considered odd. He played almost always alone, trying out shots on each hole to check his route to the greens and work out which clubs he would have to make most use of. The woods and the long irons proved to be his weapons of choice. The weather during these two weeks was pretty good, with the result that the course got drier each day and the fairways became hard and uneven while the greens were slow. By the end of the tournament, Hogan had witnessed the full gamut of Scottish summer holiday weather, but he would not have to contend with the cold misty drizzle until the tournament began.

His two qualifying rounds were safe if unspectacular. He shot a 70 and a 75 to bring him well inside the required limit of 154, but he was still nine strokes behind the leading qualifier, the holder, Bobby Locke of South Africa, who shot a 65 and a 71. In truth, Hogan's golf was worth a

Ben Hogan tees off on his way to victory in the 1953 Open Golf Championship. In the background, Hogan's caddie Cecil Timms is the more immaculately dressed .

better score, but he may well have been put off by the huge crowds who had come to see him qualify and who followed him from tee to green. Certainly his playing partner for the first round, Bill Branch, found the gallery difficult to cope with. On the very first hole his tee shot landed in a bunker and his second hit a woman spectator. His third shot went out of bounds. He shot an eight on the first hole, so it was very much to his credit that he finished with a 77, but his chances had pretty well gone from the start.

The first round of the tournament proper was not much better for Hogan, although by the end of it there had already been a certain amount of sorting out the sheep from the goats. On a day of brisk westerly wind and even a hailstorm or two, the leader was the American millionaire amateur Frank Stranahan, who shot a 70. Stranahan was playing in the tournament as a preliminary to his main event of the summer, his marriage to a fashion model, which was scheduled for 17 July. In the tradition of amateur success at the Open he played consistently well throughout the four rounds, but just failed to take home the title as an extra wedding present. Behind Stranahan on the first day was Eric Brown, the local favourite who could be as emotional as Hogan was sphinx-like. The Scot shot a 71 to be one ahead of four of the world's best golfers – Bobby Locke, the Australian Peter Thomson who would win the next three Opens after 1953, the Welsh maestro Dai Rees and the big Argentinian crowd-pleaser Roberto de Vicenzo.

Hogan shot a 73, as did the Irishman Fred Daly. The vast gallery of about 8,000 people, including Frank Sinatra, watched in awe as his woods and irons gave him the position he wanted time after time, but his putting let him down a little. Even through the hail – this is Scotland in July – he maintained his accuracy from tee to green, but many of his putts finished short. He may not have won too many friends by offering to send back to Texas for a lawn mower to cut the greens.

On the next day, the Thursday, Hogan shot a 71. The weather was a complete contrast from the day before, quite still and clear, and Hogan once again played masterful golf from tee to green. Those who watched him play suggested that until he took his putter out of the bag his golf was as good as anything that had ever been seen, but his putting was once again fallible. His round of 71 included 34 putts. Bobby Locke, who shot a 73, needed only 28 putts. So overnight at the half way mark, the lead was held by the two Brits, Dai Rees (72, 70) and Eric Brown (71, 71), one shot ahead of Roberto de Vicenzo (72, 71). Hogan was one shot further back on 144, alongside Peter Thomson and the first-round leader Frank Stranahan.

The third day was always going to be the difficult one for Hogan, because it was then the practice to play the final two rounds on the Friday. For a man with his health problems, 36 holes was always a very heavy day's work. What is more, the Scottish summer had given him a nasty head cold, and he got little sleep overnight. There were those who

Ben Hogan and his wife during the Open.

suggested that Hogan would not have the stamina to last the day, let alone catch up two shots on the leaders. But the feature of Hogan's game was his mental strength, and where others might have cracked, he simply redoubled his determination to get his hands on that claret jug.

The weather was, at least, in his favour. After all the varieties of the Scottish east coastal weather – six seasons in one day – the final Friday dawned clear and calm and conditions were ideal for low scoring. What the gallery got was not just low scores from Hogan but perhaps the finest day's golf ever seen in the Open, which may well mean the best day's golf ever seen anywhere. The crowd that followed Hogan was described by the golfer and journalist Leonard Crawley as 'the like of which I had never seen on any golf course'. They were everywhere, on the fairways, around the greens, behind the tees and even a few by the bunkers waiting for the very unlikely event that one of Hogan's shots would land in the sand. Hogan used his sand wedge very little that Friday.

His third round was a magnificent display of golf. He reached the turn in 35, one shot better than the day before, and then took a birdie three on the tenth. The course record, 69, seemed to be at his mercy as he took only two at the short thirteenth, and for the first time in three rounds managed a three at the sixteenth. At this stage, even with his putting still by no means infallible, he had taken only 60 shots to reach the seventeenth tee. However, Carnoustie is never a course you can take for granted, and even somebody playing as well as Ben Hogan could fall foul of its vagaries. His long-iron approach shot to the green was not struck quite right, and it landed in a bunker in front of the green, thus rewarding the section of the crowd that had lined the bunkers rather than the fairways all morning. He splashed out of the bunker reasonably well, and still had two shots from about 25 feet to make his par. He took three putts: the six was the only real blemish on his card all morning. Still, he finished with a 70, which meant that at lunch he was sharing the lead with Roberto de Vicenzo on 214. Behind them on 215 came the main British hope Dai Rees, Peter Thomson and the other Argentinian, Antonio Cerda, who had equalled the course record in the morning with 69.

One shot further back was the Scot Eric Brown, and two shots behind him was Frank Stranahan, the amateur enjoying his stag weekend. Realistically, any of these men could have won.

Hogan did not share this opinion. Realistically, in his view, only he could win. More to the point, only he could lose it. The championship was there for the taking. Stranahan and Rees, the latter with the local crowd urging him on, set the afternoon pace. Stranahan showed no pre-wedding nerves at all in scoring 69 to equal the course record and finish on 286. Rees, who just missed a putt for a three on the sixteenth, finished with 71 to match Stranahan's score, as did Peter Thomson, but Brown and de Vicenzo could not withstand the pressure and slipped back. De Vicenzo's 73 put him on 287, while the sometimes temperamental Eric Brown finished with a 76 for 292, bringing him level with the 22-year-old Peter Alliss, who finished in the top 10 without ever challenging the leaders. Two other Brits, Sam King and Max Faulkner, had also finished well in whatever token amounts of money were on offer, but as Hogan forged around Carnoustie for the fourth and final time only he or Antonio Cerda were left in with a chance. If they both finished on 286, there would be a five-way tie and an 18-hole playoff the following day. Clearly, Hogan did not want to have to put himself through that ordeal.

He began with four straightforward fours, if any such scores on a course like Carnoustie can be described as straightforward, and on the fifth made the move that gave him an edge on his rivals that he never lost. His tee shot at this hole ended up on the fairway, but in a terrible lie. His second shot from this awkward position finished on the edge of a bunker guarding the green, and where most men would have settled for a four, Hogan spent what seemed like minutes studying the lie, the slope and speed of the green before producing a low iron with which he chipped delicately and directly into the hole. The roar from the gallery told all his rivals in their different parts of the course that the Wee Ice Man had got the break he was looking for.

From that moment Hogan seemed to be released from any mental troubles. In his heart he knew he could not be caught, just as in their hearts his rivals knew they would not catch him. His play moved up yet another level to one of serene certainty. The length of the holes made no difference to him, the terrain was almost incidental and the raucous gallery was blocked out by Hogan's intense concentration. At the long par five sixth he was at the edge of the green in two, and a chip and a four-foot putt gave him his birdie. At the short thirteenth, a five-yard putt gave him another birdie. Only on the fourteenth hole did he take a five, but even that gave his rivals no hope. He finished in 68, a course record, and there were those who swore he could have made that 65 if he had needed to. Cerda battled gamely to shoot 71 and finish with Thomson, Rees and Stranahan on 286, but they were all four shots behind Hogan, whose four rounds had got a little better each time. 73, 71, 70, 68 – another four or five rounds and he might have broken 60. As *Golfing* magazine said, Hogan 'possesses something far above consistency. He maintains a top level of excellence as his normal standard, but apparently he can almost at will – as in his last round at Carnoustie – pull out a still higher level of brilliance that leaves everybody else looking like part of the next race.'

Hogan had won. He had his name on the jug and he could now go home to a country where they had enough sugar and milk and cheese, and deep enough baths to soak in at night. He gave the impression he would come back to defend his title the next year. 'Quitting the game?' he is quoted as saying immediately after his victory. 'No, sir. Why should I? I'm just getting to where I started out to get when I was twelve.' He also had a few of those small British balls left in his bag, which would only come in handy if he played in Britain again. At the time he was rather more complimentary about Scotland and Carnoustie than he would be once he was out of reach. 'The course was extremely tough. You need radar to play some of those blind shots,' was about as controversial as he got in the afterglow of his victory, and the newspapers responded in kind. 'Ben Hogan, tough little Texan wonder golfer, gained a stupendous victory in the Open Championship here today,' were the opening words of the *Daily Mirror*'s report, and most of the other journalists took the same

line. On his return to America he was given a tickertape parade through the streets of New York, and the golf-mad new President Eisenhower greeted him at the White House. In 1953, Hogan won the only three Majors he competed in, and even Tiger Woods has still to win all four Majors in the same year.

His final thoughts on Carnoustie were less generous. On board the ocean liner *United States*, he told the press, 'In Scotland it seems they just throw up greens and tees and cut out a narrow fairway to join them. They do nothing to the rest of the course.' The fact that golf began in Scotland in exactly that way seems to have escaped his notice, but that should not detract from Hogan's greatness as a golfer. 'There has never been a better champion,' said *The Times*. 'It's hard to say that anybody has ever been as good as Hogan at his peak,' agrees Peter Alliss.

In 1953, Hogan had reached his peak. He did not defend his Open title and never competed in Britain again. Though he played on for several more years he never won another Major. The nearest he came was losing in a playoff for the 1955 US Open, but nobody could take his 1953 triumphs away from him. When he died in 1997, aged 85, his friend and contemporary Byron Nelson said that 'in my book he is the greatest golfer that ever lived'. Not a bad epitaph.

Ben Hogan, Open Champion 1953.

10 • *The Fifth Test Match*

Saturday 15 to Wednesday 19 August

After the heroics of the Second Test at Lord's, the series against the Australians seemed determined to defy resolution. As Arthur Morris said, 'We should have won the Second Test, we should have lost the Third, and should have won the Fourth.' In the event, all three games were drawn. The Third Test, which Australia should have lost, took place at Old Trafford and, not surprisingly, the weather took a decisive hand. This was the ninth successive Ashes Test played in Manchester over half a century that had ended in a draw, a testament to the Manchester climate if ever there was one. England had brought in Edrich to open the batting with Len Hutton, but once again the selectors' nervousness about the strength of the Australian bowling meant that they picked only three specialist bowlers, the long-suffering Alec Bedser, Johnny Wardle and Jim Laker, in for the first time that summer in the place of the injured Brian Statham. The Australians brought back Hill for Ring, brought in Ron Archer for the injured Bill Johnston and Jim de Courcy, a batsman, to make his Test debut in place of the leg-spinning all-rounder Richie Benaud.

Australia won the toss, as they did in every Test that summer, and elected to bat. Bedser settled in for his customary long bowling stint, and the rest of the England attack operated around him. The weather allowed only a shortened first day, and barely 90 minutes' play on the second day. The crowds, so used to the ghastly weather of that wet summer, 'endured patiently the long idle hours after paying five shillings each at the turnstiles', to quote *Wisden*. By the end of the third day, England had made 126 for four in reply to Australia's 318, a total built around Neil Harvey's 122. Already it looked as though a draw was the most likely result, but the complete washout of the fourth day's play made it absolutely certain. The fifth and final day did allow some play, enough for England to reach 276 all out, thanks in no small part to a vigorous 44 not out from Godfrey Evans. Then when Australia batted again, with scarcely more than an hour's play left, Hutton demonstrated his captaincy skills

The England team that won back the Ashes. Back row, left to right: T. E. Bailey,
P. B. H. May, T. W. Graveney, J. C. Laker, G. A. R. Lock, J. H. Wardle (twelfth man),
F. S. Trueman. Front row, left to right: W. J. Edrich, A. V. Bedser, L. Hutton (captain),
D. C. S. Compton, T. G. Evans.

by opening the bowling with Bedser and Laker, fast medium and off
spin. Hassett hit two boundaries in Bedser's first over, but after that the
England bowlers ran riot. By the finish of the match Australia were 35 for
8, with Jim Laker having taken 2 for 11 in nine overs and Johnny Wardle
4 for 7 in five overs. Though the Test match was lost to the weather, England emerged with a psychological advantage.

Nine days later, the Fourth Test began at Headingley. England had replaced the successful Wardle with Tony Lock, now returned to fitness, and Australia had brought back Richie Benaud at the expense of Hill. Hassett won the toss yet again, and Hutton tried to bluff him by throwing the coin away in disgust. But after the recent downpours, during which rain had seeped a little under the covers, neither team wanted to bat, so Hassett called Hutton's bluff and put England in. This was the first time since 1909 that Australia had put England in to bat, and only the second time they had ever done it in England. The precedents were good: in 1909 Australia had won by nine wickets. Forty-four years on, Ray Lindwall made the most of the conditions, taking 5 for 54 in 35 overs, and fully justifying his captain's decision. England were all out for 167 within an hour of the start of the second day's play. Hutton and Compton both made ducks and only Tom Graveney, with 55, played a decent innings. 'I was proud of that 55 on a green top at Headingley against Lindwall, Miller, Davidson and Archer,' says Graveney.

When Australia batted, it was thanks mainly to Bedser, who took 6 for 95 in 28.5 overs, that Australia were restricted to 266, a lead of 99. Harvey (71) and Hole (53) were the top scorers. England fared rather better in their second innings, with Edrich and Compton both making 60-plus in between swirls of rain, but at the start of the final day their score was 177 for 5, just 78 ahead, with Compton unable to carry on batting because of a hand injury suffered the evening before. However, once again it was Trevor Bailey to the rescue. The Essex all-rounder batted for four hours and 22 minutes for just 38 runs, leaving the run-making to others. Jim Laker, with several scorching off-drives that few knew he possessed, made 48 out of a stand of 59 with Bailey, who was eventually the last man out, in the final over before tea. England totalled 275, so Australia needed 177 to win in five minutes short of two hours.

Australia had to go for the runs, so Hutton opened the bowling with Bedser and Lock. All the Australians played hard and rode their luck, notably Harvey and Hole who added 57 for the third wicket in just 30 minutes. When Bedser got Harvey lbw, Davidson came out at number five. There were 66 needed in three-quarters of an hour and still seven

Alan Davidson is well caught by Bill Edrich at slip off the bowling of Jim Laker for 22 in Australia's first innings.

wickets in hand. Australia were in the box seat. Then Hutton tossed the ball to Trevor Bailey, who had bowled very effectively off his short run during the first innings. This time Bailey decided to use his full long run, perhaps an even fuller version than usual, and took his time to set his field and plan each ball. It was a natural continuation of his efforts to abbreviate the game, which had begun when he appealed against the light two minutes before lunch, thereby successfully 'losing' an over. When he did bowl, he went round the wicket on a line wide of the leg stump. It was bodyline without the intimidation: nobody was likely to get hurt, but nobody was very likely to score many runs either. The Australians were not happy about the tactics, complaining that the over rate had been artificially slowed down, although by today's standards 12 overs in three-quarters of an hour, 16 in the hour, is not particularly slow. 'A lot of sportsmanship went out of the game in that match,' is Harvey's brief comment. When Bailey got his line slightly wrong and induced Graeme Hole to try to hit him out of the ground, Graveney took a good catch on the boundary, and the jig was up. Australia ended 30 runs short with six wickets in hand. A moral victory for the Australians, maybe, but still another drawn game.

So the two teams moved to The Oval. In the two and a half weeks between the two Tests the Australians played no fewer than five county matches, against Surrey, Glamorgan, Warwickshire, Lancashire and Essex. They drew the first three and won the final two, and many of their batsmen and bowlers had a chance to prove their worth for the final Test team. Neil Harvey hit two hundreds, Jim de Courcy one, and almost every other batsman, including the perennial drinks waiters Ian Craig and Colin McDonald, scored at least one fifty. Bill Johnston, who played four of the five matches, took 18 wickets to prove he was fit again, and when he batted scored 2, 9 and 1, not out each time. By this stage the Australians had realised that their left-arm medium-pacer had been dismissed just once all summer (c&b Vic Cannings for 8, against Hampshire on Derby Day) and had now scored over 50 runs and so was perching at the top of their batting averages. This seemed a good joke to the Aussies, and to Johnston, and from then on they tried to make sure that Johnston was not dismissed. It was not as obvious or as contrived as the Australians might make out today: Johnston scored heavily (for him) in the final few games, top-scoring with 27 not out in the first innings against the Gentlemen of England, for example. He could not have done so if he had been entirely prevented from facing any difficult bowling. However, when he reached 5 not out in the match against the South of England at the Hastings Festival on 3 September, Hassett realised that Johnston then had 102 runs for the season, and had been out just once so he declared the innings closed. Johnston had one more innings, against T. N. Pearce's XI at Scarborough a week later. As soon as he came to the wicket his partner contrived to get out, and Johnston again finished not out. The plan had worked and Johnston joined Bradman as one of only two men to that time who had averaged over 100 in an English season.

During the time between the Fourth and Fifth Tests, there was another match that attracted great public attention. On 2 August at

Crowds gather outside an electrical shop in High Holborn to listen to the BBC
commentary on the Fifth Test.

Arundel, that most lovely of cricket grounds, the Duke of Norfolk's XI
played a team led by the Duke of Edinburgh, who was still playing cricket as often as his other commitments would allow (which, in truth, was
not often, especially in Coronation Year). The match was in aid of the
National Playing Fields Association, a cause close to Prince Philip's

heart, for which they raised £3,247. The Duke of Norfolk's XI won the game, by seven runs but, unlike the Test series, the game was much more important than the result.

With Johnston fit again, the Australians left out Richie Benaud, but otherwise they fielded an unchanged team. England finally decided – in the one Test of the summer when Johnston was fully fit – that the Australian bowling attack was not so fearsome after all, and so they dropped a batsman for a bowler. Freddie Trueman came in for his first Test of the summer in place of Nottinghamshire's Reg Simpson, and the hero of Lord's, Willie Watson, made way for Peter May, the man he had displaced three Tests earlier. With the first four Tests drawn, the authorities allotted an extra day to the final Test, but this did not tempt the selectors to think defensively. The weather played its part once again, but in the end neither the extra day nor the one before it was needed.

For the fifth time in a row Hassett won the toss, and for the fourth time Australia batted first. Only once had the Australian opening pair reached 50 in the series, and they were not to do so here. In conditions that were not ideal for batting, Australia struggled against the ruthless accuracy of Bedser and, for the first time that summer, against the genuine fast bowling of Trueman. By lunch they were on 98 for 2, having lost Morris and Miller quite quickly, but the light rain that fell during the lunch break enlivened the pitch. Batting in the afternoon was a quite different kettle of fish as Trueman and Bedser rapidly got rid of Hassett, Harvey and de Courcy. At 118 for 5, Australia were in trouble. This was the cue for Graeme Hole, who was having no more than an average series and who was never to establish himself properly in the Australian side, to play his best innings of the series. He made only 37, but together with Ron Archer he wrested the initiative back from England for a while. His free strokeplay showed what might be done even on this rather doubtful surface, and when he was out, edging a catch through to Evans having been beaten for pace by Trueman, Australia had moved up to 160. On the same score Archer was out, caught and bowled by Alec Bedser. 'A little slower one,' is how Sir Alec remembers it. This proved to be Bedser's final wicket of the series, but far more significantly brought his aggregate to thirty-nine, a new Ashes record, beating the 38 wickets taken by Maurice Tate for England in the 1924/25 series. Bedser also passed Clarrie Grimmett's world Test record of 216 wickets during the summer, when he dismissed Gil Langley at Headingley, so it had been a wonderful benefit year for the man who carried England's bowling almost single-handedly between 1946 and 1953.

Archer's dismissal brought in Ray Lindwall, who once again tore into the English bowling attack. As at Lord's, his clean driving brought him a quick fifty, and in 10 minutes under two hours Australia added 115 runs for their final three wickets, of which Lindwall's share was 62. Davidson, Langley and even the eternally not-out Bill Johnston provided valuable support, while Jim Laker bore the brunt of the onslaught. His five overs cost 34 runs. Australia were finally all out for 275, which looked a reasonable score in the conditions, and there was time for England to face a couple of overs before close of play. England emerged from this little ordeal unscathed, although Hutton was lucky to survive. The fifth ball of Lindwall's over was a bouncer, which hit the handle of his bat as he fended it away, but then he had two pieces of good fortune. The ball, instead of flying straight to the slips where it would certainly have been caught, struck Hutton's cap en route, lost all its pace and dropped well short of the slip cordon. As if to prove this was his doubly lucky day, his cap came off but narrowly missed the stumps as it fell. Hutton survived two chances in one ball.

They were to prove expensive strokes of luck, for on the next morning Hutton took his score to 82, out of 154 for three. With May he added exactly 100 for the second wicket, but once they were both out England began to struggle. Compton and Graveney went cheaply and at 170 for five England had a great deal of work to do to stay on terms. Luckily, the man who was always willing to do that work, Trevor Bailey, was the next man in. It was dour stuff, but Bailey and Tony Lock stuck together to the close of the second day's play, when England were 235 for 7. Lock was dismissed very early the next morning, but Bailey ground on and on, first

Denis Compton makes the winning hit – a pull for four off Arthur Morris.

with Freddie Trueman and then with Alec Bedser. When Bedser came out to join Bailey England were still 13 runs short of the Australian total, but the last-wicket pair proceeded to add 44 precious runs. Bailey was the last man out, bowled by Ron Archer after three hours and 45 minutes at the wicket, for 64. All in all, England had batted for 142.3 overs – a run rate of 2.15 runs per over – compared to Australia's 275 in 81.3 overs, a rate of 3.38. Still, it was England who took a lead of 31 into lunch and into the second half of the game.

Huge crowds gather around The Oval's pavilion to celebrate the return of the Ashes.

The next three hours' play decided the destiny of the Ashes. Hutton gave Bedser and Trueman just a token couple of overs after lunch before bringing Lock and Laker on. Trueman, included in the side to inject real pace into the attack, had bowled only two overs and Bedser three when Hutton tossed the ball to the Surrey spinners. By that time, the Australians had already scored 19 on a fairly lifeless pitch, and Arthur Morris in particular was looking set for a big score. Unkind critics have suggested that Hutton gave Laker an over just to let his opening bowlers change ends, but if that was so, he was still shrewd enough to keep the spinners on once he had seen within the space of six balls what they were likely to do.

It was Jim Laker who began the Australian procession in and out of the pavilion. Bowling round the wicket to Hassett, it took the great Surrey off-spinner only six balls to trap the Australian captain leg before wicket. It almost looked as though Hassett had got his bat caught up in his pads trying to play a shot but, whatever the reason, he failed to get it in the way of the ball and was palpably leg before, playing back. Australia were 23 for 1, still eight runs behind England. Hole, promoted to number three in place of Miller, tried some big hitting, especially off Laker, and for a while was successful. But when Laker trapped him too, lbw for 17, the rot really set in. Harvey was bowled by Lock for one – 'There were no sightscreens at the Oval in those days, and I didn't see the ball that got me' – Miller was caught by Trueman off Laker for a duck, Morris was lbw to Lock, and de Courcy was superbly run out by Bailey, who easily beat him with a quick pick-up and throw from mid-wicket to Evans' gloves. Suddenly Australia were 85 for 6 and England had the match, and the Ashes, in their grasp. At one stage, as the Australians moved laboriously from 59 to 61, they lost four wickets in the space of 16 balls of Surrey spin. Was it the brilliance of the bowling on what was to all intents and purposes a benign pitch, or was it poor batting that undid Australia? A little bit of each is the answer. Australia's batsmen were nervous, and Lock and Laker exploited that nervousness perfectly.

This was the unlikely cue for Ron Archer to counter-attack. Helped by both Davidson and Lindwall, the 19-year-old all-rounder did his best to make a match of it. Some big hitting off both spinners, including sixes by both Archer and Davidson, left England with several men posted on the boundary, but still the Australian batsmen plundered the bowling. Davidson's six off Laker cleared the boundary by a good 10 yards, and this was at The Oval, probably the biggest Test ground in England. When the umpires took off the bails for tea, the crowd was breathless. In two hours, Australia had made 131 runs for the loss of six wickets, a hectic and, for Australia, suicidal session. Well though Archer and Davidson were batting, they would have to make many more runs to stretch the lead beyond the 100 so far achieved if Australia were to have a realistic chance of saving the game.

After tea, Archer and Davidson could not maintain their offensive. First Davidson went, bowled by Lock with the score on 135, and then Archer was well caught by Edrich at slip, again off Lock. His 49 was a great innings under the circumstances, but it did not set up a victory. In 60 minutes, with one six and seven fours, he had shown that the young blood of Australia had much to offer for the future, but not enough to relieve the present predicament. Lindwall, the belligerent old hand, hit Lock for six, but was then caught on the boundary trying to do the same to Laker, and although Langley and Johnston added a further 16 runs for the last wicket before Johnston secured his customary not out (this time with 9), Australia finished on 162 all out. Their innings had lasted only 177 minutes, and had occupied just 50.5 overs. The run rate was 3.19 runs per over, and England's bowling rate was almost 17 per hour. Lock had taken five wickets for 45 runs in 21 overs, and Laker, who took more punishment but who had made the first crucial breakthrough, finished with figures of 4 for 75 in 16.5 overs. England now had 50 minutes of the third day and all of the fourth, fifth and sixth days to score 132 to win the series. Unless a monsoon set in, it seemed that the Ashes would be coming home after 19 years.

Fifty minutes at the end of a hard day is the sort of molehill that England specialise in making into a mountain, and they put their best efforts into playing to character here. Hutton and Edrich opened circumspectly enough, but with the score on 23 Hutton hit the ball to square leg. There was an easy single there, but when de Courcy misfielded, the batsmen went for the second. De Courcy recovered quickly and his throw easily beat the helpless Hutton. Suddenly there was some alarm in the ranks. If Hutton could self-destruct so swiftly and ridiculously, then surely anything was possible and nothing could be taken for granted. But Edrich and May eased English nerves by batting out time, and overnight England were looking prosperous at 38 for 1. For Australia, the next morning would represent the final throw of the dice.

The remaining 94 runs needed for victory took over two and a half hours to compile. A huge crowd had come to see England's triumph, but they knew that the Australians would not concede victory a moment before it became inevitable. The significance of the match – and the probable result – to the nation can be gauged by the fact that on the third day the BBC had cancelled their children's television programmes to show live coverage of the match, and they then decided that the whole of the final day's play would be shown live. Today we take it for granted that

Test cricket is covered each day live on television, but in 1953, when there was only one television channel, it meant that the entire television audience would have to be tuned into the cricket, like it or not, and let Muffin the Mule go hang.

Muffin the Mule turned out to be safe on 19 August, because the match was over by 2.45. Lindwall and Johnston bore the brunt of the bowling during the morning session, and they tied down Edrich and May almost totally. They did not, however, get either of them out. Lindwall was not bowling at any great pace – he must have been exhausted by the exertions of the summer – but he still bowled with all his great skill to keep the batsmen thinking all the time. Not until the eleventh and final over of his morning spell did Edrich manage to get hold of him, hitting two consecutive bouncers for four. By the time Lindwall took his sweater he had bowled 11 overs for 22 runs, 10 of which came in that final over. Johnston was equally parsimonious, bowling 18 overs unchanged on the final morning for just 24 runs. But neither man took a wicket. The only one to fall was that of Peter May, caught by Alan Davidson behind square off Keith Miller. May had scored 37, and when he was out England were two-thirds of the way there, with 88 runs on the board and 44 more to make.

By lunch, Edrich and Compton, the great Middlesex pair, had taken the score into three figures, 101 for 2. England were nearly there. Those last 31 runs took only 35 minutes after lunch, enough time for Edrich to reach a thoroughly well-deserved fifty, and for captain Hassett and vice-captain Morris to bowl the last two overs when an English victory was assured. When Compton hit Morris to leg, and quite possibly to the boundary, for the winning run, the entire ground erupted with pent-up joy. The crowd surged on to the pitch and Edrich and Compton had to make their way back to the pavilion through the thousands of cricket lovers who pounded them on the back in congratulation and elation. Both men were as bruised as if they had been run over by a bus.

Len Hutton acknowledges the crowds at The Oval after England's triumph.

It was a scene that had been many years in the coming. The last time England had won back the Ashes had been in Australia in 1933. They had not won them in England since 1926, 27 years and a day before, in the reign of the Queen's grandfather, when Hobbs and Sutcliffe put on 172 for the first wicket to help England to overwhelming victory by 289 runs. Today's victory was equally decisive – by eight wickets – and the crowds revelled in it. They called for both teams to come out on to the balcony to receive the acclamation that was their due. Hutton, dressed in his street clothes and smoking a cigarette, waved shyly but proudly to the crowds, who would not leave the ground. Both captains were obliged to make brief speeches, the main theme being the wonderful spirit in which the series had been played. Many of the cricketers on both sides are still close friends 50 years on, so there is no doubt that the spirit was good between the two teams. However, the English tactics of slow over rates and negative bowling at times upset the Australians, and one wonders in hindsight whether both captains had ignored reality when stressing the friendly rivalry of the two sides. Perhaps this was the series in which winning became more important than taking part.

All the same, few British commentators analysed the darker side of the series. Everybody just concentrated on the wonderful achievement of winning back the Ashes in Coronation Year, and the enormous public interest in the series. As *Wisden* noted, 'Australia received some measure of compensation for losing the Ashes by taking home a record profit of over £100,000.' England's victory at The Oval was the crowning moment of even this astonishing sporting year, the day when they won back the sporting trophy that had eluded them for years. Small it may have been, but it was still probably the most important international sporting prize that Britain competed for at the time, a prize that in some strange way seemed to embody the dreams and ambitions of Britain's sporting public in Coronation Year. It was a happy ending to a glorious summer.

1953 : ENGLAND V AUSTRALIA

(5th Test) August 15, 17, 18, 19.

Australia	1st innings		2nd innings	
A L Hassett †	c Evans b Bedser	53	lbw b Laker	10
A R Morris	lbw b Bedser	16	lbw b Lock	26
K R Miller	lbw b Bailey	1	c Trueman b Laker	0
R N Harvey	c Hutton b Trueman	36	b Lock	1
G B Hole	c Evans b Trueman	37	lbw b Laker	17
J H de Courcy	c Evans b Trueman	5	run out	4
R G Archer	c and b Bedser	10	c Edrich b Lock	49
A K Davidson	c Edrich b Laker	22	b Lock	21
R R Lindwall	c Evans b Trueman	62	c Compton b Laker	12
G R Langley *	c Edrich b Lock	18	c Trueman b Lock	2
W A Johnston	not out	9	not out	6
	B 4, NB 2	6	B 11, LB 3	14
		275		162

Fall of wickets   1/38 2/41 3/107 4/107 5/118   1/23 2/59 3/60 4/61 5/61
6/160 7/160 8/207 9/245   6/85 7/135 8/140 9/144

England	1st innings		2nd innings	
L Hutton †	b Johnston	82	run out	17
W J Edrich	lbw b Lindwall	21	not out	55
P B H May	c Archer b Johnston	39	c Davidson b Miller	37
D C S Compton	c Langley b Lindwall	16	not out	22
T W Graveney	c Miller b Lindwall	4		
T E Bailey	b Archer	64		
T G Evans *	run out	28		
J C Laker	c Langley b Miller	1		
G A R Lock	c Davidson b Lindwall	4		
F S Trueman	b Johnston	10		
A V Bedser	not out	22		
	B 9, LB 5, W 1	15	LB 1	1
		306	(2 wkts)	132

Fall of wickets   1/37 2/137 3/154 4/167 5/170   1/24 2/88
6/210 7/225 8/237 9/262

† Captain   *Wicket-keeper

BOWLING

England	1st innings				2nd innings			
	O	M	R	W	O	M	R	W
Bedser	29	3	88	3	11	2	24	0
Trueman	24.3	3	86	4	2	1	4	0
Bailey	14	3	42	1				
Lock	9	2	19	1	21	9	45	5
Laker	5	0	34	1	16.5	2	75	4

Australia	1st innings				2nd innings			
	O	M	R	W	O	M	R	W
Lindwall	32	7	70	4	21	5	46	0
Miller	34	12	65	1	11	3	24	1
Johnston	45	16	94	3	29	14	52	0
Davidson	10	1	26	0				
Archer	10.3	2	25	1	1	1	0	0
Hole	11	6	11	0				
Hassett					1	0	4	0
Morris					0.5	0	5	0

Australia won the toss   England won by 8 wickets   Umpires: F. S. Lee and D. Davies

11 • *The Ryder Cup*

Friday 2 to Saturday 3 October

After the success in the recent Ashes series, the conquest of Everest by the British-led expedition and the personal triumphs of Stanley Matthews and Gordon Richards, there was an undercurrent of feeling among sports fans in Britain, that in Coronation Year, anything was possible, even winning back the Ryder Cup.

The golfing year had not been full of spectacular home successes so far, and the Open Championship had been won by the brilliant American Ben Hogan in his first appearance in the event. No golfing pundit gave Britain much of a chance against the all-powerful United States team, but in the British public's collective imagination, there was a groundswell of optimism that defied logic. Why shouldn't 1953 be Britain's year?

It had been 20 years since Britain had last won the trophy for the biennial tournament between the best golfing professionals in Britain and America. The cup had been donated in 1927 by Sam Ryder, a St Albans seed merchant and a keen, if ungifted, amateur golfer. Ryder was a member at Wentworth, and one evening in June 1926, so the story goes, he was sitting at the nineteenth hole discussing the relative merits of the British and American golfers who that day had been out on the course practising for a pre-Open Championship tournament. Who were better, the British or American golfers? Being a man of action, Ryder immediately approached several of the professionals, who thought it would be great fun to help him find his answer. These days, a date would have to be pencilled in for about three years hence, but in the 1920s professionals had less hectic diaries. The very next day, the first, entirely unofficial Ryder challenge match took place between the best British and American golfers. For Britain, Abe Mitchell, George Duncan, Archie Compston and Ernie Whitcombe were the mainstays in beating the Americans, who included Jim Barnes, Bill Mehlhorn, Emmet French and the immortal Walter Hagen, by the convincing margin of $13\frac{1}{2}$ points to $1\frac{1}{2}$.

Abe Mitchell, then aged 39 and later described by J. H. Taylor as 'the finest player who never won the Open', was persuaded to become Ryder's personal golf instructor. During his sessions out on the course with Mitchell, Ryder followed up an idea that had been put forward by George Duncan immediately after the match at Wentworth, and suggested that a permanent trophy be presented for international competition between the best golfers on either side of the Atlantic. The trophy, which cost Ryder £250, is topped by the figure of Abe Mitchell as a tribute to his part in getting the competition going. Twelve months later, a British team captained by Ted Ray (but not including Mitchell, who had come down with appendicitis on board the *Aquitania* on the journey out) competed for the Ryder Cup for the first time. Strictly speaking, they were not competing for the Ryder Cup itself, as the trophy was still unfinished, but this 1927 fixture was without doubt the birth of the tournament. The thrill of playing for their country may have been exhilarating for the British professionals who normally played just for themselves, but they failed to rise to the occasion. The match, played at Worcester, Massachusetts, proved very one-sided, with the Americans winning by 9 $\frac{1}{2}$ to 2 $\frac{1}{2}$. The concept of foursomes on the first day followed by singles on the second was established in that first tournament, and although the number of players in each team has changed, the basic structure of the Ryder Cup tournament was not altered until four-balls were added in 1963.

Despite the result, the Ryder Cup concept had proved successful and the players and spectators alike had enjoyed the friendly atmosphere of the competition. So two years later, the Cup was at stake again, this time in England. The match, played at Moortown Golf Club in Leeds, gave the British, now with Mitchell in the side, their revenge by 7 points to 5. The matches alternated between Britain and America. In 1931 (Columbus, Ohio), 1933 (Southport and Ainsdale) and 1935 (Ridgewood, New Jersey) the matches were all won by the home team, but from then on the power of the Americans began to tell and they won every contest. In 1937, back at Southport and Ainsdale, they won by 8 to 4 in what proved

Peter Alliss: over the final holes the pressure told on the rising star of British golf.

to be the last meeting for 10 years. After the war, the tournament was revived and the teams met in Portland, Oregon, in 1947. The United States won by the most lopsided score in Ryder Cup history, 11 to 1 and the only point that Britain gained was in the final singles match when Sam King beat Herman Keiser 4 and 3. In 1949 at Ganton, near Scarborough, the Americans won by 7 to 5. In 1951 the score at Pinehurst, North Carolina was 9 $\frac{1}{2}$ to 2 $\frac{1}{2}$ in favour of the Americans. By 1953, there were no active British professionals apart from Henry Cotton who had experience of winning the Ryder Cup, and interest in the competition, in America at least, was in danger of fading.

The 1953 Ryder Cup was held at Wentworth in Surrey, the birthplace if not the home of the trophy. The West Course at Wentworth was then 6,723 yards long and known as the 'Burma Road' because of its tough and demanding nature. Although it might not appear to present too many insoluble problems for the average club golfer, neither does it allow any deviation from the correct line: accurate driving is the key to a low score at Wentworth, and over the years there had been comparatively few scores under 70, a testament to the subtlety of the course as much as its length. It is a course that players need to get to know, and no doubt it was chosen in part because it was expected to give the home team an advantage. Familiarity with the Burma Road does not breed contempt, only respect.

Of the team picked for the 1953 Ryder Cup, only four had ever experienced picking up points for Britain – Henry Cotton, Dai Rees, Jimmy Adams and Fred Daly, the first Irishman to win the Open. On paper Britain had no chance whatsoever. But what did the papers know? The British team, picked very late in the day, was strong, although in the opinion of some experienced critics not as strong as it could have been. The American team, far stronger on paper and recent form, nevertheless was missing the all-conquering Open champion, Ben Hogan, who did not feel that he was physically capable of playing 36 holes in one day. All the same, there was no suggestion that this was a struggle between two second-best teams: although the Americans were favourites in the public mind and in their own minds, each American knew what an honour it was to represent his country in the Ryder Cup, and each player wanted to win, and to win well.

The British team of 10, plus Henry Cotton as non-playing captain, consisted of Jimmy Adams, Peter Alliss, Harry Bradshaw, Eric Brown, Fred Daly, Max Faulkner, Bernard Hunt, John Panton, Dai Rees and Harry Weetman. This was an interesting mix of youth and experience. The main concern for the millions of armchair selectors in pubs and editorial offices around the country was that Arthur Lees, who was having a superb year, had been left out. As Leonard Crawley later wrote (and hindsight is a wonderful thing), 'it would have been better if the selection committee had picked the form horse – Arthur Lees'. Lees was to end the year in ninth place on the PGA Order of Merit, so Crawley had a point. Still, Tom Haliburton finished in seventh place, and he was also overlooked. Sam King, the man responsible for Britain's one point in 1947, finished seventh in the Open in 1953, ahead of every Ryder Cup competitor on either side except Dai Rees, but also missed out. In those days, selection was entirely by the committee – there were no automatic places to be earned.

The highest ranked of the British team was the evergreen Dai Rees. He was already 40 years old in 1953, and despite never winning the Open championship, or any other Major title for that matter, he had been one of the leading players in Britain since he won the first of his four PGA Matchplay titles in 1936. His first Ryder Cup appearance came in 1937. He established a reputation as a great matchplay golfer, whose temperament seemed ideally suited to the Ryder Cup format. In 1953, he had finished as joint runner-up to Ben Hogan in the Open, so was on the top of his form in strokeplay as well as matchplay. He was to finish the year in third place in the PGA Order of Merit, behind only the Belgian Flory van Donck and the South African Bobby Locke.

Max Faulkner was the other main stalwart of the British Ryder Cup team in 1953. Born in 1916, he had won the Open in 1951 at Royal Portrush in County Antrim, giving him perhaps the highest international profile of any of the team. He was playing in his fourth Ryder Cup. Harry Bradshaw had never won an Open, but lost in a playoff in 1949 to the South African Bobby Locke at Royal St George's, Sandwich, when his ball landed in a bottle. Bradshaw was described by Fred Pignon in the *Daily Mail* as 'recognisable by anybody who knows the Irish'. Pignon went on to clarify this enigmatic sentence: 'Sturdy and vigorous, he smiles his way around the course.'

This was the first of Bradshaw's three appearances in the Ryder Cup, making him one of four debutants in the British team. The others were Eric Brown, Bernard Hunt and Peter Alliss, all of whom would play major roles in the drama as it unfolded over those two days at Wentworth. The 28-year-old railway fireman Eric Brown, who went on to play in four Ryder Cups and act as non-playing captain in both 1969 and 1971,

Henry Cotton, the non-playing British captain, practises his putting in case he's needed.

enjoyed his first experience in the event, but for Hunt and Alliss it was to be more traumatic. Hunt, like Brown, went on to captain teams, in 1973 and 1975, and, also like Brown, he was tall and slim, although his wavy blond hair was quite different from Brown's dark and immaculately groomed locks. Peter Alliss, also in those days tall and slim, has become the sport's leading television commentator. His father Percy had been selected for the British teams in 1929, 1933, 1935 and 1937, and Peter played for his country eight times consecutively from 1953 to 1969.

Between them, father and son played 36 Ryder Cup matches, winning a total of 16 points.

The other members of the British team were John Panton, playing for the second time; Harry Weetman, also making a second appearance, and destined to captain the side in 1965 after playing seven times in the competition; the Scottish professional Jimmy Adams, a burly, red-faced man who would have made his debut in 1939 had not the war intervened and who was now playing for a fourth and final time; and Fred Daly, the Irishman who won the Open in 1947 and who was also playing for a fourth and last Ryder Cup. Daly was dark and short, but a larger-than-life character whose attitude to golf and life was epitomised in 1950 when he had his wisdom teeth removed one morning, and that same afternoon broke the course record at Letchworth Golf Club. On the course, he would often be heard whistling to himself. Golf was not just his profession, it was his love.

Against them, the Americans had chosen a strong team, even if 50 years on not many of the names remain in the forefront of our memories. Their captain was Lloyd Mangrum. Thirty-nine years old in 1953, somewhat scruffy in his appearance, with a cigarette always between his lips, the dark and hefty Mangrum was nevertheless one of the top golfers in the world in the years immediately after the war. He won his only Major, the US Open, in 1946, and lost the 1950 US Open when he was penalised two strokes for removing an insect from his ball, in contravention of the USGA rules then in force. 'Well, I guess we'll all still eat tomorrow,' was his typically laid-back response.

The most famous name in the American side, which was without Hogan, Jimmy Demaret and Byron Nelson, was certainly Sam Snead. A couple of years older than his captain, Snead already had six Major championships under his belt, including the Open in 1946, at St Andrews. He was considered to have the perfect golf swing, and although he had a reputation for being hard to get to know, there was no doubt that in the years before Palmer and Nicklaus began to dominate the game, Snead was the most consistent winner of golf tournaments.

When he finally retired he had 84 tour victories to his name, well ahead of all his rivals. He had captained his side to victory in 1951 and was the man around whom the expected American success was going to revolve.

The United States team contained no fewer than six newcomers to the event, including four who would play just once. The two debutants who played again in later Ryder Cups were Cary Middlecoff and Ted Kroll. Middlecoff was a qualified dentist known not only for the brilliance of his golf but also for the slowness of his play. While training to be a dentist he won several amateur titles, and eventually he decided that there was more money to be made knocking golf balls into holes on greens than filling holes in teeth with amalgam. He must have been very confident in his own abilities as a golfer, because you have to look far and wide to find a poor American dentist. He already had one US Open title under his belt by 1953, and would win it again in 1956, the year after he won his only Masters title. Ted Kroll was a relaxed former amateur champion whose attitude was that 'it wasn't a matter of life and death when we played, because you weren't going to make that much money anyway. We didn't carry a briefcase with us, because we didn't need one.' A golf professional's life in 1953 was much closer to how it was in 1927 when the Ryder Cup began than to the way it became barely a decade later when the influence of television was starting to be felt.

The four one-off Ryder Cup players in the American team were Jim Turnesa, Fred Haas Jr, Dave Douglas and Walter Burkemo. Turnesa, the US PGA champion in 1952, was one of seven brothers, of whom the second eldest, Joe, had played Ryder Cup golf in 1927 and 1929. Another brother, Willie, was a Walker Cup golfer who had been British Amateur champion in 1947 and US Amateur champion in 1948. Walter Burkemo won the 1953 US PGA championship, the only Major that Hogan did not win, so he was the only holder of a Major title competing in the 1953 Ryder Cup. What's more, the PGA championship was in those days a matchplay tournament, so Burkemo was coming to the greatest international team matchplay competition as the world individual matchplay champion. Fred Haas Jr began, like Middlecoff, as a brilliant amateur golfer, and became the first man to play both Walker Cup and Ryder Cup golf (but only after Middlecoff had turned down an invitation to play in the 1947 Walker Cup because he was planning to turn professional). As an amateur, Haas staked a claim to golfing immortality by winning the Memphis Open in 1945, thus bringing to an end Byron Nelson's record of 11 consecutive tournament victories. Dave Douglas, who was in great form having recently won the Canadian Open, was one of five members of the US team who had already won, or would go on to win, the Houston Open, but in truth his career was probably the least distinguished of all the American team that year. However, he was to play a decisive role in his only Ryder Cup tournament.

The other two members of the US team were Jack Burke and Ed 'Porky' Oliver. Burke was expected to be the next big thing in American golf. Leonard Crawley wrote that 'the American side contained only two players of the highest class, namely Snead and Burke'. Although he played brilliantly in the Ryder Cup that year, and won both the US PGA and the Masters in 1956 before going on to captain the 1957 and 1973 American Ryder Cup teams, there was a feeling that Burke never quite fulfilled his potential. The 16-stone Ed Oliver, known as 'Porky' for obvious reasons, had been runner-up to Hogan at the 1953 Masters, and was in the form of his life. His career was already almost two decades old: he might have won the 1940 US Open if he had not been disqualified from the playoff for starting his final round before the designated time in order to try to beat a storm that was brewing.

There was no storm brewing, meteorologically at least, at Wentworth. The morning of 2 October dawned bright and clear. The first day's play was to be the foursomes: four matches of 36 holes each, between pairings chosen and placed in order of play by each captain without knowledge of the pairings and order of play of his opponent. So a captain could pick his pairs according to which combinations played best together, but could not know whom they would be up against. The top match pitted Harry Weetman and Peter Alliss against Dave Douglas

Max Faulkner (Britain, driving) and Sam Snead (USA) practise for the Ryder Cup
watched by a large crowd.

and Porky Oliver; the second had Eric Brown and John Panton up
against the might of Lloyd Mangrum and Sam Snead. Jimmy Adams
and Bernard Hunt were to take on Ted Kroll and Jack Burke, while the
Irishmen Fred Daly and Harry Bradshaw faced Walter Burkemo and
the dentist Cary Middlecoff. On the British side, the experienced Dai
Rees and Max Faulkner waited out the foursomes, and the Americans
rested debutants Jim Turnesa and Fred Haas. Leaving out Rees and
Faulkner was a hotly debated decision: they were the top-ranked British
players, but their record in the foursomes was not considered good
enough. They had, it is true, lost when playing together in the 1951 Ryder
Cup in Pinehurst, North Carolina, but then so had Adams and Panton.
The loss of their experience as much as their golfing skills might well
prove to be a crucial factor.

The general view of the press, before the first tee shot was hit that morning, was that if the British team were to have any chance at all they had to hold a lead at the end of the first day. The idea that they could outplay the Americans in the singles on the second day was laughable. They would have to be a point or two in credit after the foursomes to hold off the American charge on the second day. However, as Pat Ward Thomas of the *Manchester Guardian* noted, 'After studying the pairings, one can find no good grounds for optimism.' The top pair, Weetman and Alliss, were seen as Britain's trump cards, and everybody seemed to think there ought to be a point in the bag there, but there was no glimmer of hope for Brown and Panton against Mangrum and Snead. Adams and Hunt too were seen as second best, especially if Ted Kroll's putting was anything near top form. Daly and Bradshaw against Burkemo and Middlecoff was too close to call, although a good number of optimistic journalists went for the Irishmen. But even if it all went totally to plan, there did not seem to be any way the British could take more than two points out of the day, and being merely on level terms with the Americans at the end of the foursomes was not enough. Or so the pundits thought.

Luckily for sportsmen all over the world, pundits can be wrong. The first day of the Ryder Cup attracted a huge crowd of some 10,000 people, who enjoyed a day basking in glorious October sunshine (a rarity indeed, especially after the wet summer of 1953), but it ended in gloom for the home team. It seemed that any chance of a Coronation Year victory to go alongside the Ashes and Mount Everest was already lost. The Americans finished 3 to 1 up.

The top match, the one that Weetman and Alliss were bound to win, ended in a close run victory for the Americans, by 2 and 1. The *Manchester Guardian* was in poetic mood as the match began: 'The dawn had kissed the grass with heavy silver dew when Oliver drove the first ball of the match.' But poetry was not going to influence the outcome. The match would be won by the pairing that could best cope with the peculiarly unseasonal conditions. Oliver and Douglas showed some uncertainty in judging the pace of the greens on the early holes, while Alliss and Weetman seemed to have worked the course out a little better. By the eighth hole they were two up, but then things began to slip away as the Americans found their touch. Despite great chipping by Weetman, and strong all-round play, especially from tee to green, by Alliss, the pair went in to lunch one down.

During the meal it became clear just how crucial this top match was going to be. Mangrum and Snead had already established a huge lead over Brown and Panton, while Kroll and Burke seemed to have the beating of Adams and Hunt. The third American pair completed the morning round in a notional 64, and Adams and Hunt could not keep up with the pace. But if Alliss and Weetman could snatch a point, and the Irishmen take their match against Burkemo and Middlecoff (still anyone's at the halfway stage), then at least Britain would be level-pegging for the second day.

The afternoon rounds progressed for the most part entirely predictably. Mangrum and Snead, turning on the power whether it was needed or not, wiped out the hapless Brown and Panton by 8 and 7, while Kroll and Burke defeated Adams and Hunt by the almost equally crushing score of 7 and 5. The difference had been Burke's putting: on three consecutive greens he had holed missable putts, while Hunt failed from less than two feet to halve a hole they should have won. So with two matches finished, the Americans had two points safely tucked away, and Britain needed to fight all the way to stay in the hunt.

Daly and Bradshaw did just that. In a match that could have gone either way throughout the day, they held off the Americans with the steadiness of their driving and the brilliance of their approach shots to win the closest tie of the day by one hole. Burkemo and Middlecoff played very fine golf in conditions that were so good, and so unusual for Wentworth in October, that they must almost have felt more at home than the Irish pair, who were better used to battling against wind and rain than the bright sunshine. All the same, it was the Irish who took the match by one hole, to put Britain on the scoresheet at last.

Weetman and Alliss kept up with Oliver and Douglas all afternoon, although there was evidence, from Weetman's putting especially, that the pressure was telling more on the British than the Americans. The fact that the Americans had won the last five Ryder Cup competitions over an 18-year period meant not only that their team came to Wentworth expecting to win, but also that the tournament was seen as less important to the Americans than to the British. American television had all but given up on the event after a succession of one-sided matches, and of course when the competition took place in England there was no live American television coverage in those pre-Telstar years, so the whole concept was less well known, and less valued, in America than in Britain. What may have been just another little pot to the Americans was tremendously important to the British team and to the 10,000 spectators who roamed the course on both days. The size of the crowds, expected to be an encouragement to the home side, may well have worked in quite the opposite way for some of the newcomers in the British Ryder Cup side, who had never played in front of such huge galleries before. Those who have nerves to shred, prepare to shred them now.

Just when it looked as though Weetman and Alliss might catch up with their opponents, a great shot and a massive stroke of good fortune gave the Americans a three-hole lead. The great shot was a putt by Dave Douglas on the twentieth, which won a hole that they only deserved to halve, and put the Americans two up. The stroke of luck came on the next hole. Oliver sliced his drive and the ball landed at the foot of a small tree, in such an awkward position that Douglas could not even swing his club at it. The referee, Admiral Sir Charles Forbes, was consulted and, much to everybody's surprise, he ruled that the ball had landed in a rabbit-scrape, and that therefore Douglas was allowed a free drop. Douglas was able to play a good shot to the edge of the green instead of merely working the ball a little closer to the fairway, and thanks to that and another fine pressure putt by Douglas, they won another hole they might have lost.

The end came on the thirty-fifth hole, which Weetman and Alliss

Henry Cotton, apparently unaffected by the tensions of the Ryder Cup.

needed to win to stay in the match. They failed, and Douglas and Oliver had won, 2 and 1. There were handshakes all round, but the British players knew they had had their chances and failed to take them. Henry Cotton told the press at the end of the day, 'I have been kicking them in the dressing room very hard. I am ashamed they did not do better.' America were 3–1 up after the foursomes, surely an impregnable position. The journalists covering the Cup certainly thought so. British hopes of winning had, according to the *Manchester Guardian*, received 'a severe setback', which most of the other members of the press corps would have described as understatement. The Ryder Cup had gone for the sixth time, and nothing the British could hope to do on the second day could change that.

The second day, as clear and bright as the first, featured the eight singles ties. The British captain, Henry Cotton, rested Jimmy Adams and John Panton to allow Dai Rees and Max Faulkner to take their rightful places in the individual matches, while Lloyd Mangrum gave Walter Burkemo and Porky Oliver the day off, to let in Fred Haas and Jim Turnesa. Cotton decided to open with Dai Rees, to put another point on the board straight away, and to finish with Harry Bradshaw, so that there would be an experienced pair of hands on the putter if the closing holes were to prove decisive. The Americans thought that by winning the first four matches, they would make the cup safe, so put their strongest players out first. With the tournament won, it would not matter what the youngsters did at the end of the afternoon. But the best laid plans of both captains went a little bit awry.

Jack Burke, then perhaps at the peak of his game, found himself in a titanic struggle with Rees, which could have gone either way for most of the match, but Fred Daly positively slaughtered Ted Kroll by the embarrassing margin of 9 and 7. He was six up on Kroll after the first eighteen holes, having gone round in a theoretical 66, and took only 11 of the afternoon holes to clinch victory. So the first point of the day was Britain's.

The third match had been close all day. The railway fireman Eric

Brown held his own against the American captain Mangrum, but never looked like getting far enough ahead to clinch victory. In the next match, Harry Weetman was four down to Sam Snead at the half way stage, and nobody could expect to give Snead a four-hole lead and survive. Faulkner was not at his best, three holes down to Cary Middlecoff, and Peter Alliss was one down against Turnesa, despite both men taking 70 for their first 18 holes. Bernard Hunt was all square with Dave Douglas, and at the bottom of the list, Bradshaw was one up against Haas. If things didn't change, the best Britain could hope for was perhaps three points, making the final score 8 to 4 in favour of the USA and another heavy defeat for Britain. To make matters worse, Rees, who had been all square with Burke at lunch and one up at the turn in the afternoon, began to slip back. In 1953 Burke was considered the man most likely to step into Ben Hogan's shoes as the giant of golf, and although he never quite achieved the highest levels that Hogan reached, he was a formidable opponent at any time. But it was not Burke's brilliance that made the difference. It was the Welshman's putting, which until now had been so reliable, that began to let him down. Three putts at the fourteenth when he should have won the hole and three more putts at the seventeenth decided the match: Burke edged it by 2 and 1. At this stage, even with Daly's point in the bag, it looked as though Britain might lose as many as six of the singles. With nine holes to go in most of the matches, things were looking black.

Then came the most astonishing turnaround in British fortunes, which could not be put down to any one player or any one hole but which seeped into the game of every British golfer out on the course and gave the home team real hope. Suddenly there was a real chance that the Ryder Cup could come home in Coronation Year and join the Ashes in the nation's trophy cupboard. It was as if a phantom voice had said, 'Charge!' and everybody charged at once, despite the hopelessness of the situation.

Faulkner, trailing Middlecoff badly until now, fought his way back to one down, and was playing the better golf. Alliss turned on the heat and

Large crowds ring the greens at Wentworth during the Ryder Cup.

dragged himself ahead of his American opponent by one hole, and even Weetman, who at one stage early in the afternoon round had been five down to Snead, was winning holes at last. Weetman's match was in many ways the most astonishing of the singles. Snead had outplayed him for most of the day, but now in the final stretch the American's game fell apart. There was some suggestion afterwards that his wrist had been troubling him, but he never used that as an excuse. After 22 holes, Snead had a five-hole advantage, but then Weetman won three holes in a row: two down with 11 to play. Snead won the next two, so was four up at the turn, and he maintained that lead until the thirteenth, when he took a six. Weetman seized on Snead's weakness and won five holes in a row, the thirteenth to the seventeenth. Now Weetman was one up on the final tee, the first time in the match that he had been in the lead. All Weetman had to do was not lose the final hole. He didn't – a half gave him the match, and the point that should never have been there for Britain.

Eric Brown was proving to be a match for Mangrum. He had taken 69 shots for his morning round, and his afternoon round was going well. On the fourteenth tee, Brown was three up with five to play, and his was another match inexorably moving Britain's way. But at this point Mangrum turned on the power. Although Brown did not play badly, Mangrum produced three threes in succession to square the match with two to play. The balance had suddenly shifted America's way. In most years an American golfer would have been confident that a spurt like this at such a crucial time would break any British opponent's spirit, but Brown was not to be cowed. On the long seventeenth he produced a birdie four to take the hole: one up and one to play. Mangrum had to go for broke on the final hole to try to salvage a half, but drove into the rough and then misjudged or mishit his second to lie well short of the green. Brown took the safe but steady route. As his second shot landed in perfect position for his assault on the pin the roar from the crowd told him, and anybody else anywhere on the course, that the match was won. And it duly was: Brown by two holes. The fireman had proved himself in the heat of Ryder Cup matchplay.

Now Britain was square with the United States, four points all, and there were four matches still out on the course. In the first, Faulkner was struggling against Middlecoff, but not without hope. Alliss, playing the most important match of his 22 years, was one up after 12 holes of the afternoon round. Hunt was still just ahead of Douglas, and Harry Bradshaw seemed to be beating Haas. Two points needed to tie the Ryder Cup, and two and a half for Britain's first victory in 20 years. The newspaper pundits who had predicted a massacre of the innocents on singles day were being proved wrong.

To be fair to the pundits, only the most optimistic of the home supporters really felt that Faulkner could win one of those precious points. The strong push he had made in the middle part of the second round could not be maintained, and Middlecoff sat on his lead. He finished Faulkner off on the seventeenth green, after Faulkner had gambled everything on trying to bring himself back from dormy two down. He failed, and Middlecoff emerged the winner, by 3 and 1. But Bradshaw, the genial Irishman who had partnered Fred Daly to victory in the foursomes, now repeated his triumph in the singles. His victory over Fred Haas by 3 and 2 brought the overall scores level again at five-all, and the score between Ireland and the United States up to a comprehensive Ireland 3 United States 0. With the match tied, the results of the last two singles would decide the destination of the Ryder Cup. Unfortunately for Britain, the two players out on the course were the young debutants Alliss and Hunt. Henry Cotton's idea that the fate of the Cup would rest in Bradshaw's hands was upset by the comparative speed with which Bradshaw won his match.

The Cup, which at the start of Saturday's play was to all intents in its packing case and labelled up for America, was suddenly within Britain's grasp. They needed one and a half points from the final two matches to win, and as they played their final tee shots, Hunt was one up on Douglas and Alliss was one down against Turnesa. If Alliss could win the final hole and Hunt not lose it, the Cup would come to Britain. Some idea of the strain of playing the final holes of a Ryder Cup tournament, when you know that the result of the whole two days' efforts depends on your play, can be gleaned by looking at the scores made by the four remaining players on the eighteenth hole. In their morning rounds Alliss, Hunt, Douglas and Turnesa all made par fours. In this crucial second round, the same four players at the same hole made a five and three sixes. It was not just the British who were feeling the pressure.

Alliss and Turnesa played the final hole first. The entire length of the fairway and the rough around the greens was seething with spectators. Turnesa, who had the honour, looked calm enough as he drove, but his ball was obviously panicking. It flew off to the right and into the woods. Alliss came to the tee and for the moment his nerve held. His drive was perfect, well placed on the fairway. Now the chance to win the final hole and sneak a half was a realistic one. Turnesa managed to fight his way out of the woods, but was still short of the green after three shots. Alliss, as he walked up the fairway towards his ball for his second shot, was as nervous – frightened, almost – as he had ever been in his life. He needed a friend. In those days it was not the done thing for the captain to walk round with his players, or to offer encouragement during the course of a match. Fifty years on, the situation is very different, with every team player putting as much effort into supporting his team-mates' golf as he does into playing his own. 'I felt very alone,' remembers Alliss. 'I needed somebody to steady my nerves.'

His second shot betrayed those unsteady nerves. He chose the right club, but pulled his shot a little, and the ball ended up in a little dip, pin high but about 15 feet off the green. Still advantage Alliss, maybe, but if his second shot had given hints of his anxieties, his third shot proclaimed them for all to see. As he stood in the hollow, it was clear he did not know which club to use. All the papers the next day told him that he should have used his putter or a low iron, but that advice was 12 hours too late. Eventually Alliss selected his pitching wedge, and fluffed the shot completely. Now the balance had swung back towards Turnesa. But the American, too, was doing his best to lose the hole if he could. While Alliss made up in part for his terrible third shot with a fourth that put his ball no more than three feet from the hole, Turnesa three-putted from the edge of the green, to be down in six. Alliss had a simple putt for the hole and half a point. The silence of the 10,000-strong gallery was overwhelming. And Alliss missed the putt. He knocked in the rebound, so to speak, but in doing so halved the hole and lost the match. Hunt now had to beat Dave Douglas to tie the Ryder Cup.

Hunt drove well, but then decided to take Turnesa's route to the green, cutting his second shot into the trees. His third shot took him 30 feet past the hole, but Douglas, who had got to the green in two, was well short with his first putt. Then so was Hunt by about five feet, and then Douglas missed again. Hunt needed to hole his putt to be sure of a half and thus take the match. In the silence that descended on the hordes watching this crucial shot, did Hunt's thoughts stray back to the even shorter putt he had missed in the foursomes the day before? Whatever demons invaded his head, he missed again. Douglas did not. Down in five, the American took the hole and halved the match. What had looked like a final score of 6 $\frac{1}{2}$ to 5 $\frac{1}{2}$ in Britain's favour only 20 minutes earlier had finished on the same score, but in America's favour. The Burma Road had claimed two more victims, and the Ryder Cup remained in American hands.

The reports of the match were remarkably kind to the unfortunate Alliss and Hunt, offering sympathy more than criticism. 'The horror of that last hole will be remembered always,' said the *Manchester Guardian*, 'but had they not recovered with courage to winning positions after being down to infinitely more experienced opponents, we would not have blamed them.' 'In praise of the Ryder Cup team,' added Leonard Crawley in *Golfing* magazine, 'I believe they did their very best and played with the utmost resolution.' But their best had not been quite good enough. The tension had been extreme, but the American professionals had coped with it better – just – than their British opponents. Lloyd Mangrum said afterwards that he would 'never captain an American team again, because of the nine thousand deaths I suffered in the last hour'.

At least for the Americans there proved to be life after death. For Peter Alliss, despite the kindness of the newspaper reports, there was less respite. It was what he describes as 'rather a crippling thing for a young man'. He was just 22 at the time, playing in his first Ryder Cup, and 'the pressure got to us. No doubt about it. We made a total balls of it.' In retrospect it could be argued that the reason the then golden boy of British golf never quite developed in the way he was expected to, never won a Major in 20 years of trying, was partly the huge psychological blow he suffered in the 1953 Ryder Cup. 'I took it to heart a lot more than Bernard,' says Alliss half a century later. 'You felt you were responsible for the failure of British golf and the downfall of the British

Empire. It was a very emotional time.' Alliss and Hunt eventually played on a winning Ryder Cup team in 1957, when, captained by Dai Rees, Britain beat America, led by Jack Burke, by $7\frac{1}{2}$ to $4\frac{1}{2}$ at the Lindrick Golf Club near Worksop in Nottinghamshire. Alliss was the only British singles player to lose that year, and he and Bernard Hunt also lost their foursomes. Neither Alliss nor Hunt was ever actively involved in another winning Ryder Cup side, despite seven further playing appearances each, and two more by Hunt as captain. Had 1953 left such a scar, or was it merely that the cream of British golf was never as good as the cream of American golf in those years?

Coronation Year could not work its magic on our Ryder Cup golfers, although they went unbearably close. A month later there was another national sporting failure as Coronation Year came to a close, one far less expected and far more damaging to our national pride.

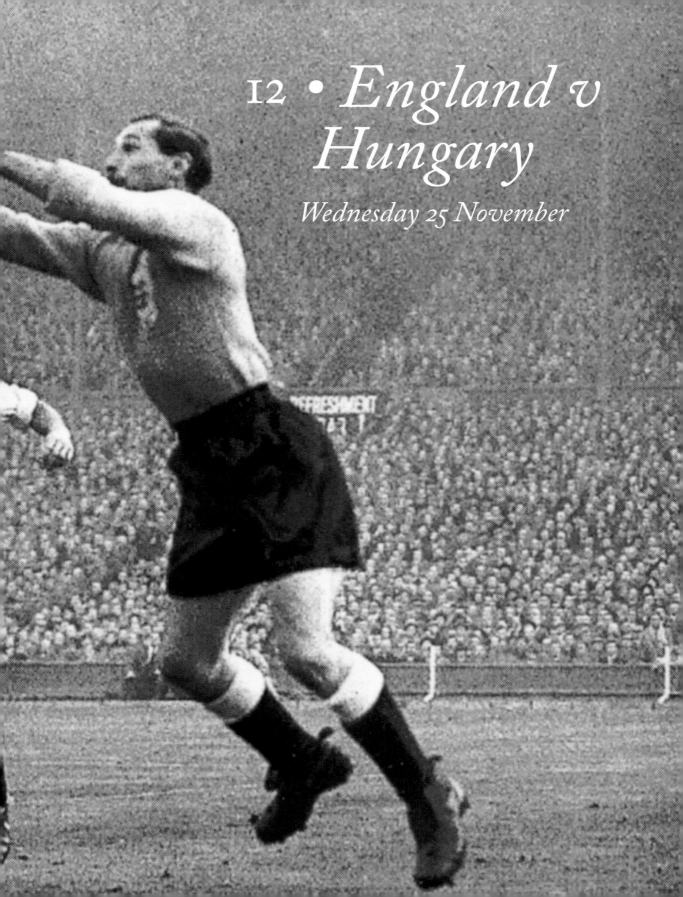

12 • *England v Hungary*

Wednesday 25 November

England is the home of football. England is where the game began, where the rules were laid down, and where all the techniques and strategies for success were worked out and perfected. The English footballer (and occasionally his Scottish, Welsh or Irish cousin) is the best in the world. It therefore goes without saying that the English football team is the best in the world. Such was the prevailing logic of the Football Association in 1953.

To their credit, two men stood out against this complacency, the long-serving FA secretary Sir Stanley Rous and the coach of the England team Walter Winterbottom. They knew that there were better teams in the world than England, and they also knew that one of them was Hungary. Sir Stanley had watched them win the gold medal at the 1952 Olympics, where they dominated every match and strolled past Yugoslavia in the final, and decided there and then that the wonder team should be invited to England, to find out how the full England side would fare against this remarkable collection of professional footballers masquerading as army officers and civil servants. What he, like everybody else, did not expect was that the Hungarians would be able to prove their superiority quite so convincingly on English soil.

English football had been shown to be vulnerable on foreign soil on several occasions since the end of the war, but never more so than in the sun of Belo Horizonte in Brazil on 29 June 1950, when the United States beat England 1–0 in a World Cup match, and put an end to England's chances of bringing home the Jules Rimet Trophy. Few people in the United States even knew that their country had a national soccer team, let alone that it could be good enough to beat a full-strength England side on neutral ground. The result might have been a one-off in terms of the United States' development as a footballing nation, but for England it was a huge disappointment and sounded a warning bell, which too few people heeded.

By late 1953, everything in the football garden was rosy again. Since their defeat against the Americans (something our golfers and tennis players but not our footballers were used to), the England team had played 25 matches, winning 14, drawing eight and losing just three: against Spain in Rio in the game that followed the Belo Horizonte loss, against Scotland at Wembley in 1952 and against Uruguay in Montevideo on the 1953 summer tour. That tour had also included a 6–3 drubbing of the United States in New York, a satisfying revenge. England had never been beaten on home soil by a team from outside the British Isles, although Austria, France and Yugoslavia had earned hard-fought draws over the past three years.

England's unbeaten home record could not last for ever, but despite the warning signs, it was not expected that the Hungarians would cause too much trouble. Yet they had beaten Yugoslavia 2–0 in the Olympic final in Helsinki the previous year, and if Yugoslavia could draw with England in England, then why couldn't Hungary go one better? If any more evidence of a decline in English football were needed, it came in the form of the match between a FIFA Rest of Europe XI and England at Wembley in October, staged to celebrate the ninetieth birthday of the Football Association. The FIFA team, captained by the great Austrian halfback Ernst Ocwirk, and containing such players as the AC Milan-based Swede Gunnar Nordahl, a pair of Yugoslavs, Zebec and Vukas, Posipal of Germany, who was then thought to be the finest centre-half in the world, and the Spain-based Hungarian Kubala was always going to be hard to beat. In the event, England held on for a tough but highly entertaining 4–4 draw, thanks to a very late penalty awarded when Mortensen crashed to the ground over Posipal's legs. It was converted with characteristic coolness by Alf Ramsey, virtually the last kick of the match.

For this fixture, the England team included Derek Ufton of Charlton Athletic, winning his first full cap at centre half. He remembers the day well. 'At the time, England were short of a centre half. Neil Franklin had gone to South America for more money, and Harry Johnston was getting old.' He was nine years older than the 26-year-old Ufton. 'When I got selected, all the press said I'd be there for the World Cup the next year.' The England team in those days would meet on the Saturday before a

Ferenc Puskas (left) and Billy Wright lead out their teams in front of the lucky 100,000 spectators at Wembley Stadium who would witness the Magic Magyars at work and play.

match, do a bit of training and play on the Wednesday. The idea was that if you kept the players away from the ball for a few days, they would be much hungrier for it on match days. This theory was followed not only by the England team, but by most of the League clubs as well. Players did a lot of running in their training and plenty of press-ups, but the only balls they used were medicine balls, which not even an English professional would try to head. The result was that, compared to their Continental counterparts, the English were extremely good at running but less adept at ball skills.

'The thing that amazed us was that when the FIFA team ran out on to the pitch, each player had a ball under his arm. We had one ball between the eleven of us. The press boys told us that the Continentals were big fat boys, and we'd win 5–1. But they played a different style of game, with Nordahl playing a deep lying role and the wingers coming inside as often as possible.' England's new centre half was used to playing a man-to-man marking game, and in the first half the English defence did just that. However, at half time they were 3–2 down, and lucky to be that close, thanks to a fortunate Jimmy Mullen goal in the forty-third minute. In the interval Walter Winterbottom asked Ufton if he would mind changing his game in the second half. 'Don't play man to man,' said Winterbottom. 'Just cover the middle for the second half, play as a deep centre half rather than marking anybody.' The media noticed the change. Roy Peskett in the *Daily Mail* noted that 'the backs were too often beaten, and Ufton, struggling hard, was far too many times left to face top-speed forwards on his own'. The manager of the FIFA XI, Dutchman Karel Lotsy, came to the same conclusion. 'I have seen English football at its best hundreds of times. This wasn't it. Their defenders were shockingly weak.'

Still, the match ended in a draw, and after the game Walter Winterbottom made a point of approaching Ufton and thanking him for making the tactical change. 'Thanks for all you've done,' was the gist of his message, 'and you will definitely play against Northern Ireland in three weeks' time.' Ufton adds, 'Walter also introduced me to the chairman of the selection committee, who also told me I'd definitely be playing against Northern Ireland.' Ufton was beginning to look forward to the 1954 World Cup but the selection committee in those days consisted of 12 men, all with individual favourites and personal axes to grind. In the three weeks between the two internationals Charlton Athletic lost heavily twice, and their centre half was never chosen for England again.

Ufton was not the only man to suffer from the ridiculous idea that 12 was the right number of heads to choose a team of 11 men. The press, for example, was crying out for the selectors to keep faith with Albert Quixall, who had made his England debut in the 4–1 victory over Wales at Cardiff on 10 October. Quixall, an inside forward with Sheffield Wednesday, was only 20 years old at the time and doing his National Service as a lance-corporal with the Royal Signals, but everybody could see he had talent. The selectors gave him three games and then he was dropped. In nine internationals in 1953, England selected 28 different players, 16 of whom were forwards. Of the 28, only two men, Billy Wright and Jimmy Dickinson, played all nine games, and 11 played only once. For four of those

(Ufton, Ernie Taylor, George Robb and Stan Rickaby), their game in 1953 was to be the beginning and the end of their international careers. No team could improve or present a realistic challenge to the rest of the world with so many changes at the whim of a committee.

The eagerly awaited Hungary match took place at Wembley Stadium on a grey Wednesday afternoon in November. The new Queen, not known as a lover of football, had left on a six-month world tour just two days earlier, perhaps timing her departure from London Airport to avoid having to sit through a football match on a cold November afternoon. A few years later, when asked by Sir Stanley Rous after a dreary Cup Final whether she thought that anybody had played particularly well, the Queen would reply, 'Yes, the band.' But on that typical early winter's day, in the absence of the monarch, it would surely be unthinkable that the Hungarians would try to upset the sporting glories of her Coronation Year.

The twelve England selectors had put together a team that they were confident about, or that at least represented a compromise majority vote. They had only one injury problem – the great Preston winger Tom Finney had a groin injury, and watched the game from the stands – but otherwise, they had the full might of the English Football League clubs to choose from. Stanley Matthews was available and was chosen, which is not such an obvious statement as it might seem 50 years on. The English football selectors, like their counterparts in many other sports, have always been wary of genius, and Matthews had been out of favour for a couple of years, only coming back into the England team for the FIFA match, largely because of Finney's injury. The two greatest wingers of their era actually played international football together only rarely. Since England lost to Scotland at Wembley in April 1951, with Matthews on the right wing and Finney on the left, they had not been seen in England colours together, and would not be again until the match against Belgium in Basle in June 1954.

The selectors opted for Birmingham's Gil Merrick as goalkeeper. This would be Merrick's seventeenth England cap, out of the last 18

Gil Merrick takes the ball, watched by full back Alf Ramsey (centre), who put many of the lessons he learned that day into good use when he began his managerial career.

games. In that time, he had conceded only 21 goals, while his forwards had scored 41. Goalkeeping in the 1950s was a different art from today. Then, the ball was a heavy leather thing that picked up any moisture on the pitch or in the atmosphere, and became a lethal weapon at the feet of a powerful striker of the ball like Stan Mortensen or Nat Lofthouse. Goalkeepers rarely wore gloves, and if they did they were woollen ones to keep out the cold, not padded and artfully shaped rubber ones to make gripping the ball easier and to dissipate the power of a shot in an ergonomically efficient manner. Merrick, then 31 years old, was at the height of his powers and unchallenged in the selectors' minds as England's best keeper. A great number of loyal First Division spectators might have thought Sam Bartram of Charlton Athletic was better – after all, it was his efforts that had almost single-handedly kept his team in the top division for over a decade – but he had lost his chance when Frank Swift had been England's first choice before the war, and now he was considered too old.

The full backs were Bill Eckersley of Blackburn Rovers and Alf Ramsey, the dour, impeccably smart Spurs defender. Both had been regular members of the national side for the past three seasons or more.

Eckersley was, like Merrick, playing his seventeenth international while for Ramsey the game represented his thirty-second England cap. The aggressive, deep-thinking Ramsey was almost 34 years old in late 1953, while Eckersley had just turned 28. Though nobody knew it at the start of the match, this game against Hungary would prove to be the final international appearance for both of them.

The half-back line was the heart of the England team, solid in defence and enterprising on the break, or so it was thought. At right half was Billy Wright, an England regular since his debut in 1946 at the age of 22. He had been captain of his country since 1948. He was the first man to play 100 games for England, and was captain 90 times in all, still a national record. His centre half was Blackpool's captain, 34-year-old Harry Johnston. Less than six months earlier he had enjoyed the peak of success when he accepted the FA Cup from the Queen, and now he was winning the tenth cap in an intermittent international career that had begun, like Wright's, in 1946. The third member of the half-back line was Jimmy Dickinson, a Portsmouth man through and through, who by the time he retired in 1965 had played 764 League games for Pompey, more for one club than anybody else in the history of the British game. He played 48 times for England between 1949 and 1956, this match gaining him, like Alf Ramsey, his thirty-second cap.

The forwards were an odd selection. On the right wing was Matthews, now almost 39, but still indisputably the best winger in Britain, and probably in the world. Inside him was his Blackpool colleague Ernie Taylor, a little man, no more than five feet four inches tall and nine stone in weight, but a prolific goalscorer in the First Division. He had already won Cup Winners' medals with both Newcastle, in 1951, and Blackpool, in 1953. In the wake of the Munich disaster in 1958 he joined Manchester United and played for them in the Cup Final that year, but could not complete a hat-trick of Winners' medals. The Hungary match was his first cap for England, at the age of 28.

Taylor was one of four changes in the forward line from the previous England game, a 3–1 victory over Northern Ireland two weeks earlier.

Out went Nat Lofthouse and Harold Hassall of Bolton, Jimmy Mullen of Wolves and Albert Quixall, and in came Taylor, Mortensen, Jackie Sewell and George Robb. Mortensen, Blackpool's Wembley hat-trick hero, was the third Blackpool man in the forward line, playing for England for the twenty-fifth time. Twenty-six-year-old Jackie Sewell, one Sheffield Wednesday man replacing another, was the youngest man in the side and was playing his fifth England game. He was considered by some to be the key man. Playing as a dual centre forward with Mortensen, 'he may prove too quick for the suspect Hungarian defence', as the *Daily Mail* put it.

George Robb, the Spurs winger, was making his debut, having been chosen at the last minute when it became clear that Finney would not be fit. Robb, a 27-year-old history teacher at Christ's College, Finchley, had won many England amateur caps, and gained his first professional cap after a great debut year in the paid ranks with Tottenham. Before the 1953/54 season, he had enjoyed several years as an amateur with Finchley, and helped them reach the third round of the FA Cup in January 1953 for the only time in their history. (They then lost 2–0 to Shrewsbury Town.) He played for Great Britain in the Helsinki Olympics (where Great Britain lost 5–3 to Luxembourg), so would have seen the all-conquering Hungarians there, but although nobody said so beforehand, it seemed a little like throwing a schoolboy to the lions to play a man who had been on the losing side to some amateur Luxembourgers barely a year earlier.

The English journalists were nevertheless confident. Charles Buchan, the doyen of football journalists, wrote in the *News Chronicle*, 'I think we have the men to beat the brilliant Hungarians.' He went on to suggest that close marking by the half backs would prevent the Hungarian forwards displaying their passing and ball-control skills, and finished with the almost heroically inept forecast, 'Do not expect a goal flood.' But Buchan was only expressing the opinion of the vast majority. Roy Peskett in the *Daily Mail* suggested that 'England could finish two or three goals to the good, and will do so if the team plays to form.' The

The England team that played the Rest of the World XI in October. Back row, left to right: Ray Barlow, Alf Ramsey, Derek Ufton, Ted Ditchburn, Gil Merrick, Jimmy Dickinson, Bill Eckersley, Jimmy Trotter (trainer). Front row, left to right: Jimmy Mullen, Stanley Matthews, Stan Mortensen, Billy Wright (captain), Nat Lofthouse, Albert Quixall, Ronnie Allen.

lone voice crying in the wilderness was that of Geoffrey Green, the highly respected *Times* correspondent, who said on the radio before the game that he thought Hungary would win 4–2. He also warned that 'one of these fine days, very soon, we shall wake up to find six goals in the back of our net'.

The Hungarians, the 'Magic Magyars', had swept everything before them since they had last tasted defeat 32 matches earlier. They had scored in every match they had played for the past six years. Under the leadership of the brilliant Ferenc Puskas, the Galloping Major with the golden left foot, they had established themselves as the best football team in the world. By the end of that November afternoon, few would doubt they were the best football team the world had yet seen. 'Look at that little fat chap,' was the comment that had entered urban mythology. 'We'll murder this lot.' Puskas was not built like an inside forward. 'Stocky' was the word usually applied to him, but only because a man could not be fat and still play football that well. Actually, in many traditional ways he could not play football that well: he headed the ball only on very rare occasions, and he was very much a left-footed only player. But it was the way he out-thought his opponents that made him so deadly. His passing was immaculate, and his ability to move into space and his quick turns, which left defenders for dead, meant he rarely had to worry about out-sprinting his man over 30 yards or going into a crunching tackle.

The Hungarian tactics were based around two men in midfield, Nandor Hidegkuti and Jozsef Bozsik. Hidegkuti wore the number nine shirt, but was in no sense a 1950s centre forward. He and Bozsik were the 2 of a 4–2–4 formation, years before the rest of Europe and the footballing world understood the advantages of this way of playing. Both had an attacking role to play, but the quiet Bozsik, wearing the number four shirt, was often treated as a standard wing half, until opponents realised their mistake, too late. The Hungarian coach, Gusztav Sebes, was the mastermind of this system, but he would never claim to have invented it. He merely built on what he had seen elsewhere, probably starting with Alex James playing the deep-lying forward role for Arsenal in the 1930s. In fact, it was more of a 3–1–2–4 system, because Jozsef Zakarias played in front of the back three, Jeno Buzansky, Gyula Lorant and Mihaly Lantos, who had the main task of marking Stanley Matthews. The back three were no footballing artists: they were the barn door that should always remain closed, the last line of defence before the Hungarian goalmouth. That Hungarian games were usually high-scoring, and the idea of a clean sheet seemed alien to them, is confirmed by the fact that 50 years later we remember the names of the constructive midfielders and the lethal finishers in the forward line more than the back three. The *Daily Mail* might well have been partly right about their 'suspect defence' but their job was to win the ball and get it upfield to Zakarias and Hidegkuti, a job they performed successfully far more often than not. Behind this trio, in goal, the Hungarians had Gyula Grosics, a very fine player. The entire Hungarian success had been built on attack rather than defence, and they needed a very good goalkeeper who was able to deal with problems that would result from the over-ambitious play of the four men in front of him. There were certainly plenty of shots at goal at both ends of the pitch when the Hungarians played, and Grosics had to work hard to keep the goals against tally at manageable levels. He was certainly no passenger, and did not deserve the cruel joke that did the rounds: 'What do you call a man who hangs around Hungarian footballers?' 'The goalkeeper.'

The front four were Puskas, Lazslo Budai, Sandor Kocsis and Zoltan Czibor. They were all brilliant players, but without doubt the one who ranked second to Puskas was Kocsis. Puskas ended his Hungarian international career with 83 goals from 84 matches, a truly phenomenal strike rate, but Kocsis went even better than that, scoring 75 goals in 68 internationals, including a world-record seven international hat-tricks. In the 1954 World Cup Finals he was the top scorer, with 11 goals in five matches, but a year earlier he was already the finished article, aged just 24, a full two and a half years younger than any of his English opponents. He was known as 'The Man with the Golden Head', which was lucky considering the total lack of heading skills shown by his captain playing alongside.

Zoltan Czibor and Lazslo Budai were the two wingers. They did not, of course, play like 1950s wingers, but more like modern wing backs, with a role that included challenging the English wingers whenever they came forward. Matthews was seen as the danger, and so two, and sometimes three men, opposed him.

The Hungarians were, of course, officially amateurs, as the *Daily Mail* rather cynically put it, 'in order to conform with Olympic Rules', and it was announced in all seriousness by their management that several of them had used some of their annual holiday allowance to take part in the game. 'Please tell the British public', continued the statement, 'that if our men lose, they will not be locked up and that there will be no by-election for Bozsik.' The Hungarian number five was a member of parliament (Communist, of course) for what was described as 'a factory district'.

At Wembley that grey afternoon 100,000 people were fortunate enough to watch this wonderful match. This number has probably quintupled over the years with people who want to say, 'I was there,' and there were another few hundred thousand who were able to watch the second half of the match live on BBC Television. All those men who had forked out a lot of money so that their wives could watch the Coronation on television were about to see a useful return on their investment (the 'Ultra Electric V80' table model cost 61 $^1/_2$ guineas, long-range model 40/- extra). The FA in their wisdom had decided not to allow the entire game to be televised, because there were Cup replays that afternoon as well, and they did not want to pull people away from those games, but at least they allowed the entire match to be shown later that evening, so that people coming home from work and hearing the result (or not hearing the result if they were very lucky) could watch the entire game. It also meant that a record of the game would survive for posterity.

The game kicked off at 2.17, just two minutes after the advertised time. By 2.18, England were one down. A pass from Bozsik to Hidegkuti was the key. The centre forward took the ball just outside the England penalty area, sold Johnston a dummy so easily you would have thought the England centre half had gone out to buy one, and blasted the ball high into the net past an astonished Merrick. The sight of the ball in the back of the net so quickly, so unbelievably quickly, was greeted with stunned silence from the capacity crowd on the terraces. Astonishment then seemed to be the order of the day for every non-Hungarian at Wembley, as over the next 89 minutes the proud English record of never having been beaten at home by a foreign side was not so much broken as shattered, ground up into little pieces and thrown out with the rubbish: and non-recyclable rubbish at that.

It was not long before Hidegkuti found the net again, only to have the goal disallowed for offside, and on 15 minutes there was a brief moment of hope for the home side when Jackie Sewell equalised. That first English goal came when Johnston intercepted the ball in the England penalty area, took a few steps and then put Mortensen through with a finely judged pass. Mortensen passed out to Sewell on the left, who hit a low hard shot past the diving Grosics. But that was as far as hope lasted. Five minutes later, a move involving Puskas to Czibor to Kocsis to the inevitable Hidegkuti, who slotted the ball home from close range, made it 2–1 to the visitors.

The Hungarians' third goal, scored in the twenty-fifth minute, was probably the best of them all. To watch the recording of the game half a century later is to become lost in admiration of the simple beauty of the move, and the lethal assurance of the finish. It also confirms how totally helpless the English team were by this time: the match was already lost, and it showed in the face and the body language of every England player. Billy Wright, the England captain, the rock around whom the team had been built for so many seasons, was the man most cruelly exposed by his opposite number, Puskas, but his flatfootedness was no more obvious than that of any of his team-mates. A flurry of passes from the back brought the ball to Czibor, who had taken up the outside-right position for the time being. Czibor made a simple pass to Puskas inside him, whereupon the Hungarian captain showed in one brief moment the gap that had opened up between English football and the best of the Continental teams. Faced with the challenge of Billy Wright, the man considered by many to be the best defender in Britain since the war, Puskas just rolled the ball backwards a few centimetres. This completely wrongfooted Wright, leaving him off-balance and the goal at the mercy of Puskas. The Galloping Major needed no further invitation. He swivelled and hit the ball into the left-hand corner of the net with such force that Merrick had no chance. Scarcely a quarter of the way through the game, the score was 3–1. It was a massacre of the innocents.

Before the half hour was reached, the rampaging Hungarians had scored another goal: this time a Bozsik free kick was diverted by Puskas past the hapless Merrick. Hungary, with a three goal lead, seemed to turn down the heat for a spell. Within minutes the debutant Robb had tested Grosics with a header, and then Mortensen, an archetypical English centre forward who never gave up, smacked in a shot to make the score 4–2. The half-time talk by Walter Winterbottom must have been interesting. Persuading all his players to come out for the second half was some sort of achievement, so demoralised did they look.

The second half was, in the event, less frenetic than the first, but no less one-sided. It only took another 10 minutes for Hungary to regain their three-goal cushion, as Merrick's shortcomings against this persistent barrage were exposed. To be fair to Merrick, the shortcomings of all the England defenders were exposed in this game, but the fifth Hungarian goal can be put down to Merrick's mistake as much as Bozsik's brilliant shot. The problem began when Czibor headed towards goal, where Merrick could only parry the ball on to the post. The ball then fell loose in the penalty area, where Bozsik pounced and thumped it into the net once again. Barely a couple of minutes later, Hidegkuti completed his hat-trick. In the grey fog of a November afternoon, the Hungarians lit up the footballing world in a way that nobody had dared imagine. Grosics in the Hungarian goal did a cartwheel to celebrate his team's sixth goal, and shortly afterwards retired with an injured arm. It was therefore the substitute goalkeeper, Geller, not Grosics, who conceded Ramsey's consolation penalty goal towards the end of the game, when Mortensen was brought down, but there was no hope that England could or would close the gap further. The final score, 6–3, reflected the fact that the Hungarians were at least twice as good as England on the day.

First reactions to the result were total admiration for the awesome display of Puskas and his team. Then came the recriminations, the wailing and gnashing of teeth at English football's lost supremacy. One of the difficulties of the contemporary observer is to distinguish the historically significant from the merely newsworthy. It might not have been evident at the time but we can see today that many of the sporting events of 1953 marked a pivotal change from the old order to the new. Stanley Matthews' Cup Winner's medal and Gordon Richards' Derby win were the last hurrahs of the old order in those sports, even if nobody thought so at the time. England's winning of the Ashes marked the beginning of a period in which they dominated the cricket field, and even Roger

Bannister's attempts on the mile record marked the start of a move towards professional athletics, professional in its attitudes and methods if not yet in its financial rewards. But at the time, nobody was able to put these events in context, because nobody could know what would happen next. The Hungary game was different. Everybody knew it marked a watershed in British football history.

Billy Wright spoke candidly immediately after the match. 'The Hungarians produced some of the finest, most brilliantly applied football it has ever been my privilege to see. They were relentless, they were superb.' The newspapers were unanimous: 'Forget the Wembley Wizards. Salute the maroon Magyar Marvels,' said the *Daily Mail*. 'Here indeed, did we attend, all 100,000 of us, the twilight of the gods,' was the more erudite comment from Geoffrey Green in *The Times*. 'The Hungarians … seemed to be playing a different game altogether,' wrote the *Daily Telegraph*. It was clear, as the *Daily Mail* said, that the Hungarians 'set the pattern for our football of the future'. A wholesale change had to be put in place.

But how had the Hungarians got so far ahead of England? Why did we not, why could we not, play like them? The main reason was that the grass roots had been ignored. It was seen to be enough that every boy kicked a ball around in the streets of the Lancashire cotton towns or played a rudimentary game of soccer in the school playground. The idea of a structured coaching system that would pick out the gifted youngsters and give them the ball skills that would allow them to compete at every level was not considered. As Gustaf Sebes told Sir Stanley Rous, 'This really is not our greatest moment. That came last year when for the second year running the Hungarian boys won the youth international tournament you started.' Britain had all the right ideas, but just did not follow them through.

The most telling comment came from the President of the Hungarian Football Association, who said at the banquet after the match, 'You had better go back thirty years to the time that Jimmy Hogan came to teach us how to play.' Jimmy Hogan? Who is he? And why had he been teaching the Hungarians how to play when he ought to have been teaching his fellow countrymen?

Jimmy Hogan (not to be confused with Jimmy Hagan, the Sheffield United forward who played once for England in 1948) was an inside forward of average ability, who, when he retired, faced the usual career dilemma of a man in his mid to late thirties with no real qualifications. Should he take a pub or should he try his hand at coaching the youngsters? He decided on the latter. Hogan was not the only ex-pro to take up coaching: by the mid-1930s there were far more men with the FA coaching qualification than there were posts available in Britain. So these men went overseas, usually on one-year contracts, and often to very far-flung parts of the globe. China, Kenya, Iceland and Paraguay were all regular destinations of these FA coaches, but their effect in many places eventually came home to haunt the home countries. The official line for FA coaches in those days (and, some would say, even today) was that the long ball was the way to move the ball up and down field and that fitness was more important than ball skills. For children, results did not matter: enjoying the game was the thing.

While this essentially amateur ethic flourished in Britain, proving the theory that football was a game for gentlemen played by hooligans, the coaches who went overseas often had very different ideas, which they could then put into practice without interference. Hogan, in Hungary, was one of many who encouraged youngsters to practise and improve their ball skills, to feel at ease on the ball, to work with others in the team and, above all, to cultivate a habit of winning. The tactics flowed from there.

Jimmy Hogan came back to England in the mid-thirties and soon became manager of Aston Villa, a position he held from 1936 to 1944. He took over when the club had just been relegated to the Second Division for the first time in its history. It took him two seasons to get it back up to the top flight, but then his career was interrupted by the war, and although Villa won the League War Cup (North) in 1944 under his guidance, when the Football League fixtures began again he had been replaced. His influence on the playing style of Aston Villa, which would

Another Hungarian goal. Dickinson, Wright and Eckersley of England are left flat-footed as Puskas (10) turns to celebrate.

have been extended through English football if he had been able to sustain their success, came to an end. That was not the end of his links with the club, though. He was not invited to the official dinner held after the England v Hungary match, despite the profuse thanks given to him by the victorious team. 'I was disappointed,' he said at the time. 'The Hungarians have invited me to a cocktail party in London tomorrow [26 October]. I am unable to accept as Thursday is one of the days when I take thirty Aston Villa youngsters in coaching classes.' 'Single-minded' is the adjective that springs to mind about Hogan. Coaching youngsters always took precedence over cocktail parties and meeting the greatest footballers in the world.

Some British footballers were aware even before 1953 how good the East European players could be. Malcolm Allison, who eventually became a very successful coach in Britain, was posted to Czechoslovakia after the war and came back saying, 'I cannot believe how good these Continentals are.' But his was one of a very few voices crying in the wilderness. It took the defeat by Hungary to remove the scales from everybody else's eyes. The most significant pair of eyes were those of England's left back that day, Alf Ramsey. The match may have been his final international as a player, but the lessons he learnt that afternoon were taken into his management career, first with Ipswich Town and then, most gloriously, with England to the World Cup in 1966.

In practical terms, the first official fall-out from the Hungary defeat was the announcement a couple of days after the match that 'the first step toward the rebuilding of English soccer' was to be made in the New Year, when the Football Association had organised a meeting of the top club managers. It was to be a brain-storming session – what is wrong with English football now, how come the Continentals are so much better than us, and what can we do about it? It is to be hoped that Jimmy Hogan was included in the Aston Villa delegation to this meeting, but one doubts it somehow.

British football was operating then, as now, under a system that tended to put club before country. While the footballing public may want England (or Scotland or Wales or Northern Ireland) to win the World Cup, the football clubs, which are where the money is, want to win club trophies and do not really care how the national sides fare. This is not how it was in Hungary in 1953. Hungary was a Communist state in which every activity was carefully controlled and its effect, both inside and outside Hungary, carefully noted. We should not underestimate the power of Communist propaganda in the success of the Hungarians. Sport fed on propaganda and propaganda fed on sport. As the Hungarian News and Information Service noted on the team's return by train to Budapest, 'the delegates of the Hungarian Working People's Party, the Government, the mass organisations, the factories and large groups of Young Pioneers greeted the heroes who had proved the high quality of Hungarian football, the strength and maturity of Hungarian sport, before the whole world'. There is little doubt that their East German neighbours noted the positive publicity that Hungary received as a result of their sports success, and took heed.

Ferenc Puskas, displaying a loyalty to his government that had entirely disappeared three years later, expressed the feelings of his team, or at least the feelings that he had been told to express on behalf of the team: 'We thank the party, the Government and our people for making it possible for us to prepare undisturbed for the greatest sporting task of our lives.' A few days later all team members were presented with decorations by the President of Hungary. 'The sportsmen, veterans of many tough battles, were deeply moved,' said the official release, 'gazing with moist eyes at the glittering Orders of Merit, which expressed the finest recognition of their country and the millions of its people.'

This was the soft human mask of Communist officialdom. Two weeks later, in the Soviet Union, there was a brief glimpse of the harder side. On 23 December the post-Stalin leadership crisis was simplified when Lavrenti Beria, Soviet Minister of the Interior and head of the police force, was tried in secret for crimes against the state, and then shot.

The newspapers were justifiably so very full of the England v Hungary football match that some may not have found room for the other England v Hungary match played the same day, but they should have done. A few hundred yards away, at the Empire Pool, Wembley, England's table tennis players took on the best that Hungary had to offer. In the final week of March 1953 in Bucharest, England won the Swaythling Cup, the top men's team trophy in table tennis, defeating the strongest European teams, Czechoslovakia, Yugoslavia and Hungary, on their way to victory. It was the first time that England had ever won the cup, and in defeating the holders, Hungary, in the final they had achieved the first great British team triumph of Coronation Year. Like football, table tennis was invented in Britain, and like football it was an Englishman, Edward Shires, described variously as a typewriting technician and a footballer, who is credited with introducing the game into Hungary around the turn of the twentieth century. For most of the time since then Hungary had dominated the sport, and in 1953 the world number one male player and world singles, doubles and mixed doubles champion was the Hungarian Ferenc Sido.

The English Swaythling Cup team consisted of four men: Johnny

Leach, Richard Bergmann, Brian Kennedy and Aubrey Simons, along with their non-playing captain Adrian Haydon, father of Ann Jones (née Haydon) who went on to table tennis and lawn tennis stardom in the next decade. Johnny Leach was without question the greatest male table tennis player ever born in Britain. He was world champion in 1949 and 1951, the last Englishman ever to win that title. After retirement, he became the voice of table tennis and 50 years on is still president of the English Table Tennis Association. His only rivals as the greatest player ever to represent England were Victor Barna, born in Hungary, and Richard Bergmann, who was born in Austria of a Polish father and an Italian mother. A prodigiously talented youth, Bergmann was part of Austria's Swaythling Cup-winning team in 1936. When Nazi Germany annexed Austria in 1938, the 19-year-old fled to England, where he served in the RAF and became a British citizen. The bespectacled Aubrey Simons, a cricketer as well as a table tennis player (he and Arthur Milton won their Gloucestershire Second XI caps on the same day), played well above himself throughout the round robin-style tournament to keep England in with a chance of the title. He also won the key opening match over Jozef Koczian in the final. The left-handed Yorkshireman Brian Kennedy was the extra player in the squad: he only played once, against Switzerland, the weakest of the teams competing for the Cup.

In the Swaythling Cup Final, between the winners of Group A, England, and the winners of Group B, Hungary, it was Hungary who were the firm favourites. England had had by far the more difficult route to the final, having to overcome the other strong team of the tournament, Czechoslovakia, in the group stages, in order to qualify. Thanks to the efforts of Bergmann, the great defender, and Simons, the inspired attacker, England edged through against the Czechs 5–4, the final deciding match between Simons and Vaclav Tereba ending at around 3.30 in the morning, with Simons victorious by 21–16, 22–20.

In many ways this final group stage match was more exhausting than the final, which England won 5–3. The reports of the match from different viewpoints make contrasting reading. The British magazine *Table Tennis Review* is justifiably ecstatic: 'At last! England made it after years of near misses. It was a glorious, exhilarating victory. We swept the world.' The crowd was overwhelmingly for the Hungarians. 'They applauded every point they won,' remembers Aubrey Simons. 'When we won a point, the only applause came from the British Embassy people.' However, even the best efforts of the crowd failed to bring victory to the glorious Hungarian People's team.

The British–Romanian Friendship Association report is a stark reminder of the political realities of the era: 'The final of the men's team competition was disputed between the teams of Britain and the Hungarian People's Republic. The experienced British formation, including two former world champions, won the game 5–3. But their victory was overshadowed by the fact that the Hungarian player Ferenc Sido outdid all the three British players, Leach, Bergmann and Simons. The teams of Czechoslovakia, Romania, China and Bulgaria made a good showing.' The reporter went on to note that 'the superiority of the sportsmen of the countries of People's Democracy proved here more categorical'. According to Aubrey Simons, the only reason an English table tennis team was allowed behind the Iron Curtain in the 1940s and 1950s was because the president of the English Table Tennis Association, the Hon. Ivor Montagu, was 'a red-hot Communist'. He was also the son of Lady Swaythling, who had presented the cup they were all playing for. 'There was a lot of poverty in Romania at the time, but we were treated like lords. We were treated better in Romania than the English Table Tennis Association could afford to treat the Romanians when they came to England.'

Eight months later, when England met Hungary at the Empire Pool in Wembley, the conditions were very different. The match was mixed, with two men and two women from each country competing. The England team consisted of Leach, Bergmann and the second most famous twins in British sport after the Bedsers, Diane and Rosalind Rowe. They were identical and could only be told apart by the fact that Rosalind was right-handed and Diane left-handed. They had won the world doubles title in 1951, and would do so again in 1954, having been runners-up in 1952 and 1953. They were the heart of the British ladies' team, which had lost in the final of the Corbillon Cup – the distaff equivalent of the Swaythling Cup – also in Bucharest in March. In addition, Rosalind was the British women's singles champion. In those days before the Chinese and Japanese came to dominate the sport, the table tennis match at the Empire Pool was as much a battle between the two greatest powers as the game at Wembley Stadium was for football.

Only the result was different. There were nine matches – singles, doubles and mixed doubles – to be played, and after the first five matches of the evening the score was even more one-sided than it had been a few hours earlier on the Wembley grass: 4–1 to the Hungarians. England then outdid even their most ardent supporters' hopes and won the last four matches on the reel to win the match 5–4. The Rowe twins were the heroines of the comeback, but Bergmann and Leach played their part too. It was nail-biting stuff, and as brilliant a display of table tennis from all players as can have been seen in Britain for many years. All too many of the newspapers ignored it, or hid the report away beneath reams of comment on the football match, at which, incidentally, both table tennis squads had been guests of honour. England had at least proved to be the best in the world at table tennis in 1953, and had done it twice. 'At least we can beat them at ping-pong,' was the newspapers' reaction the morning after the night before.

Football was the national winter sport, so football must have the final word. Roy Peskett of the *Daily Mail* later became a good friend of Derek Ufton, the Charlton Athletic centre half who probably should have played against Hungary. 'I'm sorry I got it so wrong,' he told Ufton. 'I saw them training and they didn't seem to want to run.' But the 1953 Hungarians did not need to. They were always on the ball.

13 • *The Final Days*

What else did 1953 have to offer? It had been a remarkable year right across the sporting spectrum, with some of the great contests of the century all concertinaed into a few months of Coronation Year. There could surely be nothing left to celebrate. But even outside the sporting world there were achievements to admire. On 8 September, over southern England Squadron Leader Neville Duke, in a Hawker Hunter, broke the world speed record for level flight with a speed of 727.6 mph. The record lasted only 18 days until a Supermarine Swift, another British jet flown by Mike Lithgow, moved the record up to 737.3 mph. This flight was over Libya, a venue that would not be chosen for British military test flights nowadays. Lithgow's record lasted even fewer days than Duke's, before an American 'Douglas Skyray' pushed it up to over 753 miles per hour.

The achievements of the Royal Air Force fliers meant that 1953 ended positively for British aviation, after what had been a mixed year. In civil aviation, the world's first jet airliner, the de Havilland Comet, had established a record by becoming the first jetliner to cross the Atlantic, on 29 May, the day that Everest was conquered. But this was 27 days after the dreadful crash of a BOAC Comet, G-ALYV, which broke up in a violent tropical storm in Calcutta on 2 May, Cup Final day. Newspaper headlines told the world of the 'Airliner knocked down by tempest'. There had been reports of extreme turbulence at approximately 10,000 feet in cumulonimbus clouds. Opinion was that the storm would have downed any aircraft. Thirty-seven passengers and a crew of six were lost. This was the beginning of a series of Comet crashes, which were eventually put down mainly to the little-understood problem of metal fatigue, and which effectively handed world leadership in civil jet aviation to the United States.

In October the Nobel Prize winners were announced, and among the names was that of Sir Winston Churchill, who was honoured for his writing. Churchill was unable to attend the Nobel Prize ceremony in November, so Lady Churchill accepted the literature prize on his

World heavyweight champion Rocky Marciano (right) retained his title on 24 September when he knocked out Roland LaStarza in the 11th round of their fight in New York.

behalf. The King of Sweden noted that usually it is the prize that honours the recipient, but in this case 'it is the author who gives lustre to the Prize'. The stature of Churchill in post-war Europe is hard to imagine now, but 50 years ago he was seen as the one man who had stood between Hitler and his ambitions, who had saved Europe from Nazi domination. He was more than loved, he was revered all over Europe, and although that reverence did not necessarily translate into votes for the Conservative Party he led, it certainly caused him to win awards such as the Nobel Prize for literature which, purely on merit, he perhaps did not deserve.

To return to the sporting year: some sports had lain fallow, so to speak, but even they had produced their moments. In 1953, boxing was very much a major sport throughout the world, as it was in Britain. It was still seen as a sport that young boys should be encouraged to take part in, and one in which the leading participants could be held up as role models to the youth of the nation. The world heavyweight boxing champion in 1953 was the last, and possibly greatest, white American to hold the undisputed crown, Rocky Marciano. He won the title by knocking out Jersey Joe Walcott in September 1952, and in 1953 he fought just twice. His return match against the ageing Walcott in Chicago in May ended in a first-round knockout by Marciano. Against Roland LaStarza in New York in September, the fight lasted to the eleventh round before the referee stopped the fight, with LaStarza unable to take any more punishment. Marciano would keep the title until he retired in 1956, having beaten all comers, including Britain's Don Cockell, the reigning British and Empire heavyweight champion, in May 1955.

Britain's leading boxer of the early 1950s, the middleweight Randolph Turpin, was chosen as the *Eagle* comic's Sportsman of the Year in both 1951 and 1952. However, he had a poor year in 1953. On 9 June, Turpin fought Charles Hamez of France for what the British Boxing Board of Control described as the World Middleweight Championship. The Americans and the Europeans both considered the fight to be the final decider for the right to fight an American nominee for the title, vacated by Sugar Ray Robinson, who had moved up temporarily to light-heavy-weight, but the British authorities decided it should be considered a world title bout. Randolph Turpin, as well as being *Eagle*'s Sportsman of the Year, was British, Empire and European middleweight champion, and also Empire light-heavyweight champion. In July 1951 he had beaten the apparently unbeatable Robinson on points in London to take the world title, but then lost the return bout in New York 64 days later. From that moment on, it is clear that he was no longer the same boxer.

His fight against Hamez took place in front of 54,000 people at the White City, and it proved to be both a success and a failure. It was a success because Turpin won, outpointing Mamez over the 15 rounds, but it was a failure because the fans had been led to believe that Turpin would live up to his 'killer' image and finish off his opponent very quickly. The end of the fight was greeted with boos, even though Turpin was the winner by a clear margin. Turpin's efforts throughout the 15 rounds were limited, and he seemed merely to be going through the motions, doing

enough to win but no more. 'The Sepia Slayer', as he was sometimes
billed, failed to live up to the nickname. It was in total contrast to his
performance in 1951 when he had brilliantly outboxed and outpointed
Robinson – who may possibly have underestimated his opponent – in a
sustained attack over 15 gruelling rounds. The only people who found the
Turpin–Hamez fight gruelling were the 54,000 fans who had paid good
money to watch it.

Having beaten Hamez, Turpin's next fight was against Carl 'Bobo'
Olson in New York on 21 October to settle the destination of the title
vacated by Sugar Ray Robinson. Olson, who was based in Hawaii, was
reputedly of Swedish, Portuguese and Hawaiian parentage, although how
he acquired three different strains of parentage was not explained. The
fight reporters from Britain were unanimous in considering Turpin to be
of a far higher class than Olson, and in feeling that if the mood took
him, he should win easily. Both men were 25 years old, both weighed 160
pounds and both were in their prime. It was the first world title fight
featuring a British boxer in 1953, and it should have been a good contest.
However, the newspapers were also reporting that all was not well with
Turpin's training. The *Daily Mail* noted that 'if he is still The Sepia
Slayer, the fighter with dynamite in both fists, the dynamic counter-
puncher who rocketed to world honours at 23, Randy can do it, but his
moody, aloof behaviour here, the casualness of his training, fills one's
mind with doubt.' He was right. Even though Turpin had the class,
Olson was the tougher, mentally and physically, and on the night he had
no difficulty in earning a clear points victory. There was talk of wild
women and unsuitable companions in the Turpin camp, and even Turpin
had to admit after the fight, 'If only I had been right mentally, I would
have won.' He then went on to vow that 'When I fight Olson next time,
it will be different.' Next time! What was wrong with the first time?
Olson's camp obviously shared his view, as they were in no hurry to give
Turpin a rematch, in case his mind was right next time. Turpin never
fought again for a world title, and was never again chosen as *Eagle's*
Sportsman of the Year.

Bandleader Joe Loss, Ava Gardner and her husband Frank Sinatra were among the 54,000 crowd that watched Randolph Turpin outpoint Charles Hamez on 9 June at the White City Stadium.

The demise of Turpin was the main boxing event of 1953 for British fans. Six days after Turpin's defeat at the hands of Olson, Terry Allen attempted to relieve Japan's Yoshio Shirai of his world flyweight title. Allen was a strange man. Born in 1925, he began his boxing career using his real name, Edward Govier. He joined the Navy in the Second World War, but after going AWOL he swapped ID cards with a person named Terry Allen. He carried on boxing – and living – under this borrowed name even after he was eventually arrested and sent to Egypt to serve out the remainder of the war. He boxed many times between 1943 and 1945 in Egypt, and then came back to England to continue his professional career. Allen first challenged for the flyweight world title in September 1949, and held it for four months in 1950. After losing his crown to the Hawaiian Dado Marino, he had still been rated as a leading challenger. In 15 rounds of hard slog in Tokyo, the 28-year-old Allen lost on points to Shirai, almost exactly two years after he had lost his previous title fight. The defeat marked the end of his world title challenges.

The show-jumping year, as always, culminated at the International Horse Show at the White City in July and, as usual, it resulted in a British triumph. The King George V Cup, the main individual title of the show, was won for the third time by Lieutenant-Colonel Harry Llewellyn on his famous Foxhunter. The Queen was present to hand him the trophy, as she was to hand him the team trophy, the Prince of Wales Cup, which Britain won for the fifth year running. Llewellyn had beaten three of Ireland's best competitors in the jump-off for the King George V Trophy, and in the Prince of Wales Cup, the British team beat Ireland again. Lieutenant-Colonel Llewellyn and Foxhunter, Wilf White riding Nizefela, Peter Robeson on Craven 'A' and Pat Smythe, the only female member of the team, on Prince Hal were the successful British team that year. The success was anticipated, so did not have the impact of the less-expected triumphs in football, racing, table tennis and cricket which had so brightened up the 1953 back pages. That is not to suggest that the show jumpers were any less skilled at their chosen sport than the other sportsmen and women, but merely that their success was considered less newsworthy.

The sporting year finished as it had begun, with rugby taking centre stage. On 21 November, the day the Piltdown Man hoax was revealed, Cardiff took on the touring All Blacks at Cardiff Arms Park. The Arms Park was a daunting place for any visiting rugby side, even as great a XV as the New Zealanders were. Fifty-six thousand people packed the terraces and stands to watch the ninety-eighth match ever played in Britain by the All Blacks. Of their previous fixtures, 92 had been won and only Wales (twice), England (once) and Swansea (once) had beaten them, while Ulster once managed a draw. Tradition and the bookmakers were against the home team. But Cardiff were strong advocates of open rugby, relying not on the weight of the forwards and defensive kicking but on the passing game, which in their view was more fun to play as well as to watch. In Rex Willis at scrum half and Cliff Morgan at fly half they had a brilliant hub around which to build their open game, and the All Blacks were on the defensive from the beginning.

Colonel Harry Llewellyn on Foxhunter, the combination that won the King George V Trophy in 1953, and almost every other show jumping prize in the early fifties.

It all started with a stroke of luck after only five minutes. Morgan took the ball in his own half and with a burst of speed for which he was famous ripped through the centre and punted the ball ahead. The stroke of luck came when the ball bounced back to him off one of the New Zealanders, which allowed Morgan to pass to his captain, Bleddyn Williams, who passed to Gwyn Rowlands, who kicked the ball high and across the pitch towards the All Blacks goal, where the Cardiff hooker, Judd, bundled the ball over the line. Rowlands converted to put Cardiff five points in front, a lead they never lost. The New Zealanders came back with a long penalty goal, but within two minutes of that great kick Cardiff scored their second try. This time it was Bleddyn Williams, receiving the ball from a set scrum, who kicked it ahead over the All Blacks three-quarter line for Allan Thomas to collect and send Gwyn Rowlands in at the corner. That was all the scoring, and 8–3 sounds like a dour struggle. But it was far from that, with the All Blacks pummelling away at the Cardiff defence in the final 15 minutes of the game, hoisting high kicks over their defensive line. But Cardiff hung on, and the All Blacks were beaten.

It was a great and thoroughly deserved victory, something the selectors noted when they came to pick the Welsh side to play the All Blacks a month later, once again at Cardiff Arms Park. Many of the heroes for Cardiff were included in the Welsh side – Williams, Rowlands, Morgan, Willis, and Judd among others – and the Welsh entered the game with confidence, or at least with hope. The confidence was justified. In another thrilling game, just six days before Christmas, Wales beat the All Blacks by 13 points to 8, two converted tries and a penalty goal against just the one goal and a penalty goal. New Zealand were in the box seat for much of the game, leading by 8 points to 5 with just 10 minutes to go. Then Gwyn Rowlands' magic boot came to the rescue again, kicking the home side level with a fairly straightforward but nonetheless nerve-racking penalty goal. Then Ken Jones, the Welsh winger, took an unexpected cross-kick by Clem Thomas from a line-out and raced in to score the winning try. Rowlands converted again, and Wales had won. Cardiff Arms Park went crazy for the second time in a month. Cliff Morgan remembers the day well: 'You don't forget days like that. To win those matches was something special – we didn't deserve to beat the buggers, mind.'

Morgan also sees how much the game has changed in the succeeding 50 years, perhaps more than any other sport. Rugby was amateur in those days, in spirit as well as in financial terms. 'I liked playing rugby because it was fun and good fellowship. It was a day off from the solid hard toil of the pit or the university.' The Welsh club and national sides had 'coal miners, steel workers, artists, doctors, policemen and university lecturers', and even though 'it used to cost us money to play for Cardiff', Morgan does not envy the professionals of today. 'It's harder for them now. We weren't as committed to the game. It wasn't our jobs. Today you are committed to playing well and winning. We were committed to playing well.'

That is perhaps the biggest difference between all sports in 1953 and in

Bob Stuart, All Blacks' captain, leads his team out on a cold November afternoon.

2003. Sport has now become big business. In an era when image rights have become part of a sportsman's playing contract, when losing a game can mean the loss of millions of pounds for a club and often almost as much for a player, the idea of being committed merely to playing well would be seen as letting the team down. Winning has become everything.

Perhaps 1953 showed a few signs of things to come. Britain was able to celebrate great victories that year, and there is little doubt that the sporting year would have been less memorable if Bolton had held on for victory, even if Matthews had made or scored half a dozen goals in a losing cause. It would have meant less if Gordon Richards had once again missed out in the Derby, even if his defeat had been at the hands of the Queen's horse Aureole. We would not have remembered the 1953 Australian cricketers so fondly if they had not so obligingly been not quite good enough, and the Welsh rugby XV would not still be having reunion dinners every year if they were commemorating a narrow defeat.

And what if Hillary and Tenzing had had to turn back a couple of hundred feet from the summit of Everest?

Sporting history is all about victory, not defeat. Grantland Rice, an American, was the man who noted that the One Great Scorer 'marks – not what you won or lost – but how you played the game', which was the basis of sports ethics for a hundred years or more. Now the philosophy is 'Winning isn't everything, it's the only thing.' Professional sport is serious business, but unlike business you cannot have more than one winner. Ford, General Motors, BMW, Renault and the rest can divide up the motor car market and each have a decent share, but nobody can divide up the FA Cup, the Ashes or the Ryder Cup. Either you win or you lose.

We look back on 1953 with affection because victory featured more often than defeat, at least for British sports fans. We also look back with affection because it seems such a different place. There were still people who played both cricket and football for England, for goodness' sake, and schoolteachers who could be picked to play football against Hungary. Nobody, not even Stanley Matthews, Gordon Richards or Ben Hogan, became a millionaire by virtue of sporting expertise, and yet sport was still a true leveller, allowing all people to watch and play on equal terms. Coronation Year was probably a watershed for several sports and several sportsmen, but few if any noticed at the time. Yes, it was the final flourish for Gordon Richards and the only Cup Winner's medal for Matthews. Yes, Everest was climbed and yes, Ben Hogan's Open was a one-off. But in many other sports there was no watershed, just a natural progression from the amateur ethic to the professional over half a century or more. Len Hutton did not retire for another couple of years, Bannister did not achieve the four-minute mile until 1954 and major changes like open tennis, one-day cricket and professional rugby were still many years ahead.

Coronation Year was just a perfect background for great sporting achievements, and, happily, British sportsmen delivered some of them. The British people were in celebratory mood all year, and it was our great good fortune that our sporting heroes gave us all something else to celebrate.

Bibliography

The following books, magazines and newspapers were among those that provided me with valuable reference material during my research for this book:

Newspapers
(mainly from the British Newspaper Library, Colindale; all published in London except where indicated):
Daily Mail
Daily Mirror
Daily Telegraph
Evening News
London *Evening Standard*
Manchester Guardian
News Chronicle
News of the World
St Petersburg Times, Florida
Sporting Life
Staffordshire Sentinel
Star
Sunday Express
Sunday Pictorial
The Times

Magazines:
Athletics Weekly
Charles Buchan's Football Monthly
Cricketer
Golfing
Eagle
Illustrated London News
Motor Sport
Table Tennis
Table Tennis Review

Books:
The Ascent of Everest, John Hunt (Hodder & Stoughton, 1953)
The Ashes Crown the Year, Jack Fingleton (Collins, 1954)
Athletics Facts And Feats, Peter Matthews (Guinness, 1982)
Bloodstock Breeders' Review, 1954

British Hit Singles, Paul Gambaccini, Tim Rice, Jonathan Rice (Guinness, 1989)
Coronation Everest, Jan Morris (Burford Books, 2000)
The Four Minute Mile, Roger Bannister (Lyons & Burford, 1994)
Golfer's Handbook 1995 (Macmillan, 1995)
Guinness Record of the F.A. Cup, Mike Collett (Guinness, 1993)
High Adventure, Edmund Hillary (Hodder and Stoughton, 1957)
The Horseman's Year 1954, ed. W.E. Lyon (Collins, 1954)
International Rugby Championship 1883–1983, Terry Godwin (Collins, 1984)
International Who's Who of Sport, ed. Peter Matthews (Guinness, 1993)
Lester Piggott, Julian Wilson (MacDonald Queen Anne, 1985)
One Hundred Greatest Golfers, Peter Alliss (MacDonald Queen Anne, 1989)
Our Everest Adventure, John Hunt (Brockhampton Press, 1954)
Oxford Companion to Sports and Games, ed. John Arlott (OUP, 1976)
Pro-Golf, European Tour Media Guide, (PGA, 1998)
Sixty Seasons of League Football, R.C. Churchill (Penguin, 1958)
The Sport of Queens, Dick Francis (Michael Joseph, 1957)
Sports Report, ed. Eamonn Andrews and Angus Mackay (Heinemann, 1954)
Stanley Matthews, David Miller (Pavilion, 1989)
The Story of the Football League, ed. Charles Sutcliffe (Football League, 1938)
Wisden Book of Test Cricket, Bill Frindall (MacDonald Queen Anne, 1979)
Wisden Cricketers' Almanack 1954, ed. Norman Preston (Wisden, 1954)
World Championship Boxing, Ian Morrison (Guinness, 1990)

Other media:
British Paramount News
Pathé News
Many different sporting websites were used to check small details.